The Structure and Development of the Common Market

Also by

A. E. Walsh & John Paxton

Trade in the Common Market Countries

The Structure and Development of the Common Market

A. E. Walsh M.B.E.
John Paxton Ph.D

HUTCHINSON OF LONDON

HUTCHINSON & CO (*Publishers*) LTD
178-202 Great Portland Street London W1

London Melbourne Sydney
Auckland Bombay Toronto
Johannesburg New York

First Published 1968

382.9142
W 2 2 3 s

© A E Walsh & John Paxton 1968

This book has been set in Times Roman,
printed in Great Britain on Antique Wove paper
by Balding & Mansell Ltd,
of London and Wisbech, and bound by
Wm. Brendon & Son Ltd, of Tiptree, Essex

09 085480 2

TO LILIAN & JOAN

Contents

Acknowledgements	vii
Preface	viii

1	Post-war Europe.	1
2	The Treaty of Rome explained.	17
3	The Institutions of the European Communities.	37
4	The Tariff Structure of the Common Market.	43
5	Agriculture	56
	(a) The Original Idea.	58
	(b) The Commission's Proposals.	64
	(c) The Constitutional Crisis.	69
	(d) The Final Breakthrough.	75
6	Sales and Turnover Taxation in the Common Market.	83
7	Competition—Cartels and Exclusive Dealing Agreements.	100
8	Industrial Property—Patents and Trade Marks.	110
9	Social Security in the Common Market.	115
10	Mobility of People and Capital.	129
11	A Common Transport Policy.	133
12	The European Coal and Steel Community.	135
13	The European Atomic Energy Community.	154
14	Agreements of Association.	169
15	The Financial Organisation of the Community: Development Fund and Investment Bank.	185
16	Economic Growth in the Common Market.	190
Bibliography		203
Appendices		
	(a) Who sells most to the Common Market Countries and Britain.	205
	(b) Who makes most in the largest sectors of industry in the Common Market.	217
	(c) Some Comparative tables on consumption of products in Common Market.	223
	(d) Population of the Common Market—country, age and sex.	227

Acknowledgements

Over many years we have received considerable help, encouragement and advice from various officials of the Commission of the European Economic Community in Brussels and from the Press and Information Department of the Community in London. We should particularly like to thank them for their help to us in preparation of this volume.

We should also like to thank Dr. Walter Rosenberger of Keesing's Contemporary Archives and Dr. S.H. Steinberg of The Statesman's Year-Book for help and encouragement. To officials of the National Farmers' Union our thanks for helping us to clarify the British point of view on Agriculture and also our thanks to our indexer Mrs. D. Fetherstonhaugh.

Preface

In setting ourselves the task of writing this book, we felt that the first ten years of the existence of the Common Market provided enough material for a work in which could be set in juxtaposition the most important of developments which have followed the original drafting of the Treaty of Rome. Future historians will give different values to the events of those ten years. The next ten years will provide material for them for a long time to come.

The Treaty of Rome is one of the most remarkable documents in the social and economic history of the western world.

History is replete with attempts at federation in its widest meaning and with the obstacles which federation raised for the statesmen who undertook the task uniting countries and states in geographical proximity or with common interests. Those obstacles have frequently concerned the powers to be given to the central government and those to be retained by the member-states.

No attempt at federation in the past, whether successful or not, can be compared with the magnitude of the task which faces Europe today. The countries of Europe have taken a thousand years to mould the present pattern of their maturity.

The first task facing the signatories of the Treaty of Rome was to set up the Customs Union of the Six for industrial goods and for agricultural products. The latter proved far more complex than the former but agreement has eventually been achieved.

The European Economic Community is much more than a customs union. It is explicit in providing for complete economic union so that goods, people and capital will be able to pass over the national boundaries of the member-countries as freely as they can move inside any one country today.

At the time of writing this book, the European Economic Community has solved the major problems of the *Customs Union* and is now grappling successfully with the requirements of *Economic Union*. After these, on the distant horizon, lies *Political Union*. That will be for future writers. This work is but an interim report.

CHAPTER 1

Post-War Europe

If history demands a date for the most important event in the movement which led to the creation of the European Economic Community that date might well be Tuesday 9 May 1950. It was on that day, at 4 o'clock in the afternoon, that the French Minister of Foreign Affairs, Monsieur Robert Schuman, announced at a press conference that his Government had decided to place the entire complex of coal and steel production in France and Germany under a common High Authority in an organisation which would also be open to participation by other West European countries.

If history demands names with which to associate the process of crystallising out the solution containing all the ingredients of a new order in Europe, these names are certainly Jean Monnet and Robert Schuman. Monnet was an administrator. Administrators need politicians to put forward their ideas. Throughout the entire period of the chain of events from which the European Economic Community evolved, it is the partnership between Monnet, the administrator, and Robert Schuman, the politician, to which must be attributed the responsibility for the preparation of the plan and for its launching.

Throughout the long period of the instability of successive governments in France from 1945 onwards and their short and tempestuous lives, the name Schuman persists, once as Premier for a short time, but for almost all the time as Foreign Minister. Even the Bidault Government, which was in office at the time of the announcement of the Schuman Plan, only lasted until June 24th 1950; but Schuman still remained Foreign Minister in the subsequent governments.

Although he was neither by temperament nor by political education a believer in economic determinism, it was Schuman, above all his contemporaries, who demonstrated that while economic motives had for generations supplied the reason and the temptation to resort to war to settle national aspirations economic motives and resources could equally be orientated towards making war impossible.

The war left behind in its aftermath many Europeans with faith that they had a part to play in making a further war between France and Germany 'not merely unthinkable but materially impossible' and that, if a start could be made by the pooling of coal and steel production in the area in which nature had laid the resources but in which political conflict had divided them there might be created in Europe a new order in which motives and the resources for war would no longer exist.

Of these Europeans, it was Robert Schuman who recognised that he had the talent, and, as Foreign Minister of France, the power to change the face of Europe. Fortune was perhaps kind to him in the response which his ideas evoked from other European statesmen and in the chords which his bold and imaginative plan struck in the minds of men at the particular time and in the particular conditions which were rife in Europe. This is how history is often made.

Jean Monnet by contrast was an administrator. He was neither a member of the French Government nor of the French National Assembly. He was Director-General of the French Reconstruction Plan and as such he had, since the Liberation, achieved an almost unique international reputation and influence, despite the fact that his primary concern was with the French economy.

To Monnet must be credited the working out of the Schuman Plan. Of Monnet, Schuman declared that he played a predominant role from the very beginning in the conception of the plan and in elaborating the text of the treaty under which the European Coal and Steel Community was formed.

The Schuman Plan has something at once banal and romantic in the manner of its unfolding. Once completed, the problem was to get it adopted. M. Bidault, the Prime Minister, had as late as April 1950 made some suggestions for another scheme for co-ordinating economic and defence action between the United States and their allies. This idea had found no response in the United States but it made it difficult for Bidault to follow it up with ideas for a totally different plan.

Monnet had, however, a powerful ally in Robert Schuman, the Foreign Minister. Both sought the same solution to Europe's difficulties. Both saw that political unity must be sought as the result of economic unity and that the formation of a Franco-German Coal and Steel pool was the first stage towards greater achievements in the future.

Events moved quickly in the last stages in the preparation and presentation of the Plan.

On the fateful days which preceded M. Schuman's announcement

Post-War Europe

of the plan to set up the European Coal and Steel Community, it fell to Monnet to bring the project to its definitive stage and to set in motion the machinery which he had so skilfully devised.

On 4 May 1950 he called the men who had been collaborating with him in its preparation to a meeting in the rue Martignac in Paris— M. Clappier, permanent head of M. Schuman's Ministry, M. Jacques Gascuel, M. Hirsch and M. Uri. The 'conspirators' agreed upon their respective roles for the drafting and presentation of the announcement of the project. On 8 May all the drafts which had been used in its preparation were destroyed. On the morning of 9 May the text of the announcement was finally completed and it was left to M. Clappier to take it personally to M. Schuman to expound at a Cabinet meeting which was being held that day at the Elysée Palace. Would M. Schuman be able to persuade his ministerial colleagues to listen to what he had to say? M. Monnet and his team waited impatiently by their telephones. No news came. M. Monnet telephoned the Elysée; he thought that the Cabinet might have broken up before reaching M. Schuman's exposition.

The minutes of Cabinet meetings remain secret and one can only surmise the course of the discussions. Only a few ministers besides the Prime Minister, M. Bidault, and M. Schuman himself, had any prior knowledge of the subject. For the others it must have been a complete surprise.

As they listened to M. Schuman, few of them can have grasped the full significance of what he was saying. Few can have realised that afternoon that they were listening to a project which would have a profound effect upon history of Europe and affect the destinies of millions of people. This was not just another occasion for a routine exchange of ideas to be conducted through conventional diplomatic channels, but a solemn declaration to which France would be irrevocably committed. Probably no one who did not take part in the deliberations of that meeting will ever know all the facts.

Suffice it to say that M. Schuman secured the Cabinet's agreement to the form and text of the announcement which he submitted, and went straight to a press conference which, such was his confidence of his success, he had called in advance, and made his announcement.

His declaration had the effect which he had sought, in France and abroad. The surprise element had been complete. The psychological impact was immeasurable. Certainly M. Schuman had secured the support of Germany for the German Chancellor had on 8 May referred to the project as 'magnanimous' and on 13 May he described it as an act of historical significance. It seems doubtful, however, that Adenauer was told precisely of the form and text of Schuman's announcement before the morning of 9 May. The British Government did not know what was coming, nor, indeed, did the U.S. Secretary of State, Mr. Dean Acheson, who was in Paris on 8 May. In one master stroke, Robert Schuman had enabled France to gain the initiative in European affairs and a new era in Europe had begun.

The march of events after M. Schuman's announcement on 9 May 1950 was swift. On 20 June 1950 delegates from the Governments of France, Germany, Belgium, Luxembourg, the Netherlands and Italy met in Paris. They started work at once on drafting a treaty and 10 months later, on 18 April 1951 the draft treaty establishing the European Coal and Steel Community was signed and ready for ratification. It was put to the vote in the Parliaments of the six countries and ratified. Britain had been invited to take part in the discussions but declined. The Prime Minister, Mr. Attlee, told the House of Commons that Britain could not agree to the fundamental condition that she should commit herself in advance to be bound by the future decisions of a higher coal and steel authority.

The European Coal and Steel Community was formed without Britain. The treaty came into force on 25 July 1952 and the High Authority, which had been installed in Luxembourg, assumed its duties.

* * *

The history of the coal and steel industries in France and Germany forms a significant part of the history of the two countries themselves and in particular of those areas on their joint frontier which had been for so long in dispute—the Saar Basin with its coal mines and Lorraine with its resources of iron ore.

In modern times no one European country has had within its own borders a balanced supply of iron ore and coking coal. Even the return of Lorraine to France in 1919, although it altered the pattern of Germany's coal-ore balance, did not have the effect which was expected, because Germany had for years been organising her industry, as had other steel producing countries including Britain, on the basis of rich imported ores from other countries.

Indeed the interdependence of the European countries on one another for both coal and iron ore had brought about all kinds of international integration in the industry. This integration was particularly evident between France and Germany between the wars when industrial collaboration was the only way of maintaining coal and steel equilibrium in the face of all the political upheavals of the period.

For obvious reasons, this process of integration became one of enforced collaboration during the Second World War. It is not surprising therefore that when all the turmoil of the immediate post-war years had passed, there existed, at all levels in France and Germany, a framework of personal relationships upon which collaboration directed to peaceful industrial purposes could be constructed. Though the factories had been destroyed, the men who had run and directed them in peace and in war remained.

It is impossible to say exactly who first had the idea of a Franco-German Iron and Steel Pool. According to Bernard Lavergne it came originally from Hugo Stinnes, the coal and steel magnate of the Ruhr, in 1931. Paul Wergner in his biography of Konrad Adenauer says that as far back as 1923 at the time of the French occupation of the Ruhr, Adenauer, then Mayor of Cologne, had believed in the unification of the heavy industries of France and Germany.

The concept of the European Coal and Steel Community—and, as we shall show later, the European Economic Community, (the Common Market)—is a political one. The Schuman Plan on which it was based was approved by the French Cabinet 'as a first step in the federation of Europe'.

When the war in Western Europe ended in 1945, victors and vanquished alike were in a state of utter political and economic exhaustion. Physically, Britain had suffered grievously, but not in the same way as the Continental countries. She was operating under a system of stringent controls and regulations imposed to mobilise her resources for total war. The unwinding of these controls was a tedious and frustrating process which necessitated prolonging almost all the restrictions to the re-opening of external trade that the war had made necessary.

In Europe conditions were infinitely worse. Physical damage had paralysed roads and railway transport and most of the large factories. From 1940 to 1944 Germany had made herself into the axis upon which the entire production of the countries of Western Europe turned. Everything short of the necessities of life itself (and often even these) which these countries produced flowed into Germany to meet her demands for food and war materials.

The defeat and collapse of Germany brought in their train nothing less than the complete collapse of the framework of economic links which Germany had built up during the war and there was nothing left to take its place. It is estimated that in 1945, pig iron production in the countries that now form the Common Market, was less than one third the level of 1939 and coal production even less.

Such chaos demanded palliative measures. The first of such measures to relieve the desperate economic situation in the worst-hit countries was provided by UNRRA, the United Nations Relief and Rehabilitation Administration, which, by its charter, was designed primarily to help the peoples in countries which had opposed the German axis nations before and during the war.

The first positive step to revive international industrial economic relationships was the Anglo-American loan agreement of 1946 by which Britain received a nett sum (after provisions for the repayment of outstanding lend-lease claims) of £1,300m. from the United States. One of the conditions of this loan was a return to convertibility of currency. In her attempt to carry out this condition Britain vitiated the purpose of the loan and dissipated much of the loan itself.

The period between the summer of 1946, when the bulk of American assistance to Europe virtually came to a standstill and the winter of 1947, when Britain brought matters to a head by informing the United States that she could no longer maintain her share of the combined military and economic aid to support the Greek Government against Communism, was a period of great confusion in Europe. Communism was rapidly gaining ground. The consolidation of the Communist domination in Eastern Europe was having its effect on the Communist parties in Western Europe. The Communist Party had become the strongest party in France and Italy was expected to move in the same direction.

America reacted quickly to a situation which had been brought about by the failure of the West to assess the magnitude of the task of rehabilitating Europe. On 12 March 1947 President Truman announced the Truman Doctrine which warned the Soviet Union against further political pressure in South East Europe. In June 1947 General George C. Marshall, newly appointed Secretary of State, announced his plan, which was later approved by Congress, for large scale economic help to the European countries to finance the purchase abroad of the machinery and equipment which they needed but which they lacked the dollar resources to pay for.

The Marshall Plan was described at the time as the blood transfusion which sustained the weakening European economies and gave them strength to work their own recovery.

To administer the aid given under the Marshall Plan the Organisation for European Economic Co-operation was set up by the signing of the Convention for European Economic Co-operation on 16 April

1948. Under this Convention the member governments pledged themselves 'to combine their economic strength, to join together to make the fullest collective use of their individual capacities and potentialities, to increase their production, develop and modernise their industrial and agricultural equipment, reduce progressively barriers to trade amongst themselves, promote full employment and restore or maintain the stability of their economies and general confidence in their national currencies'.

O.E.E.C. comprised the following countries: Austria, Belgium, Denmark, France, Germany, Greece, Iceland, Ireland, Italy, Luxembourg, the Netherlands, Norway, Portugal, Sweden, Trieste, Turkey and the United Kingdom.

Even with such massive external assistance, which by June 1950 had amounted to some £3,300m. the efforts to restore economic health in Western Europe was subjected to strain and pressures. Inflation, rising prices and devaluation were discounting much of the value of the external aid.

Nevertheless by the end of 1949 European currencies were sufficiently aligned to allow a start to be made on dismantling the complicated structure of bilateral trade and payments and to return to a system of multilateral clearing of payments.

From 1948, when it began, to 1956 O.E.E.C. had achieved most of its major objectives. In addition to the arrangements through the European Payments Union for multilateral clearing it had succeeded in getting some 90 per cent of European trade freed from quota restrictions. The countries with moderate import tariffs considered, however, that they could not proceed with the elimination of their remaining quotas until a start had been made on the reduction of tariff disparities.

In 1948, shortly after the signing of the Convention setting up the O.E.E.C. the first moves designed to achieve political federation in Europe became apparent. At The Hague Congress, in May 1948 leading Europeans, Bidault, Blum, Churchill, de Gasperi, Monnet, Spaak, van Zeeland and others called for measures which could lead to the political and economic integration of Western Europe. As a result in 1949 the Council of Europe was inaugurated in Strasbourg.

The Council of Europe has two political chambers, a Committee of Ministers, usually the Foreign Ministers of the member States and a consultative assembly of Representatives, made up of members of the Parliaments of the member States.

The Council of Europe never assumed or was given any legislative authority. Within its corridors of power, there have been consultation and pressure, proposal and counter-proposal, but none of these met the aims of the European federalists.

Political debate was no substitute for action. Even during the first year of the existence of the Council of Europe, the real movement towards European integration began to emerge.

If political unity could not be achieved as a primary aim in Europe there were statesmen who felt that, if a basis for economic integration would be found, political unity would follow.

Prominent amongst them was Monsieur Spaak, the Foreign Minister of Belgium. In the autumn of 1955 a Committee was appointed under the chairmanship of Monsieur Spaak to consider a plan for a Common Market. At the deliberations of this committee a United Kingdom delegate attended as observer.

Between 1952 and 1957 the door to Britain's close participation in the moves towards European integration was wide open. This is the period of lost opportunity. A Free Trade Area would have been possible then but for Britain's reluctance to help O.E.E.C. to move towards tariff reductions. By the time the Spaak Committee had prepared its plan for the Common Market opinion was hardening. Britain faced with the choice of coming in or staying out made her disastrous decision to remain aloof.

For all practical purposes the decision to form the European Economic Community was taken at the Messina Conference held in June 1955 and attended by Ministers from France, W. Germany, Italy, the Netherlands, Belgium and Luxembourg. The Treaty itself was signed in Rome on 25 March 1957.

Between these two dates, there was considerable activity on the part of the other member countries of O.E.E.C., led by Britain, to avoid being left out of the new economic order in Europe. Negotiations were opened in March 1957, to form a Free Trade Area made up of the six members of the Common Market and of seven European countries, Britain, Norway, Sweden, Denmark, Switzerland, Austria and Portugal.

In the light of all subsequent developments it seems strange that it was the Customs Union aspect of the European Economic Community that dominated the scene of these negotiations. The Free Trade Area was to be an association of the European Economic Community and the seven European countries not included in the Community, in which all the disciplines of the Treaty of Rome were to be observed by the Common Market while the other countries maintained a large measure of independence including freedom for their own external trade policies. Tariffs on goods passing from one Free Trade Area country to another were to be abolished progressively. The Common Market common external tariff against all other countries not members of the Free Trade Area was to go ahead as laid down in the Treaty.

Such advantages as for instance, duty free imports of food, raw materials and manufactured goods from the Commonwealth as were enjoyed by Britain were to remain. It was said of Britain at the time that she was seeking the best of both worlds. 'With its different institutional structures, inspired by a different purpose yet performing some of the same tasks, the Free Trade Area would have been likely to exert a weakening influence on the Common Market' (The Economist, 25 April 1959).

The plan for a Free Trade Area of the Six and the Seven non-member countries was worked out in London during 1956 and a decision to open discussion was taken in 1957. In October 1957, O.E.E.C., including France, approved the principle of a Free Trade Area. On 17 October 1957 the Council of O.E.E.C. passed a resolution in which it declared its determination to secure the establishment of a European Free Trade Area which, taking into consideration the objectives of the European Economic Community, would take effect parallel with the Treaty of Rome. To this resolution France subscribed.

West Germany wanted a Free Trade Area. So did the Netherlands and, to a lesser extent, Belgium. The German Foreign Ministry had certain reservations because it did not want to upset its new relationships with France. Italy was somewhere half way between the two. France paid lip service to the O.E.E.C. Plan but, because her trade policy was protectionist and because she was beginning to see the prospects of putting a curb on West Germany through her dominant position in the European Economic Community she showed signs in January 1958 of her intention to sabotage the Free Trade Area idea. One of France's Junior Ministers, M. Maurice Faure, was strongly pro-Free Trade Area. Opposed to him was the head of the Economic side of the French Foreign Ministry M. Wormser who, throughout the whole period of discussions relating to Britain's place in Europe, has been a most formidable adversary.

The French pinned their faith on the problem of 'Origin' as the most plausible grounds in which to oppose a Free Trade Area, on the pretext that the privileges enjoyed within the Commonwealth would distort conditions of competition for the Common Market and make it difficult to prevent many Commonwealth products which enjoy duty free entry into Britain from getting into Europe by the back door. For over a year the French delegation raised one technical objection after another to the system which was emerging from the negotiations and which is now successfully used in Efta.

Challenged on this, the Community produced the Ockrent Report which, while reaffirming that the Community was determined to arrive at an agreement for a Free Trade Area associated with the Community on a multilateral basis nevertheless reiterated many of the supposed difficulties. France then fell back upon her second line of defence by raising every conceivable obstruction on the step-by-step examination of the difficulties which Britain wanted to make.

Looking back in these negotiations for a Free Trade Area, it must be admitted that Britain's position was weak and her approach naïve especially in view of the relative isolation of France at that time. It is not surprising that Britain was suspected of wanting to set up an organisation which at best was regarded as defensive and which, at worst, could seriously undermine the purpose of the European Economic Community and its disciplines.

At the end of 1958, the political game came into full play and M. Soustelle speaking for the French Government at a Press Conference abruptly denounced the whole plan and the negotiations were immediately broken off.

THE EUROPEAN FREE TRADE ASSOCIATION

In May 1959 Sweden took the first steps towards forming a Free Trade Area of the Seven European countries which had attempted to set up a Free Trade Area with the European Economic Community. Sweden invited Austria, Denmark, Norway, Portugal, Switzerland and the United Kingdom to discussions in Stockholm for this purpose.

On 20 November 1959, these seven countries agreed the Stockholm Convention setting up the European Free Trade Association (Efta) to come into effect on 1 July 1960.

The main purpose of the Convention was to stimulate trade between the member countries by giving 'Area tariff treatment' to industrial goods traded from one member country to another. For this purpose, the protective tariffs for elimination were all customs duties which had not been declared as revenue duties. Agricultural products are excluded from the Efta Convention.

The essential difference, in terms of its existence as a Customs Union, between the Common Market and Efta is that while the Treaty of Rome lays down a common external tariff to be levied on all goods coming from non-member countries, the members of Efta maintain their own existing levels of tariffs towards goods coming from the rest of the world.

By a series of tariff reductions between 1960 and 1966, Efta became a completely free trade area for trade between its members on 1 January 1967 with the exception of special provisions for delayed tariff reductions by Portugal.

One of the many obstacles which were raised by France in the 1958 negotiations for a Free Trade Area in Europe concerned the question of origin. How would it be possible so to define the origin of goods as to ensure that the elimination of tariffs within the area did not open a back door for goods from outside the area to get through the tariff wall?

This difficulty was met in the Efta Convention by the simple expedient of specifying origin criteria. Goods entitled to free entry can conform to one of three conditions. They can qualify (1) by having been produced wholly within the Area of Efta; (2) by having been produced within the area by a qualifying process specified in the Process List; (3) or, in place of (2) by containing not more than 50 per cent by value of non-Area materials, except for textiles which were excluded from the percentage criterion.

Very few of the disciplines of the European Economic Community were written into the Efta Convention. Indeed, apart from the elimination of customs duties between the member states of Efta there is no provision for integrating them economically in the way in which the Treaty of Rome integrates its six members. Nor have the Efta countries any aims of political union. The Secretariat of Efta consists of an organisation with offices in Geneva.

In the summer of 1961, the British Government decided upon two steps towards overcoming the difficulties with which the economy has been beset since the end of the second world war. The first step was the programme of the Chancellor of the Exchequer, Mr. Selwyn Lloyd to improve the balance of payments situation which was experiencing one of the crises which have been phenomena of the post war period. The second was the announcement by the Prime Minister, Mr. Harold Macmillan, that an attempt was to be made to negotiate Britain's entry into the Common Market.

This decision called for consultation with the Commonwealth countries and three Cabinet Ministers were nominated to visit all the

Commonwealth countries to smooth the part of the Government in preparation for its discussions with the Six.

On the whole, the reaction of the Commonwealth countries was luke warm. Most feared the effects of the common agricultural policy of the Common Market on their exports of foodstuffs and of the loss of Commonwealth preference for much of their other exports to Britain.

In the event, on 10 August 1961 Britain, joined by Denmark, requested negotiations aimed at membership of the European Economic Community and on 8 November 1961 negotiations started in Brussels.

The talks were long, difficult and often acrimonious. Britain made every concession that she deemed possible in the light of her obligations to the Commonwealth and to dependent territories, The story is told of a journalist who at one point asked a French delegate how the negotiations were going. The Frenchman replied 'Terrible. Things couldn't be worse. The English are agreeing to everything.'

By the end of 1962, agreement had, in fact, been reached on all but a hard core of problems. It was agreed that the enlarged Community would help the temperate Commonwealth countries (Australia, New Zealand and Canada) in a broadly based move towards world-wide agreements to include price and production policies, minimum and maximum quantities to enter international trade and special safeguards for developing countries. The main subjects left for agreement concerned processed foodstuffs (canned and dried fruits), safeguards for New Zealands exports of dairy produce, and Britain's request for zero tariffs on certain important raw materials, notably aluminium, zinc, lead, wood pulp and newsprint.

At this point in the discussion, on 14 January 1963, President de Gaulle made one of his customary 'ex cathedra' announcements and said that Britain was not ready for membership of the European Economic Community and on 29 January 1963 on the initiative of the French the Brussels negotiations were abruptly broken off, in much the same manner as the Free Trade Area negotiations had been broken off in Paris four years earlier.

The following is a short chronology of the principal events connected with the European Communities:

1946 19 September Winston Churchill, in Zurich, urges Franco-German reconciliation within 'a kind of United States of Europe'.

1947 5 June General Marshall proposes American aid to stimulate recovery in Europe.

Post-War Europe

	29 October	Creation of Benelux—economic union of Belgium, Luxembourg and the Netherlands.
1948	16 April	Convention for European Economic Co-operation signed—the birth of O.E.E.C.
1949	5 May	Statute of the Council of Europe signed.
1950	9 May	Robert Schuman makes his historic proposal to place French and German coal and steel under a common Authority.
1951	18 April	The Treaty setting up the European Coal and Steel Community (E.C.S.C.) is signed in Paris.
1952	10 August	E.C.S.C. High Authority starts work in Luxembourg under its first president, Jean Monnet.
	10 September	E.C.S.C. Common Assembly holds its first session in Strasbourg, and elects Paul-Henri Spaak as its first president.
1953	10 February	E.C.S.C. common market for coal, iron ore, and scrap is opened.
	1 May	E.C.S.C. common market for steel is opened.
1954	21 December	An association agreement between United Kingdom and E.C.S.C. is signed.
1955	1–3 June	Messina Conference: the Foreign Ministers of the Community's member states propose further steps towards full integration in Europe.
1957	25 March	Signature of the Rome Treaties setting up the Common Market and Euratom.
1958	1 January	The Rome Treaties come into force: the Common Market and Euratom are set up.
	9 February	E.C.S.C. transition period ends—full operation of common market for coal and steel.
	19–21 March	First session of the European Parliament—Robert Schuman elected president.
1959	1 January	First tariff reductions and quota enlargements in the common Market. Establishment of common market for nuclear materials.
	20 November	European Free Trade Association convention signed between Austria, Denmark, Norway, Portugal, Sweden, Switzerland and the United Kingdom.
1960	10–12 May	Community decides to speed up its timetable for implementing the Common Market.
1961	9 July	Greece signs association agreement with E.E.C. (entry into force 1 November 1962).

14   The Structure and Development of the Common Market

18 July	The six Community countries issue Bonn Declaration aiming at political union.
1 August	The Republic of Ireland applies for membership of the Common Market.
10 August	Britain and Denmark request negotiations aiming at membership of the Common Market.
8 November	Negotiations with Britain open in Brussels.
15 December	The three neutrals, Austria, Sweden and Switzerland, apply for association with the Common Market.
1962 14 January	Community fixes basic features of common agricultural policy, and regulations for grains, pigmeat, eggs and poultry, fruit and vegetables, and wine.
9 February	Spain applies for association with the Common Market.
2, 5 March	Britain applies for membership of the E.C.S.C. and Euratom.
30 April	Norway requests negotiations for membership of the Common Market.
15 May	Community decides on second speeding-up of Common Market timetable.
16 July	Conclusion of 1960–62 negotiations for worldwide tariff cuts in G.A.T.T. Community substantially reduces common external tariff.
30 July	First regulations implementing the common agricultural policy come into effect.
1963 14 January	President de Gaulle declares that Britain is not ready for Community membership.
22 January	Franco-German Treaty of Co-operation signed in Paris.
29 January	British negotiations with Six broken off.
1 July	Signature of Yaoundé Convention, associating 18 independent states in Africa and Madagascar with the Community for five years from 1 June 1964.
12 September	Turkey signs association agreement with Community (entry into force 1 December 1964).
23 December	Common farm-policy regulations for rice, beef and dairy products agreed.
1964 14 April	Council of Ministers accepts Commission's

		proposals for fighting inflationary trends in Community.
	4 May	Kennedy Round negotiations open in Geneva.
	23 September	Common Market Commission bans Grundig-Consten exclusive-sales agreement as contravening monopoly rules.
	1 November	Common policy regulations for beef, dairy products and rice come into effect.
	9 December	First meeting of the Parliamentary Conference of members of European Parliament and parliamentarians from Yaoundé associated states.
	15 December	Council adopts the Mansholt Plan for common prices for grains.
1965	31 March	Common Market Commission proposes that, as from 1 July 1967, all Community countries' import duties and levies be paid into Community budget and that powers of European Parliament be increased.
	8 April	Six sign treaty merging the Community Executives.
	31 May	Common Market Commission publishes first memorandum proposing lines of Community policy for regional development.
	1 July	Council fails to reach agreement by agreed deadline on financing common farm policy; French boycott of Community Institutions begins seven-month-long crisis.
	26 July	Council meets and conducts business without French representative present.
1966	17 January	Six foreign ministers meet in Luxembourg without Commission present and agree to resume full Community activity.
	3 May	Common Market Commission publishes memorandum on legal means of forming 'Community law' companies.
	7 May	Medium-term Economic Policy Committee publishes first five-year outline program, which is adopted by Council on 8 February 1967.
	11 May	Council agrees that on 1 July 1968, all tariffs on trade between the member states shall be removed and that the common external tariff

should come into effect, thus completing the Community's customs union. It agrees also on the completion of the common farm policy by the same date.

13 July European Court of Justice upholds principle of Commission's ban on Grundig-Consten agreement.

16 July Nigeria signs an association agreement with the Community.

24 July Common prices for beef, milk, sugar, rice, oilseeds and olive oil agreed by Council, enabling free trade in agricultural products by 1 July 1968.

10 November British Prime Minister Harold Wilson announces plans for 'a high-level approach' to the Six with intention of entering E.E.C.

1967 January–March Mr. Wilson and Foreign Minister George Brown visit Rome, Paris, Brussels, Bonn, The Hague and Luxembourg and discuss the possibility of British membership.

2 May Mr. Wilson announces in the House of Commons that Britain is preparing a formal application for membership of the E.E.C.

11 May Britain lodges formal application for membership of the European Economic Community.

CHAPTER 2

The Treaty of Rome Explained

European history is, as every schoolboy knows to his cost, littered with Treaties. Some have altered the political and economic face of Europe. Most have been signed following a period of war and the aim has been that the vanquished should not regain its former power.

In our lifetime another Treaty has been signed and mention of it has already entered the history books. This Treaty has as its aim the raising of living standards for European peoples.

On 1 January 1958 the Treaty of Rome establishing the European Economic Community came officially into force.

This chapter deals with the principal provisions of the Treaty setting up the European Economic Community or Common Market. Subsequent chapters deal in greater detail with developments and interpretation of the Treaty from 1 January 1958.

The final drafts of the Treaty had been completed by the intergovernmental committee in Brussels on 9 March 1957, and the Treaty was signed in Rome by Belgium, France, West Germany, Italy, Luxembourg, and the Netherlands on 25 March 1957. The signing ceremony took place at the Palazzo dei Conservatori on the Capitoline Hill. The signatories being Signor Segni (then Italian Prime Minister); Dr. Adenauer (then Federal German Chancellor); the Foreign Ministers of Belgium (then M. Spaak); France (then M. Pincau); Italy (then Dr. Martino); Luxembourg (then M. Bech); and the Netherlands (Mr. Luns); The West German State Secretary for Foreign Affairs (Professor Hallstein, representing the then Foreign Minister, Dr. Von Brentano, who was on a visit to Australia).

Between July and December 1957 the Treaty was ratified by the Parliaments of all the six member-countries.

The Treaty, which was concluded for an unlimited period, consists of 248 Articles, 15 Annexes, 4 declarations of intention, and 3 protocols.

In the preamble to the Treaty, the six signatory countries declared their intention of establishing 'the foundations of an enduring and closer union between European peoples' by gradually removing the economic effect of their political frontiers. It was agreed that a common market and a common external tariff (Customs union) would be established for all goods; common policies would be devised for agriculture, transport, labour mobility, and important sectors of the economy; common institutions would be set up for economic development; and the overseas territories and possessions of member-States would be associated with the new Community. All these measures had one 'essential aim'—the steady improvement in the conditions of life and work of the peoples of the member-countries.

The tasks of the Community were defined in Article 1 of the Treaty as 'the achievement of a harmonious development of the economy within the whole Community, a continuous and balanced economic expansion, increased economic stability, a more rapid improvement in living-standards, and closer relations between the member-countries'.

INSTITUTIONS

A system of institutions is laid down in the Treaty, and they consist of:
- (a) The Assembly
- (b) The Council of Ministers
- (c) The Commission
- (d) The Court of Justice

and, acting in a consultative capacity
- (e) The Economic and Social Committee.

The power of decision is entrusted, in the main, to the Council of Ministers with the Assembly exercising political power over the other institutions of the Community. As the economic and political character of the E.E.C. develops the Assembly will obtain greater power and delegates chosen from the Parliaments of the member-states make up the Assembly. These institutions are discussed in greater detail in Chapter 3.

One of the principal characteristics of the process of creating a Common Market is its irrevocable character. This constitutes an important safeguard for the smaller member-countries in as much as their sacrifices in adjusting themselves to the new conditions do not involve the risk of a complete standstill and a subsequent return to the previous status after a period of time.

The Common Market was planned to be established in three

The Treaty of Rome Explained

stages within a transitional period of 12 years which could be extended to 15 years, i.e. completion will be by 1970 at the earliest and 1972 at the latest.

Within the basic 12-year period there are three stages, each lasting, in principle, four years. However at the end of the first four years if the Council of Ministers and the Commission had not unanimously agreed that the objectives of that stage had been essentially accomplished, the stage would automatically have been extended for one year. At the end of the fifth year there could be another one-year extension on the same condition, whilst at the end of the sixth year a further extension could be granted only if a request by a member-state for such an extension was recognised as justified by an ad hoc arbitration tribunal of three members appointed by the Council of Ministers. In deciding whether the objectives of the respective stages had been essentially accomplished, and the obligations under the Treaty carried out, no member-country could prevent a unanimous decision by basing its protest on non-compliance with its own obligations.

The second and third stages could have been either prolonged or shortened by unanimous decision of the Council of Ministers, subject to the maximum limit of 15 years for the whole transitional period.

The member-countries co-ordinate their economic policy to the extent required for achieving the aims of the Treaty. The institutions of the Community ensure that the internal and external financial stability of the member-countries was not endangered. Any discrimination against nationals or companies of other member-countries is prohibited, except in the special cases expressly laid down in the Treaty.

THE BASIS OF THE ECONOMIC COMMUNITY

The European Economic Community is based on a Customs Union covering the whole trade of member-countries and entailing (a) a prohibition on imposing import or export duties or similar levies between member-countries; (b) the introduction of a common tariff on imports from non-Community countries; (c) the abolition of all quantitative import and export restrictions and other similar measures between member-countries. The free exchange of goods within the Community applies not only to goods produced in the member-countries but also to those which have been imported by a member-country from outside the Community, and on which Customs duties have been paid on entry.

Internal Tariffs Tariff restrictions on trade between member-countries will be abolished entirely by the end of the transitional period at the latest. During the transitional period, national tariffs (those in force on 1 January 1957 being taken as the basis for calculation in each case) would be reduced by 10 per cent. three times in each of the first two stages, and by the remaining 40 per cent during the third stage. In fact the reductions are taking place much quicker than initially envisaged as will be seen in Chapter 4.

External Tariffs A common tariff on imports from non-Community countries will be established in full not later than the end of the transitional period. As a general rule, the final tariff for each product will be the arithmetical average of the corresponding national tariffs in force on 1 January 1957. National tariffs which vary initially by no more than 15 per cent from the average tariff will be replaced by the latter within four years; in other cases the gap will be reduced by 30 per cent after four years, by 60 per cent. after eight years, and will be eliminated entirely by the end of the transitional period. Certain exceptions to these general provisions were permitted and are explained in greater detail in the chapter dealing with tariffs.

Quantitative Restrictions It was planned that all quantitative restrictions on trade within the Community would be progressively eliminated by a series of quota increases. (This procedure differed from the one applied by the O.E.E.C., which provided for the immediate complete removal of import quotas in respect of a growing range of individual products.)

Thus, one year after the coming into force of the Treaty, 1 January 1959, the member-states converted all their existing bilateral import quotas into global quotas in favour of all other member-countries, without any discrimination between them. All these global import quotas were to be increased annually by at least 20 per cent as regards their overall value, and by at least 10 per cent as regards each individual product; bigger increases were made in the case of quotas amounting initially to less than 3 per cent of the domestic output of a given product. While Governments had a certain amount of discretion as to the incidence and timing of quota increases, they were nevertheless required to work towards the ultimate objective, viz. that by the end of the tenth year each individual quote should be equivalent to at least 20 per cent of the national production of the article concerned.

Special provisions regulated the position of those member-countries that had already introduced high global import quotas on the coming into force of the Treaty, or had gone beyond the obligations assumed within the then O.E.E.C. as regards the liberalisation of imports. If the Commission found that the imports of a certain commodity into a member-country during two successive years had been below the respective import quota, the quota was abolished altogether.

Quantitative restrictions on exports had to be abolished by the end of the first stage at the latest. Member-countries were nevertheless permitted to impose import, export, or transit restrictions or prohibitions which were justified for reasons of public morality, public order, public security, or on similar grounds, provided there was no arbitrary discrimination or any concealed restriction of trade. In fact, all quotas on industrial imports from member-countries were abolished on 31 December 1961.

As regards certain State monopolies in the member-countries which might have led to restrictions in intra-Community trade with effects similar to quota restrictions, the Treaty provided that all such monopolies had to be gradually changed so that at the end of the transitional period any discrimination between nationals of member-countries as regards both purchases and supplies ceased. If a certain product was subject to a commercial State monopoly in one or several member-countries, the Commission could then authorise the other member-states to take certain protective measures.

Agriculture Agricultural products are included in the Common Market (unlike such organisations as Efta) although the Treaty envisaged a special regime to apply in view of the different social structure of agriculture in the various member-countries, where it made it difficult to introduce a completely liberalised market. The history of the development of the thought and action on the Common Agricultural Policy down to the break-through on 24 June 1966 is given in Chapter 5.

Labour, Settlement, Services and Capital The free circulation of labour, services, and capital, as well as the right to settle, work and trade anywhere in the Community, is to be fully established by the end of the transitional period.

Labour As soon as the Treaty came into force, the Council of Ministers decided by simple majority voting what measures were necessary to ensure complete mobility of labour within the Community, including (i) the abolition of all discriminatory measures between nationals of member-countries; (ii) the right to apply for jobs anywhere within the six countries, and—on terminating any employment—to stay on in the country concerned under conditions to be fixed by the Commission. Measures taken by the Council of Ministers include provisions (i) for the dissemination of information about available jobs and labour, as well as other procedures to meet supply and demand under conditions which avoid serious danger to the standard of living and employment in the various areas and industries; (ii) for the removal of administrative difficulties; and (iii) for close collaboration between national labour organisations. Also the Council of Ministers have to decide on social security arrangements applicable to conditions of full mobility of labour.

Right of Settlement All restrictions on the right to settle freely in any member-country, or the right of nationals of any member-country to set up agencies, branches, or subsidiary companies in the territory of another, are to be gradually removed during the transitional period. The right of settlement includes the right to engage in any economic activity and to establish or manage companies and other enterprises.

The Treaty stated that before the end of the first stage of the transitional period the Council of Ministers would work out a general programme to remove from existing restrictions every kind of activity, and to determine the various stages of implementation. All decisions relating to the execution of this general programme, or for the abolition of restrictions on specific activities, would be taken by the Council of Ministers.

The Council are also drawing up rules for the mutual recognition of diplomas, certificates, and other qualifications, and for the co-ordination of existing regulations in the member-countries concerning the practice of professions.

Services All restrictions on the offering of services by insurance companies, banks, finance houses, the wholesale and retail trade, and by members of the professions will gradually be removed within the Community during the transitional period. Before the end of the first stage the Council of Ministers drew up a general programme to implement this principle.

Capital Existing restrictions on the movement of capital between the Community countries are planned to be progressively removed. As far as is necessary for the proper working of the Common Market, restrictions on current payments relating to the movement of capital (e.g. interest, dividends, rents, premiums) should have been completely abolished not later than the end of the first stage of the transitional period. The aim was that decisions by the Council of Ministers on the abolition of capital movement restrictions would be taken by unanimous vote during the first two stages, and by a qualified majority thereafter but progress has been slow in this field.

The only exceptions from the general rule of the eventual free movement of capital within the Community will apply in the following cases: (a) loans directly or indirectly intended to finance the Government, public institutions, or organs of local government of one member-country could be issued or sold in another member-country only with that country's consent: (b) member-countries while generally forbidden to introduce any new restrictions concerning capital movements, would be entitled to take protective measures within certain limits if such movements were likely to disturb their economies—the application of these protective measures being, however, supervised by the Commission.

As regards capital movements between member-countries and non-Community States, the Council of Ministers lay down all the measures required for controlling such movements and the foreign exchange policies connected with them, with the aim of achieving the highest possible degree of liberalisation. Council decisions in these matters will require unanimity. In the event of different degrees of liberalisation of capital movements and foreign exchange policies between one member-country and another leading to abuses of the regulations then existing, a member-country affected by such abuses is able to take suitable measures to stop them after consulting with the other member-countries and the Commission. Measures of this kind, however, might be subsequently amended or abolished altogether by decisions of the Council.

Transport The Council of Ministers will establish a joint transport policy and common rules for international transport within or through the Community, covering rail, road, and inland water transport. It will also lay down the conditions under which transport undertakings of one member-country will be permitted to operate in another. These decisions will have to be taken unanimously in the first two transitional stages and by a qualified majority thereafter, but unanimity will still be required after the second transitional stage whenever the Council's decisions related to principles of transport policy and might seriously impair the standard of living and employment in certain areas.

The extension of suitable common rules to sea and air transport, and the procedure applying in these cases, will be a matter for the Council to decide and such decisions requiring unanimity.

The Treaty laid down that all freight rates which discriminated as to the national origin or destination of the goods transported would be suppressed by the end of the second stage of the transitional period, whilst all special rates or privileges granted by a member-country for the purpose of helping or protecting specific undertakings or industries would have to be ended at the beginning of the second stage, unless specially authorised by the Commission. Two years after the coming into force of the Treaty, and after hearing the views of the Economic and Social Committee, the Council issued general regulations so that the Commission could take the necessary individual decisions after hearing the views of all the member-countries concerned.

In taking its decisions, the Commission take into account not only the requirements of an adequate location of industry but also the needs of less developed areas; the problems of areas which have suffered greatly through political conditions; and the effects of the various rates and tariffs on the competitive position between various kinds of transport.West Germany is authorised, notwithstanding the provisions of the Treaty, to take any measures required to compensate the areas affected for economic disadvantages arising from the political division of Germany.

However general agreement on Transport policy has not advanced at the pace envisaged in the Treaty.

A consultative committee of experts appointed by member-Governments was set up to advise the Commission on all transport questions.

ECONOMIC AND SOCIAL POLICY OF THE COMMUNITY

To ensure free and equal competition within the Community, common rules and policies were introduced in the member-countries as summarised below.

COMMON RULES

Cartels and Monopolies Any agreement or association preventing, restraining or distorting competition within the Community is forbidden, e.g. agreements or associations directly or indirectly fixing prices; regulating or controlling production, investment or technical development; sharing markets; requiring the acceptance of additional goods besides those needed by the customer; or providing for discriminatory conditions of supply. Exceptions were only permissible if such agreements contribute to production, distribution, or technical or economic progress, and if (i) an adequate share of the benefits arising therefrom is passed on to the consumer; (ii) the restrictive effect is not greater than was necessary for the purpose; (iii) the agreements do not open the way to monopolistic practices. The

The Treaty of Rome Explained

abuse by any or a number of enterprises enjoying a dominant position in a given market within the Community is also forbidden.

The plan was that during the early period anti-monopoly rules would be enforced nationally on the basis of detailed reports by the Commission to member-governments. Within three years, however, international rules and directives having the force of law throughout the Community would be issued by the Council of Ministers; those decisions would require a unanimous vote. If no such rules and directives had been issued by the Council within the three-year period, it would be able to make them thereafter by a qualified majority, on a proposal of the Commission and after consulting the Assembly.

Although the member-countries themselves would initially enforce anti-cartel and anti-monopoly regulations, the Commission had certain supervisory functions immediately after the coming into force of the Treaty. Specifically, the Commission could note violations of anti-cartel or anti-monopoly rules and could authorise a member-country whose interests were affected to take the necessary protective measures.

These principles apply not only to private industry but also to public enterprises, as well as to enterprises enjoying special or exclusive rights and privileges. State monopolies of a fiscal character and similar undertakings will, in principle, also come under the Treaty. The rules governing competition are examined in more detail in Chapter 7.

Dumping Dumping practices by any member-country within the Common Market are prohibited. If, during the transitional period, the Commission find that a member-state has engaged in such practices, it can make 'suitable recommendations' to the country concerned with a view to ending them. If the country concerned nevertheless continues such practices, the Commission can authorise that the other member-country or countries affected take the necessary protective measures, details of which would be laid down by the Commission.

State Subsidies Unless otherwise provided by the Treaty, State subsidies, of whatever kind, which distort or threaten to distort competition are prohibited. Nevertheless, certain subsidies are permissible notably subsidies of a social character; relief after natural catastrophes; subsidies given to certain areas in West Germany as compensation for the economic disadvantages caused by the division of Germany; special aid for under-developed areas or for projects of common European importance; and aid for the development of certain branches of the economy, provided it does not affect trade conditions in a manner detrimental to the common interest.

The Commission also examine all existing subsidies falling under this provision, in co-operation with the member-countries. And where it found that they were incompatible with the principles laid down in the Treaty, or were abused, it has ordered their abolition or amendment. If the country concerned does not carry out the Commission's decision within the stipulated period, the Commission itself or any other member-country affected can immediately appeal to the Court of Justice.

All member-countries are obliged to inform the Commission in advance of any proposed introduction of amendment of such subsidies; if the Commission considers these measures incompatible with the Treaty it can apply the procedure mentioned above.

Approximation of Laws By unanimous vote, the Council of Ministers can issue rules for the approximating of such existing legislation in member-countries which directly affects the setting-up or working of the Common Market.

ECONOMIC POLICY

The aim of the Treaty is that member-countries will harmonise their general economic, foreign exchange, and foreign trade policies.

General Economic Policy The general economic policies of member-countries is regarded as a matter of joint interest, and the countries concerned consult each other as well as the Commission on the measures which should be taken to meet changing circumstances. Such measures can be laid down by a unanimous vote of the Council of Ministers.

Balance of Payments Although each member-country remains automonous in currency matters and has sole responsibility for the maintenance of equilibrium in its balance of payments, combined with the maintenance of a high degree of employment and stable prices, all members co-ordinate their general economic and foreign exchange policies to the extent necessary for the efficient working of the Common Market. This co-ordination includes co-operation between their Economic Ministries and Central Banks. A Monetary Committee was set up with the task of supervising the exchange and financial positions of member-countries and of making regular reports to the organs of the Community.

Each member-country should conduct its foreign exchange policy in harmony with the common interest. All payments relating to the exchange of goods and services and the movement of capital, as well

The Treaty of Rome Explained

as the transfer of interest, dividends, rents, wages, salaries, etc., to other member-countries, should be permitted as far as such transactions were liberalized under the Treaty.

If a member-state is threatened with serious balance-of-payments difficulties the Commission is required to conduct an inquiry without delay. It can then propose to the Council of Ministers measures whereby the rest of the Community might help the member-state concerned, such 'mutual help' including the provision of limited credits by the other member-countries. If the latter refuse to give such aid, however, the organs of the Community will permit certain protective measures in favour of the country affected. Member-countries are, nevertheless, able to take the necessary protective measures on their own initiative, and without waiting for the Commission's decision, if they are threatened by a sudden balance-of-payments crisis; in such eventualities the Council might, however, subsequently demand that the country concerned should amend, suspend, or abolish the measures in question.

External Trade Policy A common external trade policy will be established by the end of the transitional period; pending this, member-countries are required to co-ordinate their trade relations with non-Community countries. The Commission is working out proposals for the procedure to be applied during the transitional period with a view to the eventual unification of external trade policies, and will submit these proposals to the Council of Ministers for the latter's approval. In harmonising their trade policies during the transitional period, member-countries will endeavour to unify their liberalisation lists vis-a-vis non-Community countries at the highest possible level, on the basis of recommendations by the Commission. One of the biggest efforts to achieve these ends was E.E.C. negotiating as a group at the Kennedy Round discussions of G.A.T.T. As an important aspect of this process of co-ordination, the export subsidy policies of the member-states is to be harmonised before the end of the transitional period.

The common external trade policy after the end of the transitional period will cover the application of a common customs tariff; the joint conclusion of trade and customs agreements; the unification of trade liberalisation measures; the working-out of common export policies; and the joint application of protective measures, e.g. against dumping or subsidies by non-community countries.

For trade and customs negotiations with non-Community countries the task of the Commission is to initiate discussions with the consent of the Council of Ministers, and to be in continuous consultation with a special committee appointed by the Council for this purpose; any agreements reached would need confirmation by the Council, which would be the organ for officially concluding agreements on behalf of the Community. This procedure applied to all Customs negotiations from the coming into force of the Treaty, and to all trade negotiations from the end of the transitional period.

During the transitional period member-countries consult each other in all matters relating to international economic organisations, with a view to harmonising their actions, and attempt to pursue a common policy as far as possible. Thereafter they would act in agreement throughout.

In formulating their joint trade policy, member-countries take into account the favourable results which the abolition of customs duties within the Community are expected to produce in increasing the competitive power of their industries.

SOCIAL POLICY—CREATION OF EUROPEAN SOCIAL FUND

General Provisions The Commission has promoted the co-ordination of the social policies of member-countries, with particular reference to employment, labour legislation, conditions of work, vocational training, social security, prevention of industrial accidents and occupational diseases, health protection, trade union rights, and collective bargaining between employers and employed. The Commission carries out this task by means of inquiries, recommendations, and consultations, and deals with both internal problems and questions raised by international organisations. Before making any recommendations, the Commission listens to the opinion of the Economic and Social Committee. The Commission also reports on social developments within the Community in its annual report to the Assembly. The latter body can request the Commission to make reports on special problems of a social nature.

Wages and Social Insurance Contributions The Treaty laid down the principle of equal pay for equal work and that this should be generally applied during the first transitional stage (this, in fact, was not achieved.) A special protocol annexed to the Treaty dealt with Social Security contributions in France.

European Social Fund A European Social Fund was established to facilitate employment and the mobility of labour within the Community. This Fund refunds to any member-country 50 per cent. of the cost incurred by that country, or its public bodies, for the following purposes: (a) re-training workers who had become unemployed as a result of the Common Market for another occupation, provided

The Treaty of Rome Explained

they had worked at least six months in their new jobs; (b) moving workers who had been compelled to change their residence (as a result of the setting-up of the Common Market) to other localities, provided they had been employed at their new places of residence for at least six months; (c) special subsidies paid to workers who were temporarily forced to work short time, or who had been temporarily thrown out of work, through changes in production by the undertaking employing them, and which had been paid to enable the workers concerned to maintain their standard of living pending the restoration of their full employment. The 50 per cent refund is dependent on (i) the workers affected having been fully employed again by the undertaking concerned for at least six months, and (ii) the Government concerned having previously submitted an approved re-organisation scheme to the Commission.

The Fund is administered by the Commission, assisted by a Committee consisting of representatives of member-Governments and trade unions. The Fund's budget is part of the Community's general budget, and is prepared by the Commission and needs the approval by the Council of Ministers. All regulations for the working of the European Social Fund, and for laying down in detail the terms on which it will aid member-countries, are issued by the Council of Ministers on proposals of the Commission, and after consulting the Economic and Social Committee and the Assembly. The Council of Ministers also lay down general principles for a joint policy in vocational training, designed to contribute to a harmonious economic development both in the individual member-countries and in the Common Market as a whole.

THE EUROPEAN INVESTMENT BANK

The Treaty stated that the European Investment Bank would be set up as an independent legal entity, its members consisting of the countries signatory to the Treaty. The Bank would promote a common investment policy within the Community and would, on a non-profit basis, grant loans or guarantees for (i) projects in underdeveloped regions; (ii) the modernisation, re-organisation, or extension of industries which were difficult to finance on a purely national basis; and (iii) new industries of joint interest to several member-countries which, because of their size or special character, would be difficult to finance by a single member-country.

The Bank's capital would be 1,000,000,000 E.P.U. units ($1,000,000,000), of which France and West Germany would each contribute $300,000,000, Italy $240,000,000, Belgium $86,500,000, the Netherlands $71,500,000, and Luxembourg $2,000,000. Member-countries would be required to pay in 25 per cent of their capital shares, in five equal instalments, within $2\frac{1}{2}$ years after the Treaty entered into force; of each payment, 25 per cent would be in gold and the remainder in the national currency.

The Bank could also borrow in the capital market, but if this were not possible on reasonable terms, it could request member-countries to grant it special loans for financing specified projects. Such request could only be made, at the earliest, four years after the Treaty came into force, and the loans might not exceed a total of $400,000,000, or $100,000,000 borrowed in any one year. They would bear 4 per cent interest per annum unless the Board of Governors fixed another rate.

The Bank—the statutes of which were annexed to the Treaty—would have (a) a Board of Governors, consisting of the members of the Council of Ministers; (b) a Board of Directors, comprising 12 members and 12 alternate members who would be appointed by the Board of Governors for five years. The Board of Directors would be independent of the member-governments and would comprise 3 members and 3 alternate members nominated by France, 3 each by West Germany, 3 each by Italy, 2 each by the Benelux countries jointly, and one each by the Commission. There would also be a steering committee consisting of a chairman and 2 vice-chairmen, appointed by the Board of Governors on the recommendation of the Board of Directors.

Examples of the achievements of the Bank are given in Chapter 15.

ASSOCIATION OF OVERSEAS TERRITORIES WITH COMMON MARKET—SPECIAL DEVELOPMENT FUND FOR OVERSEAS TERRITORIES

The overseas territories of Belgium, France, Italy, and the Netherlands were allowed to be associated with the Community. A special convention annexed to the Treaty laid down the details of this association for the initial five-year period.

The main principles of Association were that the products of the overseas territories would enter the Community on equal terms with those of the member-states, and each territory would extend to all the other member-countries any concessions applying to the country with which it was specially connected. Whilst Customs duties between the overseas territories and member-countries would, in general, be gradually removed under the five-year convention, and quantitative import restrictions progressively abolished, the overseas territories would nevertheless be allowed to continue to impose Customs duties

The Treaty of Rome Explained

required for the development of their industries and the financing of their public expenditure. Such duties, however, would be progressively reduced vis-a-vis other member-countries to the same level applicable to goods imported by the territory concerned from the member-country with which it was specially connected—thus abolishing any discrimination against the other member-countries.

As regards existing individual import quotas of the overseas territories, these would be converted into global quotas for the benefit of all those member-countries (and their overseas territories) with whom the territory in question was not specially connected. (Thus, in a French overseas territory there would be a global import quota for imports from, e.g. Belgium, Germany, Italy, and the Netherlands, in place of previously existing individual import quotas from each of these countries.)

Overseas Development Fund The five-year convention provided for the setting-up of a special Development Fund for the overseas territories, with a total of $581,250,000. Of this sum, France and West Germany would each contribute $200,000,000, Belgium and the Netherlands each $70,000,000, Italy $40,000,000, and Luxembourg $1,250,000. The Fund was allocated to the overseas territories of the four member-countries concerned as follows: France $511,250,000; Netherlands $35,000,000; Belgium $30,000,000; and Italy $5,000,000.

Details of the contributions and allocations for each of the five years were agreed as follows:

CONTRIBUTIONS

Years	First	Second	Third	Fourth	Fifth
Percentage	10%	12·5%	16·5%	22·5%	38·5%
Countries:		in million dollars (E.P.U. units)			
Belgium	7	8·75	11·55	15·75	26·95
W. Germany	20	25	33	45	77
France	20	25	33	45	77
Italy	4	5	6·60	9	15·40
Luxembourg	0·125	0·15625	0·20625	0·28125	0·48125
Netherlands	7	8·75	11·55	15·75	26·95

ALLOCATIONS

Years	First	Second	Third	Fourth	Fifth
Percentage	10%	12·5%	16·5%	22·5%	38·5%
Overseas territories of:		in million dollars (E.P.U. units)			
Belgium	3	3·75	4·95	6·75	11·55
France	51·125	63·906	84·356	115·031	196·832
Italy	0·5	0·625	0·825	1·125	1·925
Netherlands	3·5	4·375	5·775	7·875	13·475

Applications for the financing of projects out of the Development Fund are made by the responsible authorities of the member-countries and overseas territories concerned. The Commission then draws up annually the general programme of proposed investments on which the Council of Ministers make the final decisions, on the principle of a rational geographical distribution of the projects to be financed. These projects comprise, in particular, hospitals, technical training and research institutions, institutions to increase employment, and investment projects connected with productive development.

Association of Other Countries It was also provided that member-countries might offer participation in the Community to certain independent countries such as Morocco, Tunisia, and Libya, and to the Autonomous territories of the Netherlands Antilles and Surinam.

GENERAL FINANCE

The member-states contribute to the Community budget in the following proportions: France, Italy and West Germany, each 28 per cent; Belgium and the Netherlands, each 7·9 per cent; Luxembourg 0·2 per cent.

The budget is prepared by the Commission, which also investigates the possibility of replacing the contributions of member-countries by independent resources, notably receipts from the common tariff. (The agricultural crisis of 1966 in which France partially withdrew from E.E.C. working committees was caused by the problems of control of Community funds arising from the common external tariff.) The budget is submitted for approval first to the Council of Ministers and then to the Assembly. In the case of any modifications proposed by the Assembly, the Council of Ministers, in consultation with the Commission, makes the final decision.

GENERAL PROVISIONS AND SAFEGUARDS

Safeguarding Clauses With the consent of the Commission, member-countries are able during a limited period to deviate from the provisions of the Treaty in order to meet special difficulties which are caused to some of their industries during the gradual introduction of the Common Market.

A member-country which is, for example, in serious and persistent difficulties is entitled during the transitional period to take special steps to safeguard its economy or the economy of certain areas; in such a case the Commission decides without delay about the measures which it considered necessary, and at the same time lays down the conditions of their implementation.

Member-states are also allowed to take special measures for the protection of their interests in the sphere of defence or in the event of war.

Membership and Association   The Treaty applies to Algeria and the French Overseas Departments under special conditions.

Any other European country can apply for membership of the Community; the terms of its admission, and any consequential amendments of the Treaty which might become necessary, would be agreed between the original member-countries and the applicant country.

Agreements can also be concluded with another country or group of countries for their association with the Community, based on certain mutual rights and obligations, joint action, and special procedures. Similar agreements of association could be entered into with international organisations.

ANNEXED PROTOCOLS

The following protocols were annexed to the Treaty:

(1)   A protocol containing the statutes of the European Investment Bank.

(2)   A protocol sanctioning the continuation of trade between West and East Germany as a German internal matter. It laid down that each member-country would inform both the other members and the Commission of any agreements relating to its trade with East Germany; that member-countries would ensure that the implementation of such agreements were not contrary to the principles of the Common Market; and that they would accordingly take suitable measures to avoid any damage to the economies of the other member-countries. It was also laid down that member-countries would be prepared to take suitable measures to prevent difficulties for themselves arising from the trade of another member-country with East Germany.

(3)   A protocol allowing France to maintain for the time being the system of export subsidies and import duties in the franc area. This system would, however, be reviewed annually by the Commission and the Council of Ministers.

(4)   A protocol stipulating that the Italian 10-year plan for industrial expansion (the 'Vanoni Plan') would be taken into account in the policy of the Community.

(5)   A protocol providing for certain protective measures for the agriculture of Luxembourg.

(6) A protocol allowing the continuation of special tariffs for imports by member-countries from certain other countries with which they maintained particularly close political or economic relations—e.g. imports into the Benelux countries from Surinam and the Netherlands Antilles; imports into France from Morocco, Tunisia, and the former Indo-Chinese States (Cambodia, Laos, and Vietnam); and imports into Italy from Libya and the former Italian Somaliland.

(7) A protocol providing that tariffs for imports from the other member-countries into Algeria and the French Overseas Departments would be regulated in due course.

(8) A protocol on oil products allowing member countries to maintain their Customs duties on such products vis-a-vis other member-countries for a period of six years.

(9) A protocol confirming that the Netherlands would ratify the Treaty only in respect of its European territory and Dutch New Guinea.

(10) A protocol allowing West Germany to import certain quantities of bananas below the common Customs tariff.

(11) A protocol containing special provisions for the import of coffee into Italy and the Benelux countries.

(12) A special declaration on Berlin was annexed to the Treaty, reading as follows: 'The Governments of Belgium, West Germany France, Italy, Luxembourg, and the Netherlands, having regard to the special position of Berlin and the need for the free world to support it, and wishing to reaffirm their association with the population of Berlin, will support within the Community all measures required to ease the economic and social situation of the city, to further its reconstruction, and to secure its economic stability'.

(13) Seven lists covering the items for which special maximum levels would be provided in the common Customs tariff were also annexed to the Treaty, together with a list dealing with agricultural products.

AGREEMENT ON COMMON INSTITUTIONS

Among the subsidiary conventions and protocols also signed at Rome on 25 March 1957 was an agreement laying down: (a) that there should be one Assembly common to the three European Communities (i.e. the Economic, Atomic Energy and Coal and Steel Communities); (b) that there should be a Common Court of Justice and (c) that the E.E.C. and Euratom should share a single Economic and Social Committee.

The Treaty of Rome Explained

SEAT OF INSTITUTIONS

A Treaty for the merger of the separate executives of the three Communities—the Commission of the E.E.C., the High Authority of the E.C.S.C., and the Commission of Euratom was signed by the member-countries on 8 April 1965 and this took place on 1 July 1967. The decision to merge the institutions was generally felt to be the prelude of the merger of the Communities themselves.

The main difficulty in agreeing on the merger had been to find a formula agreeable to Luxembourg which sought to maintain both its political status as a Capital of Europe and the material advantage of being the headquarters of the Coal and Steel Community. It was agreed, however, that Brussels, Luxembourg and Strasbourg would remain the working seats of the Community as long as no final choice of a single capital had been made. Brussels would be the seat of the new single Community Executive and the consultative bodies attached to it; meetings of the Council of Ministers would be held there except in April, June and October when Luxembourg would be the meeting-place.

Luxembourg would retain the Secretariat of the European Parliament and the Court of Justice and would also become the seat of other legal and quasi-legal bodies which might be set up including any body with legal jurisdiction in the patents field.

Strasbourg continued to be the meeting-place of the European Parliament.

Luxembourg became the seat of the financial institutions such as the European Investment Bank which was formerly in Brussels.

Under the Treaty certain other services would be transferred to or remain in Luxembourg such as the Community Statistical Offices which were divided between Brussels and Luxembourg, the joint publications office, services dealing with workers' health and the dissemination of scientific data from Euratom.

CHAPTER 3

The Institutions of the European Communities

We have mentioned earlier that, in April 1965, the Six member-countries signed a Treaty providing for the merger of the three executives of the European Coal and Steel Community, the Common Market and Euratom into one Commission and for a single Council of Ministers. Within two years of the merger it was envisaged that a single Treaty would replace the Paris and Rome Treaties.

The Institutions of the European Community are: The *Assembly* or European Parliament which consists of 142 members elected by the national Parliaments of the member-countries and comprising 36 members each from France, West Germany and Italy, 14 each from Belgium and the Netherlands and 6 from Luxembourg. The members are divided into four political groups—Christian Democrats, Socialists, Liberals and the European Democratic Union and the groups sit together in the Chamber irrespective of nationality. The election of members is determined by the national rules of each member-country, but it was agreed that the Assembly would later draft proposals providing for the introduction of a uniform electoral procedure in all member-countries. Plans were, in fact, drawn up in 1960 which envisaged members' direct election to the Assembly by universal suffrage.

The European Economic Community shares the Assembly with the European Coal and Steel Community and Euratom.

The Assembly meets once a year in October to discuss the annual reports of the Commissions of E.E.C. and Euratom and the High Authority of the E.C.S.C. It has the power to enforce the resignation of the Commissions and the High Authority, such decisions requiring a two-thirds majority of the votes cast as well as an ordinary majority of its total membership. The Assembly also discusses the Community budgets and is empowered to propose amendments. It has to be consulted on certain proposals of the Commissions, the High Authority and the Council of Ministers implementing essential principles of the Treaties; and is entitled to meet in extraordinary session if a majority of members demand it, or at the request of the Commissions, High Authority or of the Council of Ministers.

The Councils of Ministers are the only Community Institutions whose members directly represent the member governments. Representatives of the national governments sit in the Council and for major decisions the Foreign Ministers are generally present but the actual Minister of say, Agriculture or Transport or Economic Affairs is generally present for the subject under discussion. The Councils consist of one representative each from the Governments of the member-countries and it takes decisions in one of three ways: either unanimously, by simple majority, or by a weighted majority according to the various circumstances laid down in the Treaties. The unanimity requirement applied particularly in the early stages of the Community's existence.

Decisions requiring a simple or a qualified majority are in most cases taken only on a proposal made by the Commissions or High Authority and generally any such proposal would not be amended by the Council except by unanimous vote. (This provision was aimed at conferring great responsibility upon the Commissions and safeguarding the stability of their activities; this method has met with some difficulty largely because France and the E.E.C. Commission clashed over the Common Agricultural Policy which is discussed in some detail in Chapter 5). The role of the E.C.S.C. Council of Ministers was mainly limited to giving an opinion before the High Authority takes decisions; on certain fundamental questions, however, the approval of the Council is required before decisions become binding. The E.C.S.C. Council's decisions were mainly taken by majority vote. For E.E.C. and Euratom the Councils of Ministers took the final policy decisions, but they did so only on the basis of proposals from the respective Commissions.

The Commissions of the E.E.C. and Euratom had nine members jointly appointed by the member-Governments for four-year terms and eligible for re-appointment. The members, chosen on the basis of their general capability, are completely independent and neither solicit nor accept instructions from their Governments and are, in fact, the senior members of the Community's Civil Service. No country can have more than two of its nationals on the Commission.

The Commissions were collegial bodies and take their decisions by simple majority vote. Their main tasks were to supervise the application of the Treaties, and of measures adopted within its framework; to take part in the shaping of Council and Assembly decisions by

The Institutions of the European Communities

making proposals to the Council, which the latter could not amend, except by unanimous vote; to formulate opinions and recommendations on matters within the scope of the Treaties; to take those decisions for which authority had been conferred upon them; and to publish annually a general report on the activities of the E.E.C. and Euratom.

The *High Authority* of the Coal and Steel Community was composed of nine members appointed for six years, and could not include more than two members of the same nationality and it was 'responsible for assuring the fulfilment of the purposes stated in the Treaty.' Its members exercised their functions in complete independence in the general interests of the Community, and neither solicited nor accepted instructions from any Government or from any organisation; they were forbidden to exercise any business or professional activities, paid or unpaid, or to acquire or hold, directly or indirectly, any interest in any business related to coal and steel during their term of office, or for a period of three years thereafter.

Eight members of the High Authority were appointed by the Governments of the member-states by agreement among themselves, and these eight elected the ninth member by a simple majority. The members designated remained in office for six years. One-third of the members were re-elected every two years. The President and Vice-President of the High Authority were elected for two years, from among the members of the High Authority, and were eligible for re-election. The High Authority acted by majority vote.

The various means by which the Council of Ministers, and the Commission guide the work of the Community are defined as follows:

(a) *regulations*, which are compulsory and directly applicable to any member-state;

(b) *directives*, which are binding on the recipient State in respect of the result to be attained, but allowing it to choose ways and means of achieving that end;

(c) *decisions*, which are obligatory on the parties concerned; and

(d) *recommendations and opinions*, which have no binding force.

(Of the millions of words that have been written and spoken about the Community considerable comment has been made, and sometimes banner headlines printed, concerning ideas put forward under (d) *recommendations and opinions* which have subsequently been ignored and forgotten. This has sometimes led to some confusion in the public's mind).

The new Commission combining the institutions of the E.E.C., E.C.S.C. and Euratom) which took office on 1 July 1967 consisted of 14 members — three each from France, West Germany and Italy, two each from the Netherlands and Belgium and one from Luxembourg. When the Communities themselves are merged, or on 1 July 1970 at the latest, the number of members will be reduced to nine.

The Court of Justice, like the Assembly, is common to the three Communities and superseded the then existing Court of Justice of the European Coal and Steel Community. It consists of seven members jointly appointed by the member-Governments, holding office for six years and eligible for re-appointment. There are also two Advocates-General.

The functions of the Court are to safeguard the law in the interpretation and application of the Treaties, to decide on the legality of decisions of the Council of Ministers or the Commission, and to determine violations of the Treaties. Actions can be brought before the Court either by a member-country, or by the Councils of Ministers, or by the Commission, or by any person or legal entity affected by a decision of the Community. Action is based on the contention that the Councils or the Commission were not empowered to take a decision; have violated essential rules of procedure; have violated a Treaty or any rule implementing it; or have abused their discretionary powers. In addition *the Economic and Social Committee* is common to the Economic Community and Euratom and consists of representatives of all sections of economic and social life, such as employers' organisations, trade unions, and similar bodies. Its members, appointed for four years by a unanimous decision of the Councils of Ministers, are drawn from the member-countries in the following numbers: France, Italy, and West Germany, 24 each; Belgium and the Netherlands, 12 each; Luxembourg, 5, making a total of 101 members.

The Committee assists the Councils of Ministers and the Commissions in an advisory capacity, and has to be consulted in those cases specifically laid down in the Treaty. *The Consultative Committee* with 51 members carries out similar tasks for the E.C.S.C.

The Scientific and Technical Committee This body assists the Euratom Commission in an advisory capacity and consists of 20 members. In addition there are a number of other consultative bodies which aid the Community's work such as the Monetary Committee,

The Institutions of the European Communities

the Short and Medium-term Economic Policy Committees, the Committee of Central Bank Governors, the Budgetary Policy Committee, the Transport Committee, the Administrative Commission for the Social Security of Migrant Workers and the Nuclear Research Consultative Committee.

The Structure and Development of the Common Market

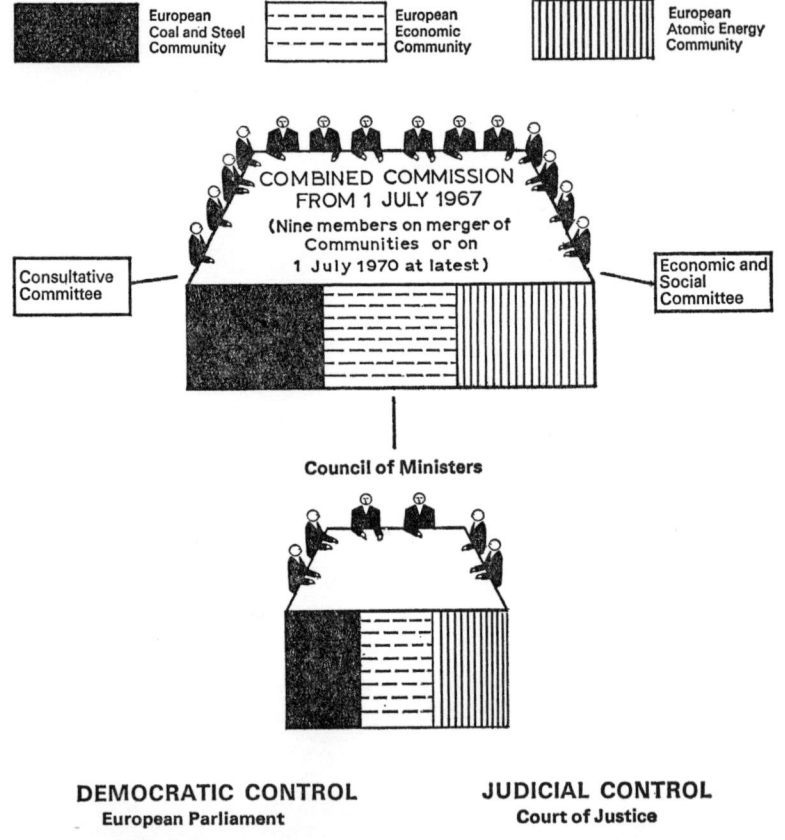

CHAPTER 4

The Tariff Structure of the Common Market

The first task of the Treaty of Rome was to set up the Customs Union. Its chapter on this lays down the principles, firstly, for the elimination of customs duties as between the member-states and, secondly, for the establishment of a common customs tariff for everything they buy from outside the Common Market.

For all practical purposes, 1968 can be regarded as the year for the final completion of the Customs Union of the Six members of the European Economic Community. Leaving aside the associate countries, Greece and Turkey whose moves towards full participation in the Customs Union provisions of the Community are spread over a longer period and the other Associated Territories, the European Economic Community will, by mid 1968, enjoy complete free trade within its own frontiers and will be protected by the common external tariff against all countries which have not signed the Treaty of Rome or treaties of association.

The table on p. 44 shows the dates on which the progressive changes in both the internal and external tariffs were originally planned and the dates on which they were actually implemented by the accelerated stages of the transitional periods.

With the free trade within the Common Market fully established by mid-1968 the pre-Common Market tariffs of the Common Market countries towards one another become a matter for history rather than for economic research.

It is, therefore, with the common external tariff of the Six that we are concerned in this chapter.

The Treaty lays down that, with a few exceptions, the duties under the common customs tariff should be at the level of the arithmetical average of the individual duties applicable in the four customs territories covered by the Community (Germany, France, Italy and Benelux).

In practice, the common external tariff is higher and more restrictive than the average incidence of the 1957 tariffs. A weighted

		Moves in Internal Tariffs for Common Market Countries trading with one another.		Moves towards Common External Tariffs for Common Market Countries trade with other countries.	
		Per cent of national tariffs laid down in the original planned transitional period.	Actual per cent of national tariffs applied under the accelerated time table for the transitional period	Per cent alignment of national tariffs towards the common external tariff—planned.	Per cent alignment of tariffs—made.
	Treaty came into force 1 January 1958				
Stage 1	1959 1 January	90%	90%		
	1960 1 July	80%	80%		
	1961 1 January	—	70%		
Stage 2	1962 1 January	70%	60%	30%*	30%*
	1 July	—	50%		
	1963 1 July	60%	40%		
	1964 —	—	—		
	1965 1 January	50%	30%		
Stage 3†	1966 1 January	40%	20%	30%	30% Common external tariff effective.
	1967 1 July	—	15%		
	1968 1 July	—	nil		
	1969				
	1970				

†In Stage 3 remaining duties were due to be removed at the latest by 1 January 1970.

*Where the difference between the national and the common tariff was 15 per cent or less the common tariff was adopted at the end of Stage 1.

average would have been lower than an arithmetical average because Germany and Benelux, both low tariff territories, accounted together for 60 per cent of the imports of the Six.

Moreover, the method used in fixing the levels of the common external tariff was deliberately weighted the other way by means of the device of using levels based upon the 'legal' or authorised import tariffs instead of the lower rates that were actually being applied for French import duties for certain items for the purpose of calculating the arithmetical averages. The items for which this device was used are those in List *A* of the Treaty. For example, France's import tariff for plastic materials on the basis of chemical derivatives of cellulose (ex B.N.39.03) was mainly 20 per cent. For the purpose of calculating the arithmetical average of the common external tariff for this item, List *A* fixes 30 per cent as the duty to be taken into account for France. For pianos the French import duty of 24·4 per cent became 30 per cent in List *A* for the purpose of increasing the average of the common external tariff. This device for inflating the

The Tariff Structure of the Common Market

arithmetical averages was used for some 50 items of chemical, paper, textile and engineering products.

A second device (Article 19 paragraph 3a) covered a wide range of chemical products which allowed the so-called average to be inflated by raising certain Benelux tariffs not exceeding 3 per cent to 12 per cent so as to allow an upper limit of 25 per cent for the common tariff on these items.

Both these devices could be said to have been contrived to give France a higher degree of protection than she would otherwise have enjoyed under a strictly calculated arithmetical average. They would also be in Britain's favour as members of the Common Market because in some of the items in question the United Kingdom Tariff is 33 per cent and the reductions to bring Britain in line with the common external tariff are less than they would otherwise have been.

Over the spectrum of the common external tariff of the European Economic Community, as might reasonably be expected from any system based on averages, the rates of duty are fairly consistent. Rates of less than 10 per cent or more than 20 per cent are the exceptions, for industrial goods. There is an absence of such tariff peaks as appear in the United Kingdom scales as are due to the high level of duties on synthetic and artificial silk; and on other goods which fell under the original Safeguarding of Industries legislation of 1921.

Certain exceptions to the general principle of fixing the tariff levels were permitted: (a) on a certain number of commodities, fixed duties would replace the arithmetical average (some of these were laid down specifically in the Treaty, others were settled by negotiation between the member-countries during the first stage); (b) in the case of a wide range of raw materials, the common tariff would not exceed three per cent; (c) in the case of a wide range of semi-manufactured goods it would not exceed 10 per cent; (d) in the case of a range of inorganic chemical products, it would not exceed 15 per cent; (e) in the case of a range of organic chemical products, dyestuffs, and artificial fibres it would not exceed 25 per cent; (f) a member-country finding itself in special difficulties could be authorised by the Commission to delay the reduction or increase of certain tariff items for a limited period, but this would only apply to items which represented not more than 5 per cent of the total value of that member- country's imports from non-Community countries.

Member-countries might be permitted by the Community to import at tariff rates below those of the common tariff, or duty free, certain goods up to a fixed quota in the following cases: (a) if the supply of the member-country concerned was traditionally dependent to a considerable extent on imports from non-Community countries, and if production within the Community was insufficient to cover that country's requirements; (b) if any change in the sources of supply, or an insufficient supply within the Community, involved serious disadvantage to the manufacturing industries of the member-country concerned; (c) if the quantity of imports under this exemption was not so large as to cause the risk of a diversion of economic activities to the member-country concerned (i.e. because of its lower tariffs) to the disadvantage of other member-countries; (d) if, in the case of food products, such imports would not result in a serious disturbance of the market.

Rates in the common Customs tariff can be altered or suspended either as a result of negotiations with non-Community countries in return for concessions by those countries, or because the Community considers such action necessary for reasons of its own economic policy.

The adjoining Table shows, for a representative list of industrial goods the E.E.C. External Tariff, and for purposes of comparison, the United Kingdom full rates; and the Commonwealth Preference rates, most of which now apply equally to imports from the other Efta countries because all tariffs in Efta have been eliminated.

This table also shows the Quantity or Value of United Kingdom imports and the respective proportions of those imports which come in under the full rates or duty free as of Commonwealth or Efta origin.

The European Economic Community is, of course, a member of GATT (General Agreement on Tariffs and Trade) and in the nineteen years of GATT's existence probably the most significant landmark was agreement on the 'Kennedy Round' in May 1967. GATT came into being 'to seek a world trading system based on non-discrimination and aimed at higher living standards to be achieved through fair, full and free exchange of goods and services'.

Forty-nine countries took part in the Kennedy Round negotiations and it is interesting to note that member-states of the E.E.C. negotiated as one. These countries represented 80 per cent of world trade and as a result of these protracted discussions which originated with the passing of the U.S. Trade Expansion Act 1962, tariff cuts averaging 35 per cent and in some cases reaching 50 per cent have been agreed on industrial goods. The timing of the cuts varies between states but the rough plan is to reduce by five equal instalments ending on 1 January 1972. This procedure will be adopted by the United

The Tariff Structure of the Common Market

States but the E.E.C., United Kingdom, Sweden and Switzerland will reduce by two-fifths on 1 July 1968 followed by further instalments on 1 January 1970, 1971 and 1972. By the summer of 1968 therefore 40 per cent of the tariff cuts will have taken place under the Kennedy Round for intra-European trade.

Apart from the material advantages the real importance of the Kennedy Round to E.E.C. was that it demonstrated that the Community could negotiate as a single unit with the rest of the world on vital economic matters. Lengthy bargaining took place between the Six before arriving in Geneva for the Kennedy Round and the effect of the tariff cuts will be felt over a long period to come and although it allows for greater competition this should also lead to greater efficiency. The tariff-cutting spread over the period to 1972 will provide the economies of all the trading countries with a stimulus not unlike that which the E.E.C. have received from reduction of duties within the Community.

The following are some of the most important tariff changes in the Common External Tariff of the European Economic Community arising from the Kennedy Round:

Product	Present Tariff per cent	1972 Tariff per cent
Motor Cars and Parts	22	11
Aircraft Engines and Parts	10–15	5–7$\frac{1}{2}$
Textile Machinery	8–15	4–7$\frac{1}{2}$
Photographic and Cine Equipment	12–18	7–13
Rubber Belting, Tyres, etc.	12–18	6–10
Hand Tools	9–14	5–9
Agricultural and Horticultural Machinery	9–10	4–7$\frac{1}{2}$
Leather	6–10	3–8
Mechanical Handling Equipment	8–11	4–9
Furniture	17	8$\frac{1}{2}$
Cigarettes	180	90
Whisky, Gin and Beer		One-fifth reduction

The average depth of the cut is 36% on £603 million worth of dutiable exports to the Common Market.

TARIFF LEVELS

	E.E.C. Common External	U.K. Full	U.K. Efta and Preferences
BASE METALS			
Iron and Steel	%	%	
Blooms and Billets	10	10	Free
Iron and Steel coils for re-rolling	10	10	Free
Iron and Steel Wire rod	10	10	Free
Iron and Steel Bars and Rods	10	10	Free
Angles of Iron and Steel	10	10	Free
Universals over 4·75m.	10	10	Free
Plates 3–4·75m.	10	10	Free
Plates under 3m.	10	10	Free
Other coated Iron and Steel Plates under 3m.	10	10	Free
Hoop and Strip	10	10	Free
Iron and Steel Wire	10	10	Free
Weldless Tubes and Pipes	14	20	Free
Welded Tubes and Pipes	14	20	Free
Tube and Pipe Fittings	14	$17\frac{1}{2}$	Free
Non Ferrous Metals			
Copper, unwrought	Free	Free	Free
Nickel, unwrought	Free	Free	Free
Aluminium, unwrought	10	Free	Free
Lead, unwrought	6	7s. 6d. ton	Free
Zinc, unwrought	7	30s. 0d. ton	Free
CHEMICALS AND CHEMICAL PRODUCTS			
Mineral and Chemical Fertilisers			
Nitrogenous	10	Free—$33\frac{1}{3}$	Free
Phosphatic	6	$17\frac{1}{2}$	Free
Potassic	0–3	Free	Free
Paints and Varnishes	9–20	2s. 6d. gal.	2s. 6d. gal.
Synthetic Organic Dyestuffs	17–20	10–$33\frac{1}{3}$	Free
Soaps	19	15–25	Free
Surface-acting Washing preps.	17	Free–10	Free
Pharmaceutical Products.			
Medicaments	17–34	10	Free
Insecticides,	8–15	10	Free
PULP AND PAPER			
Paper			
Newsprint	7	Free	Free
Other Printing and Writing Paper	15–18	$16\frac{2}{3}$	Free
Kraft Paper and Paperboard	18	15	Free
Machine made Paper and Paperboard	18	$16\frac{2}{3}$	Free
Fibre boards and Building boards	15	20	Free

The Tariff Structure of the Common Market	49

U.K. IMPORTS

tons	% from E.E.C.	% from Efta	% from Commonwealth	% from Rest of World
	25	36	11	28
	45	55	—	—
	32	62	1	5
	60	17	—	23
	7	82	—	11
	35	39	—	26
	81	16	—	3
	37	11	20	32
	81	7	—	12
	26	46	1	27
	55	17	—	28
	50	21	—	29
	26	20	—	54
	7	2	47	44
	1	20	54	25
	3	23	53	21
	3	—	90	7
	5	3	60	32
	92	1	—	7
	100	—	—	—
	53	—	—	47
	39	8	19	34
	44	43	—	13
	34	—	—	66
	44	11	6	39
	46	23	2	29
	65	—	—	35
	—	37	57	6
	6	66	20	8
	—	45	20	35
	11	71	8	10
	4	72	12	12

TARIFF LEVELS

	E.E.C. Common External	U.K. Full	U.K. Efta and Preference
PULP AND PAPER contd.	%	%	%
Pulp			
Mechanical Wood Pulp	6	Free	Free
Chemical Wood Pulp Diss. grade	6	Free	Free
Sulphate Wood Pulp	6	Free	Free
Sulphite Wood Pulp	6	Free	Free
FACTORY PLANT AND EQUIPMENT			
Industrial Machinery			
Power Gen. M/c other than electric	14	$17\frac{1}{2}$	Free
Heating and Cooling Equipment	11–13	15	Free
Pumps and Centrifuges	10–18	$15–17\frac{1}{2}$	Free
Production Machinery			
Paper and Pulp Machinery	12–14	$17\frac{1}{2}$	Free
Textile Machinery	10–14	15–20	Free
Machine Tools for Metal working	6–12	10	Free
Printing and Bookbinding M/c	6–14	$15–17\frac{1}{2}$	Free
Construction and Mining Machinery	9–15	15	Free
Food Processing M/c	13	$12\frac{1}{2}–17\frac{1}{2}$	Free
Engineering Supplies			
Grinding and Polishing Wheels and stones	10	$10–17\frac{1}{2}$	Free
Abrasive Cloths and Paper	11	10–20	Free
Refractory Products (not construction)	12–18	$10–33\frac{1}{3}$	Free
Manufactures of Asbestos	20	10–20	Free
Ball Bearings	18	20	Free
Rubber Belting	15	10	Free
Leather Belting	10	15	Free
ELECTRICAL PLANT			
Electric Power M/c	12–17	$10–17\frac{1}{2}$	Free
Apparatus for Elec. Circuits	16	20	Free
Electrical Equipment			
Insulated Wire and Cable	17	20	Free
Electric Lamps	15–18	$20–33\frac{1}{3}$	Free
Thermionic Valves & Tubes, Transistors	16–20	$33\frac{1}{3}$	Free
Batteries and Accumulators	17–20	$15–33\frac{1}{3}$	Free
Electrical Measuring and Control. Instruments	15	$33\frac{1}{3}–50$	Free
Automotive Elec. Equipment	14–22	30	Free–20
Electro-Mech. Hand Tools	14	$17\frac{1}{2}$	Free
TRANSPORT EQUIPMENT			
Passenger Motor Cars	29	30	20
Lorries and Trucks	28	30	20
Bodies and Parts of Motor Vehicles	19	30	20

The Tariff Structure of the Common Market 51

U.K. IMPORTS

	% from E.E.C.	% from Efta	% from Commonwealth	% from Rest of World
	—	85	9	6
	—	40	34	26
	—	68	11	21
	1	71	14	14
	34	11	5	50
	39	25	8	28
	31	26	2	41
	45	26	5	24
	46	24	3	27
	50	15	—	35
	60	11	—	29
	20	3	2	75
	58	17	2	23
	*	*	*	*
	*	*	*	*
	*	*	*	*
	*	*	*	*
	31	20	—	49
	*	*	*	*
	*	*	*	*
	33	18	4	45
	30	10	3	67
	38	12	—	50
	68	2	4	26
	40	5	2	53
	*	*	*	*
	24	13	7	56
	31	2	3	64
	42	14	—	44
	83	10	2	5
	82	3	—	15
	62	2	1	35

*Breakdown figure not available from the same source.

The Structure and Development of the Common Market

	TARIFF LEVELS		
	E.E.C. Common External	U.K. Full	U.K. Efta and Preference
TRANSPORT EQUIPMENT contd.	%	%	%
Motor Cycles	26	20	20
Bicycles	21	20	Free
Tractors, other than Road	12–20	20	Free
MECHANICAL HANDLING EQUIPMENT			
Mech. Handling M/c	14	15	Free
PHOTOGRAPHIC & OPTICAL GOODS, SCIENTIFIC INSTRUMENTS & SUPPLIES			
Binoculars, Microscopes, etc.	15–20	50	Free
Photographic Cameras	18	40–50	Free
Cine Cameras and Projectors	16–19	33⅓–50	Free
Medical Instruments, n.e.s.	16	20–50	Free
Electro-Medical Apparat.	16	20–50	Free
PLASTICS			
Products of Condensation	15–22	10–33⅓	Free
Products of Polymerisation	19–23	2s. 6d. gal.	Free
Regen. and Deriv. of Cellulose	19–23	20–33⅓	Free
Plastic Manufactures	17–23	20–33⅓	Free–22
OFFICE EQUIPMENT			
Typewriters	16	20	Free
Calculating and Accounting Machines	11–14	10–17½	Free
Statistical Machines, Card or Tape	11	17½	Free
Other Office Machines	15	10–17½	Free
TOOLS AND IMPLEMENTS			
Tools for Hand and Machine use	12–16	15–17½	Free
TEXTILES AND CLOTHING			
Cotton Fabrics, Woven Grey not merc.	15	17½	Free
Cotton Fabrics, Woven other than Grey	15	17½	Free
Woollen Fabrics, Woven	16–20	17½	Free
Linen Fabrics, Woven	21	17½	Free
Synthetic Fibre Fabrics, Woven	21	24–80	⅝ of full rate
Artificial Silk Fabrics, Woven	20	24–80	Free
Knitted Fabrics	16–20	22–33⅓	⅝ of full rate
Lace, Embroidery, Ribbons	23	25	Free
Clothing of Textile Fabrics not knitted	20	22–33⅓	20–30
Clothing, knitted	21	20	Free
Footwear	20	10–20	Free

The Tariff Structure of the Common Market 53

U.K. IMPORTS

% from E E.C.	% from Efta	% from Commonwealth	% from Rest of World.
58	—	—	42
66	10	—	24
49	2	8	41
50	20	3	27
33	6	7	54
27	7	5	61
20	23	—	57
27	12	6	55
61	15	—	24
45	8	14	33
47	8	5	40
20	5	6	69
36	15	12	37
79	6	3	12
38	23	2	37
50	1	1	48
17	4	—	79
30	27	5	38
—	3	56	41
46	9	24	21
67	6	7	20
31	5	3	61
53	13	4	30
64	10	2	24
17	15	52	16
20	52	10	18
14	9	63	14
21	12	56	11
36	5	29	30

TARIFF LEVELS

	E.E.C. Common External	U.K. Full.	U.K. Efta and Preference
HOUSEHOLD AND CONSUMER DURABLES	%	%	%
Domestic Electric Appliances	19	17½	Free
Sewing Machines	12	15	Free
Glass Tableware	24	30	Free
Pottery	27	5	Free
Furniture	18	20	Free
MISCELLANEOUS METAL MANUFACTURES			
Cutlery	16–17	20	Free
Hand Tools	16	15–33⅓	Free
Nails, etc.	16	20	Free
Nuts and Bolts	16	20	Free
Locks	17	20	Free
Safes	17	15	Free
Chains	16	25–33⅓	Free
Springs	17	20	Free
TELEVISION AND RADIO			
Television Receivers	22	20	Free
Radio Receivers	22	20	Free
MISCELLANEOUS MANUFACTURES			
Watches	13	33⅓	22 (Free from E
Gramophones, Tape Recorders	19	10–20	Free–22
Gramophone Records, Tapes	17	15	10
Pianos and other String Musical Instruments	18–22	33⅓	22
Toys and Games	19–25	25	Free
Pens, Pencils and Fountain Pens	16	20	Free

Because of the large number of sub-divisions, particularly in the U.K. Customs Tar figures are approximate. Where possible the rate quoted is that of the items with the import totals. For textiles and clothing generally the rates quoted are those cover natural fibres, e.g. cotton, wool etc. and not those containing man-made fibres.

Sources: Common External Tariff of E.E.C., U.K. Customs Tariff, Commodity O.E.C.D.

The Tariff Structure of the Common Market 55

U.K. IMPORTS

% from E.E.C.	% from Efta	% from Commonwealth	% from Rest of World
51	12	16	21
34	6	25	35
41	18	7	34
50	16	—	34
22	26	—	52
35	10	34	21
*	*	*	*
50	37	—	13
18	12	—	70
*	*	*	*
*	*	*	*
*	*	*	*
*	*	*	*
63	10	—	27
25	7	37	31
5	85	1	9
33	27	—	40
18	2	—	80
*	*	*	*
11	2	42	45
19	5	8	68

down figures not available from the same source.

CHAPTER 5

Agriculture

By 1 July 1968 the European Economic Community will have put into effect a common farm policy, centrally financed from a single fund. This policy involves:
(a)   common marketing policies with free trade throughout the Community and common price levels for all major products.
(b)   a common policy for external trade, replacing the previous complex and varying national structures of tariffs, quotas and minimum prices by a single Community system of variable import levies and minimum import prices and tariffs, and
(c)   a common policy to raise the efficiency of Community farming.

Since 1962 the common agricultural policy has been introduced by stages, and it now covers approximately 85 per cent of the Community's total farm output, including grains, rice, pigmeat, beef and veal, eggs and poultry, milk and dairy products, fruit and vegetables, wine, sugar and vegetable fats and oils. Other products still to be brought under the common farm policy are tobacco, hops, flowering bulbs and fish. The common policy has been adapted to the particular requirements of the various product groups; in some cases, such as grains, it involves considerable market intervention; in others, such as wine, it is applied mainly through the enforcement of quality standards.

The task of agreeing a common policy for agricultural products has been long and at times tortuous. It has involved several 'crises' and on occasions the clock has had to be put back so that 'deadlines' could be met. Agricultural products were specifically mentioned in the Treaty of Rome (see page 21) and the landmarks in progress towards the Common Agricultural Policy are:

1960: The first proposals by the E.E.C. Commission for a common agricultural policy were placed before the Council of Ministers.

14 January 1962: The Council of Ministers agreed the fundamental outline of a time-table to implement the policy and also agreed on

Agriculture

establishing marketing organisations for grains, pigmeat, etc.

30 July 1962: The marketing organisations for grain etc. were set up but agreement was not reached on prices.

29 July 1963: President de Gaulle threatened severe consequences for the European Economic Community if agreement was not reached on the remaining farm organisations and the Agricultural Fund by December 1963.

23 December 1963: Agreement was reached on the majority of marketing organisations and the broad rules of the Agricultural Fund.

15 December 1964: West Germany agreed to common grain prices. Earlier President de Gaulle had threatened to boycott the E.E.C. if agreement was not reached.

1 July 1965: France withdrew from E.E.C. working committees ostensibly because of disagreements on implementation of Agricultural Fund.

31 January 1966: Agreement reached with France whose representatives returned to the conference table, and work restarted on negotiating a common agricultural policy and industrial customs union.

11 May 1966: Agreement was reached on the Agricultural Fund and for completing the agricultural common market by 1 July 1968 subject to further agreement on meat, milk, fruit and vegetables as well as on foreign trade policies, notably in the Kennedy Round.

24 July 1966: Final details of the E.E.C. Common Agricultural Policy agreed.

A pamphlet published in November 1966 by the National Farmers' Union of London called 'British Agriculture and the Common Market' opens with the following paragraph:

'The agreements concluded by the six member-countries of the European Economic Community at their Council sessions in July 1966 mark the virtual completion of the framework of the common agricultural policy; over 85 per cent of farm produce is now covered by marketing organisations of one sort or another'

and it goes on in a later chapter:

'It can be accepted that the agricultural objectives of the Rome Treaty are broadly similar to those of the British Agriculture Acts. These acts aim at the maintenance of a stable, efficient and prosperous agricultural industry: the principle objectives for agriculture in the Rome Treaty are to increase productivity, to secure a fair standard of living for the farming population, to stabilise markets, to guarantee regular supplies and to ensure prices for consumers. There is, however, a wide difference between the methods by which we seek to attain these objectives and those applied in the E.E.C.'s common agricultural policy'

The agreement for the first stage of a common agricultural policy for the E.E.C., which was adopted by the Council of Ministers on 14 January 1962, was signed by the French Foreign Minister, M. Couve de Murville, subject to the approval of the French Cabinet; this was given on 17 January, and the agreement was meant to come into force on 1 July 1962, but only became effective on 30 July.

THE ORIGINAL IDEA

Policy Objectives The main objectives of the common policy for agriculture were outlined as follows:

(a) to balance supply and demand within the Community and externally by influencing supply by such measures as more regional specialisation, stockpiling, and structural reforms, and increasing demand by improving the quality of products.

(b) to provide farmers with a fair income by structural and regional improvements, the consolidation of holdings, electricity supplies, better transport and farming methods, information services, and education.

(c) to stabilise the market by protecting farmers from speculative price fluctuations while not insulating them from the influence of long-term movements in world markets.

(d) to ensure equitable supplies to consumers by enabling the processing industries to find external outlets at reasonable or competitive prices, and by preventing prices from being fixed on the basis of marginal production costs.

Products The regulations adopted by the Ministers applied to grain, pigmeat, eggs, poultry, fruit and vegetables, and wine. Fundamental decisions were also taken on the remaining major farm products (rice, beef and veal, dairy produce, and sugar) and a time-table was set for the publication of the full regulations on all these items in 1962. The products covered constituted over 46 per cent of the total inter-Community trade in farm produce.

Transition Period A seven year transition period pending the full implement of the common policy was fixed from 1 July 1962 to 31 December 1969, but a decision to shorten this period to six years could be taken in the third year.

Quality Standards Common quality standards would be progressively applied to fruit and vegetables marketed within the producing

Agriculture

member-states. The exporting member-states would exercise a quality control before products were exported to another member-country. A quality and grading certificate would accompany the goods, for checks by the importing country. Quantitative import restrictions would be abolished for graded products as follows:
(i) 'Super' Grade by 1 July 1962;
(ii) Grade I by 1 January 1964;
(iii) Grade II by 1 January 1966.

Harmonisation of Prices All prices, except for maize, were to be harmonised between an upper limit based on present German prices and a lower limit based on French price levels. Separate Community marketing organisations would be set up for wheat, coarse grains, sugar, and dairy produce, and there would be detailed intervention in the internal markets of the Community and external protection in the form of variable levies.

'Target' prices would be fixed annually for all these products, while for grain there would also be 'intervention' prices at which the marketing organisations would buy up supplies in order to guarantee to producers sales at a price as close as possible to the target price. Intervention prices would be target prices less a fixed percentage determined by each country between a minimum of 5 per cent and a maximum of 10 per cent. During the transition period adjustments would also be made where prices varied between different regions of member-states. 'Threshold' prices would be fixed as a sort of minimum import prices for grain, and would be the target price in the area of the greatest deficiency (i.e. with the largest imports) less the cost of transport from the point of entry.

For beef, pigmeat, poultry, and eggs there would be no target prices and no intervention prices and therefore no guaranteed prices and the system would be based on arrangements for protection from world markets. Minimum import prices would, however, be fixed as 'Sluice-gate' prices for pigmeat, eggs, and poultry—in the last two cases for trade with non-member-countries only, and in the case of pigmeat also for intra-Community trade.

Fruit, vegetables, and wine would be subject to supervision of quality. The common organisation would also introduce a minimum price system applicable to non-member-countries. Where the Community markets suffered from, or were threatened by, serious dislocation due to imports from non-member-countries, these imports might be suspended or subjected to a uniform compensatory levy charged on entry by all members.

Safeguard Clause An escape clause covered all products subject to the agricultural policy. Under the clause a member-country might close its frontiers immediately if imports from other member-states jeopardised its home production, but it must then immediately inform the E.E.C. Commission, which would decide within four days whether the closure was justified; there would be no appeal against its decisions except to the Court of Justice. In the case of cereals the time-limit would be extended from four to ten days, while for vegetables and fruit no country could take unilateral action and imports must be continued while the countries concerned appealed to the Commission. This last decision was taken after a lengthy debate during which the Italian delegation pointed out that their fruit and vegetables might rot at the German frontier if they were stopped while high-level decisions were taken on import suspension.

Management Committee Five Management Committees would be set up respectively for grain, pigmeat, eggs and poultry, fruit and vegetables, and wine. They would consist of representatives of the member-states presided over by a member of the Commission, who would have no vote.

Where appropriate, the Commission would consult the relevant committee on the draft of a proposed measure; decisions of the committee would be taken by qualified majority vote. The Commission would then decide on the measures to be taken and these would be immediately applicable. If they were at variance with the opinion given by the committee, the Commission might postpone their application for a maximum of one month, during which period the Council of Ministers, acting by qualified majority, could take a different decision. This procedure would apply to such matters as fixing the lump-sum figure which in effect determines the margin of Community preference, and to the arrangements to avoid diversion of trade in the grain sector.

The Agricultural Fund The common agricultural policy would be financed by a Guidance and Guarantee Fund whose revenue for the first three years would consist of financial contributions by member-states. The Fund's total revenues would be fixed annually by the Council and would consist in the first year as to 100 per cent from national budgets; in the second year as to 90 per cent would come from national budgets and 10 per cent from levies on imports from non-member countries; and in the third year as to 80 per cent from the national budgets and 20 per cent from such levies.

Before the end of the third year the Council would lay down rules to ensure gradual progress towards a common market system. When the common market stage was reached receipts from the levies on

Agriculture

imports from non-member countries would go to the Community and be used to cover Community expenditure.

The Fund would be used for three main functions:
(i) the subsidising of export from high-cost produces;
(ii) market intervention to ensure stability of prices;
(iii) to aid the modernisation of farms (e.g. by subsidising lower interest rates or by extending periods of credit), such help being exclusive of aid to farms from the Social Fund of the European Investment Bank.

Levies The system of levies (under which consumers in the importing country make up the difference between lower world prices of imports and those of the home agricultural market) would apply to the grain, pigmeat, eggs, and poultry sectors, for which it would supersede all national measures of protection at the frontier. During the preparatory stage a system of intra-Community levies would also be in force, but to maintain a preference for member-countries the amount of these levies for their products would be lower.

Grain The amount of the levies on soft wheat and coarse grains from non-member countries would be equal to the difference between the most favourable c.i.f. price for the product and the threshold price of the importing member-state. For intra-Community trade the amount thus calculated would be reduced by a lump sum.

For hard wheat the member-countries producing such wheat would fix the levies for it in accordance with a similar procedure, the threshold price being fixed at a level at least 5 per cent higher than that for soft wheat. The amount of the intra-Community levy in the case of a member-state not providing hard wheat would be the same as that imposed upon imports from non-member countries.

For a number of products of grain processing such as malt, gluten, bran, feeding-stuffs, etc. the levy would contain a first element corresponding to the price difference for the basic products and a second element to allow for the need to protect the processing industry; this latter portion would, however, be progressively reduced in the case of the intra-Community levies.

Animal Products For animal products such as pigmeat, poultry and eggs, the system of levies would be similar but not uniform because the present level of protection of the three products also differed, viz. the production of eggs was protected only by tariffs in all member-countries, pig breeding was often further protected by measures such as quotas, minimum prices etc. and the import of poultry was free except in France.

The levy for the three products would comprise three parts (1) an amount corresponding to the difference in the cost of feeding-stuffs; (2) an amount to replace the Customs duties in respect of both member and non-member countries (towards non-member-countries this amount would rise by 2 per cent annually until it reached a level of 7 per cent—the same duty therefore for the three products); (3) an amount to replace quota protection (this part could be applied anywhere for pigmeat but for the import of poultry only in France. It would take account of the difference between the average market prices in the importing and in the exporting member-country during a reference period).

After intensive negotiations within the Council of Ministers on the detailed regulations implementing the common agricultural policy, it was announced in Brussels on 2 June 1962 that full agreement had been reached and that the first stage of the common farm policy involving the creation of common marketing organisations for cereals, pigmeat, eggs, poultry, fruit and vegetables, and wine would come into operation on 30 July 1962.

Dr. Sicco Mansholt, Vice-President of the E.E.C. Commission and the member in charge of agriculture, gave details of the new policy at a press conference on 27 July 1962. Describing the entry into force of the common agricultural policy as an event 'of great importance not only for Europe but for the whole world,' Dr. Mansholt explained that the Commission would have to establish every day c.i.f. prices in the Community for the agricultural products involved, taking into account all the information coming in from the ports, from world markets, from the trade, and so on; it had to be able to take common decisions extremely quickly so that the policy could be put through. Although there would be unforeseen difficulties, Dr. Mansholt expressed confidence that in view of the co-operation already developed all problems could be solved. He added that he did not think there would be great changes in the first year because of the standstill of prices.

* * *

The next important step in establishing the Common Agricultural Policy was to obtain agreement on common cereal prices. This was achieved on 15 December 1964 after much indecision and disagreement. One of the principal points of issue was the wide difference between the prices of wheat in France and in West Germany, the official price payable to French farmers being much lower than that which German farmers were guaranteed by their Government; while the French Government was unwilling to agree to a marked upward revision of the wheat price for fear of possible inflationary effect, the West German Government objected to a sizeable reduction in the receipts of German farmers, which might have cost them the electoral support of the agricultural community.

France, moreover, having a substantial grain surplus, was concerned about finding additional export markets in other member-countries, especially West Germany, which hitherto had obtained a large part of her import requirements from overseas.

An important step towards a solution to the cereal price problem was a set of proposals presented by the E.E.C. Commission to the Council of Ministers in November 1963. These had been worked out by Dr. Mansholt and subsequently became known as the 'Mansholt Plan'. It was a modification of these proposals that was adopted by the Council of Ministers in December 1964.

The Mansholt Plan

The Council of Ministers would fix basic target prices for the whole Community for soft and hard wheat, rye, barley and maize, starting with the 1964–65 selling season. The target price for soft wheat (the most important single product) would be DM 425 (approximately £38. 12s 6d. per ton. Subsequently the Council would set the basic prices for each year's harvest by 1 August of the previous year.

During the Common Market's transition period the unfavourable effects of this once for all move on the income of farmers in certain member-countries would be fully compensated by appropriate financial aid from the Community. Starting in 1966, however, this aid would gradually be replaced by Community measures to improve farming efficiency and living standards. In addition to the basic target price, the proposals included a series of intervention or support prices based on selling prices in the main consuming areas after allowances had been made for transport costs. The plan also provided for the setting up of quality standards, rules for estimating monthly price variations and rules for fixing the threshold price in areas having no target prices.

The Commission's proposals meant a reduction of all grain prices in Germany by between 11 and 15 per cent; in Italy of wheat and rye prices by 11 per cent; and in Luxembourg by 16 per cent for wheat and 8 per cent for rye. Thus a loss of farm income would result in these countries.

For France there would be a rise in most grain prices—8 per cent for wheat, 16 per cent for barley, 1 per cent for maize; for Italy an increase of 23 per cent for maize and 15 per cent for barley; and for the Netherlands one of 6 per cent for wheat and 8 per cent for barley.

It was emphasised that whereas change in prices would be fully reflected in farmers' incomes, any calculation of their incidence on consumer prices would have to take into account processing and distribution costs; on this basis prices would only fall or rise by one third or one quarter of the actual increase or decrease in grain prices. Thus the overall rise in consumer prices for bread, pasta, pigmeat, eggs and poultry might reach 3 per cent in France, 5 per cent in the Netherlands and 1–2 per cent in Italy.

The estimated losses to farmers arising from the price changes would be as follows: Italy $65m; Luxembourg $900,000; West Germany $140m.

The aim of the Commission's proposals for wheat prices was to maintain the Common Market's import needs at about their 1956–57 to 1958–59 volume of 10,000,000 tons annually. It was specifically expected that the proposed increase in French prices would not encourage a serious increase in the amount of land under wheat. Discussions on the 'Mansholt Plan' took place from May 1964 onwards and it was not until after a meeting of the West German Cabinet in late November that Herr Schmücker, the West German Minister of Economic Affairs was able to inform the Council of Ministers on 1 December that his Government would accept a unified grain price, proposing DM 440 a ton for soft wheat against the DM 460 originally demanded by West Germany and the DM 425 envisaged in the Mansholt Plan. These proposals became the basis of the eventual agreement.

At the December 1964 meeting of the Council of Ministers it was also requested that the E.E.C. Commission should present proposals on how the common agricultural policy should be financed for the period 1965–1967 and that these proposals should be presented by 1 April 1965.

* * *

THE COMMISSION'S PROPOSALS

The Commission accordingly submitted its proposals to the Council. These covered not only the renewal of levies on agricultural goods but also proposed that both these levies and industrial import duties should be paid into the E.E.C. fund. *As these receipts represented enormous amounts and constituted the E.E.C.'s financial resources, the Commission proposed that the European Parliament should be strengthened by being given powers to determine the Community's revenue, and that it should also receive wider powers over the Community's budget.*

The Commission's proposals were grouped as follows:

Agriculture

(1) A new regulation on the financing of the common agricultural policy;
(2) Arrangements for replacing the financial contributions of member-countries by the Community's own resources;
(3) Amendments to Articles 201 and 203 of the Treaty.

The Commission considered that these proposals which were not confined to agricultural matters and were intended to make the Community financially autonomous, would mark an important and decisive step forward towards European integration, inasmuch as the Community would then have financial resources of its own and its expenditure would be governed by decisions taken at Community level, in which the European Parliament would play an important part.

Proposed New Agricultural Regulation

The Commission considered that the introduction of the single market system on 1 July 1967, would involve the common financing of refunds on agricultural exports to non-member countries and of measures to regulate markets under the common organisation, since such expenditure would be the financial consequence of agricultural policy decisions taken by the E.E.C. as a whole. Arrangements should therefore be made to enable the Guarantee Section of the Fund to finance measures other than those already provided for, should such measures be decided upon under the common organisation of markets.

The Commission also considered that, if they were to be regarded as the responsibility of the Community as a whole, the measures to be financed should be based, at the single market stage, on precise and comprehensive rules, particularly as regards commercial policy. Because refunds on exports to non-member countries, measures taken to regulate markets, and other measures would be financed in their entirety by the E.E.C., methods would have to be worked out of checking that expenditure conformed to Community rules.

According to the Commission's proposals, financing of the common agricultural policy through the European Agricultural Guidance and Guarantee Fund would be built up after 1 July 1965, in two stages:
(i) from 1 July 1965 to 30 June 1967 the transitional system provided for would be maintained; and
(ii) from 1 July 1967 the single market system would be in operation.

During the transitional period (i above) the contribution of the

Fund (Guarantee Section) would be fixed for 1965–66 at four-sixths of the eligible expenditures, and for 1966–67 at five-sixths.

The expenditure of the Fund would be covered by contributions determined according to the following scale:

	1965–66	1966–67
	Per cent	Per cent
Belgium	7·96	7·96
Germany	32·35	30·59
France	32·35	30·59
Italy	18	22
Luxembourg	0·22	0·22
Netherlands	9·12	8·64

At the single market state (ii above) the Fund (Guarantee Sections acting in accordance with Community rules, would finance refund) on exports to non-member-countries, measures taken to regulate markets, and other measures decided by the Council by a qualified majority on a proposal from the Commission. When the single agricultural market became effective, the proceeds of agricultural levies would automatically accrue to the Community. The Commission considered, however, that, in view of the degree of market integration attained by 1 July 1967, *it would be important that, with effect from that date, the proceeds from agricultural levies as well as puties on imports from non-member countries should accrue to the Community as revenue in its own right, since the place where the levies and duties would be collected and the place where imports would be consumed would be less likely to lie within the same member-country. The replacement of member-countries' financial contributions by the Community's own resources appeared desirable because, if the Community was to develop smoothly, the removal of obstacles to intra-Community trade could not be confined to agricultural produce. If there was to be a coherent economic policy, not only agricultural levies but also Customs duties on industrial products would have to be abolished on 1 July 1967.*

The Commission pointed out that a problem which confronted all Customs unions would arise in the Community: the place where levies and customs duties were collected would correspond less and less with the place at which the imported goods would be consumed, and the Commission had therefore made its proposals for financing of the common agricultural policy part of the whole financial and institutional balance of the E.E.C.

The Commission recalled that different scales were used to calculate the financial contributions of member-countries to the Community budget—there being one scale for the operation budget,

Agriculture

another for the Social Fund, and another for the Agricultural Fund. The Commission made estimates of the percentages of total expenditure for 1967 which each country would have to pay according to these different scales. These percentages or weighted scales were estimated to be: for Belgium 8·14 per cent; for Germany 29·88 per cent; for France 29·79 per cent; for Italy 22·88 per cent; for Luxembourg 0·21 per cent; and for the Netherlands 9·10 per cent.

Contributions for 1967 For the year 1967 the Commission proposed maintaining the weighted scale. The budget would be reckoned in two equal parts:
(i) During the first half-year on the basis of financial contributions from member-countries;
(ii) During the second half-year on the basis of the Community's own resources.

Member-countries would pay to the Community the agricultural levies and a part of the customs duties collected in their respective territories, the total amount of such payments being equal for each country to its contributions in the first half-year. The Commission would then note the percentage of the proceeds of levies and Customs duties left to each member-country.

Contributions in 1968–71 During the following four years (1968–71) the percentage of receipts remaining with the member-country would be reduced by one-fifth each year. In this way all the revenue from levies and Customs duties would accrue to the Community after 1 January 1972.

(If in 1967, for example, a country had to allocate 60 per cent of its total receipts from Customs and levies to the Community, that country would have to pay 68 per cent in 1968 (60 plus one-fifth of 40), 76 per cent in 1969, etc.)

Total Revenue and Expenditure, 1967 and Expenditure 1967 and 1968 Total revenue from levies and Customs duties was estimated at $2,300,000,000 per annum. The total expenditure that the Community would have to meet, if the Commission's proposals were adopted, was estimated at $1,237,000,000 for 1967 and $1,758,000,000 for 1968.

The Commission proposed a limited increase in the European Parliament's powers under Article 201 of the Treaty of Rome so that wider powers of control over the budget would be accompanied by wider powers to determine the Community's revenues.

Taking into account the ideas put forward by the Parliament itself on 12 May 1964, the Commission sought to introduce an arrangement effecting a certain balance between the powers of the Parliament, the Council of Ministers, and the Commission. It therefore proposed certain amendments to Article 203 of the Treaty dealing with Budget procedure, as follows:

(i) Any amendments made by the Parliament to the draft budget prepared by the Council would be deemed to have been approved unless the Council, within twenty days, modified them by a majority of five-sixths; if, however, the Council and the Commission agreed on changes to the Parliament's proposals, they could be adopted by a smaller majority of four-sixths.

(ii) The Commission shall study the conditions under which the financial contributions of member-states provided for in Article 200 may be replaced by Independent Community revenue.'

(iii) The Commission would submit proposals to the Council, which would refer them to the Assembly. The Council would take its decisions by unanimous vote, but a qualified majority would be sufficient if the Assembly had rendered an opinion supporting the Commission's proposals by a two-thirds majority of the votes cast constituting an absolute majority of its members. The provisions adopted by the Council would have to be approved by the member-countries according to their respective constitutional rules, until such time as the members of the Assembly were elected by direct universal suffrage.

(iv) The financial year should run from 1 January to 31 December, and the preliminary draft budget should be laid before the Council by the Commission not later than 15 September, of the year preceding that to which it referred. The Commission would at the same time send the preliminary draft to the Assembly, and the draft budget would be laid before the Assembly not later than 15 October.

The Commission considered that the new budget procedure would be a step towards full budgetary powers for the European Parliament, which it would exercise when elected by direct universal suffrage.

Dr. Hallstein, the President of the Commission, had informed the European Parliament, at its session of 22–26 March 1965, that the Commission intended to submit to the Council proposals on financing the Common Agricultural policy and the provision of independent revenue for the E.E.C. The Parliament adopted a resolution approving the principle that the proceeds of agricultural levies and duties on imports from non-member countries should accrue to the Community, but urged that the burdens should be fairly shared; it also expressed the view that the creation of independent revenue for the Community should be conditional upon transfer to the Parliament of power to fix revenue and expenditure.

The Netherlands States-General (Parliament) adopted on 16 June

1965, by an overwhelming majority, a resolution which emphasised: (a) the need for the common agricultural market and the common industrial market to come into effect at the same time; (b) the essential condition that, as the creation of the Common Market's own revenue resources necessitated a change in the Community's budgetary procedure, an effective sharing of the powers of decision and control with the European Parliament should be simultaneously introduced; (c) the desirability of a beginning being made in granting legislative powers and the right of veto to the Parliament; (d) that, to strengthen parliamentary democracy in the E.E.C., the holding of direct elections to the Parliament was urgent.

The E.E.C. Commission's scheme was considered by the Council of Ministers at a meeting in Brussels which opened on 28 June 1965, under the chairmanship of M. Couve de Murville, the French Foreign Minister.

M. Couve de Murville immediately rejected the Commission's proposals, maintaining that political conditions had been imposed by the Commission which were totally unacceptable to France, and that the sole question to be settled was the renewal of levies after the expiry of the existing agricultural finance regulations on 30 June.

THE CONSTITUTIONAL CRISIS

Dr. Luns, the Netherlands Foreign Minister, on the other hand strongly urged the adoption of the Commission's proposals, being supported by Dr. Schröder and Signor Fanfani, the West German and Italian Foreign Ministers. M. Spaak, however, expressed the view that the renewal of the agricultural finance regulations must be decided by 30 June as demanded by France, while the other points raised by the Commission could be dealt with at a later date.

Professor Hallstein, on behalf of the Commission, defended its proposals by reason of its authority to pursue economic integration under the Treaty and under subsequent Council regulations on agriculture. He nevertheless indicated the Commission's willingness to reconsider its proposals, but M. Couve de Murville refused to agree, although the other Foreign Ministers were in favour of continuing the debate.

Discussions of the Agriculture Ministers on 21 June, under the chairmanship of M. Pisani (France), on farm finance questions likewise remained indecisive; and after further talks by the Foreign Ministers on 30 June Herr Lahr (West German State Secretary for Foreign Affairs) stressed that the German delegation continued to insist on all the three aspects of the Community's policies—finance for the Agricultural Fund, direct revenues for the Community, and increased budgetary powers for the European Parliament—being decided together. M. Couve de Murville, in reply, gave a warning that if the 30 June deadline for deciding on the renewal of the financial regulations were not met, France would consider that formal commitments were no longer respected, and this would have serious consequences.

Although Dr. Hallstein, Signor Fanfani, Dr. Schröder, and Dr. Luns stressed their willingness to reach agreement and to continue the talks, another serious disagreement arose subsequently during discussions on the extent of the national contributions of member-countries to the financing of the common farm policy—the French delegation demanding a firm commitment for the period 1965–70, while the Italian delegation refused to accept such a commitment without obtaining a clearer picture of the burdens which it would involve for all the countries concerned.

Shortly after midnight on 1 July M. Couve de Murville declared that agreement was impossible and proposed that the Council should adjourn. In spite of suggestions that the clock be 'stopped' and that the Commission be asked to work out immediately a compromise proposal for further consideration, the discussion ended without result in the early hours of 2 July.

Following the temporary breakdown of the talks, the French Government announced on 5 July 1965, the withdrawal of its representatives from the Commission's working committees on agriculture, foreign relations, and the association agreement with Nigeria then under negotiation; the chief French Representative to the European Communities (M. Jean-Marc Boegner) was recalled to Paris on 6 July, and France boycotted a meeting of the Common Market representatives in Geneva on 6 July called to co-ordinate the tactics of the Six in the 'Kennedy Round' trade negotiations. M. Giscard d'Estaing failed to attend a meeting of Finance Ministers in Stresa in July and at the next meeting of the Council of Ministers on July 26–27 France was not represented—officials at the Quai d'Orsay defining the French boycott as the 'policy of the empty chair'.

Prior to this Council meeting, and in an effort to help solve the crisis, the Commission had published a memorandum on 22 July 1965, dealing with the problems which had caused the crisis. The Commission proposed in this memorandum that:

(a)   Independent revenue for the E.E.C. should be postponed until 1970, as 1967 was not acceptable to all member-countries;
(b)   Between 1967 and 1970 a compensation fund should be

Agriculture

created to redistribute, among member-countries, the duties collected at points of entry. The common external tariff would become effective from 1967 and redistribution of duties would be essential because the points of entry would not always be in the country of use or consumption;

(c) The existing system of financing farm policy would remain in effect until the time that the Agriculture Fund progressively took over the financing from member-countries;

(d) A decision on these proposals should be made by 1 November 1965;

(e) The new finance regulations should be linked to enforcement of common policies for sugar, fats and oils, fruit and vegetables, on which no agreement had so far been reached;

(f) A ceiling should be placed on the financial cost to Italy;

(g) when agreeing the final stages of the agricultural policy as from 1 July 1967, the complete elimination of Customs duties between member-countries and the introduction of the common external tariff on all goods entering the E.E.C. should be introduced on the same date.

The memorandum was discussed by the Council after M. Spaak had raised the question whether in France's absence the meeting was legally constituted. The Council decided that it would discuss the memorandum but left open the question whether it was to take material decisions.

During the autumn of 1965 much diplomatic activity took place in an effort to encourage France to return and take a full part in the Community's proceedings. On 30 November a further request by the 'Five' lead to discussions between Signor Colombo, President of the Council and M. Couve de Murville in Rome. Two days following the second ballot in the French presidential election the French Government accepted an invitation to meet the Council of Ministers in Luxembourg in January 1966 to try to reach a settlement.

The Council's Luxembourg meetings were devoted almost entirely to the discussion of the French requests concerning the non-application of majority decisions and the role of the Commission, a satisfactory solution of which the French Government had made a condition for resuming its active participation in the E.E.C.

It will be seen that 'procedures' and aspects of politics play a greater part in the Luxembourg Agreement than the subject of Agriculture but it was on the question of Agriculture that France took her political stand and therefore the subject must be included here.

Explaining the French objections to the principle of majority decisions, M. Couve de Murville said that in questions of vital interest only unanimous agreement was politically conceivable. Without pressing for an amendment of the Treaty the French Government therefore suggested a political agreement among the member-countries whereby the Council would abstain from deciding by majority vote if any member should so request it because of the vital importance of the question for his country.

The other members refused any formal settlement which would involve giving a member-country a permanent right to veto; they felt, however, that this was in practice largely a false problem, since unanimity would always be sought on major issues.

The solution eventually agreed upon was announced in a communique at the end of the second session on 29 January 1966, as follows:

(a) 'When issues very important to one or more member-countries are at stake, the members of the Council will try, within a reasonable time, to reach solutions which can be adopted by all members of the Council while respecting their mutual interests, and those of the Community, in accordance with Article 2 of the Treaty. (This article aims at approximating the economic policies of E.E.C. members to create a common market.)

(b) 'The French delegation considers that, when very important issues are at stake, discussion must be continued until unanimous agreement is reached.

(c) 'The six delegations note that there is a divergence of views on what should be done in the event of a failure to reach complete agreement.

(d) 'They consider that this divergence does not prevent the Community's work being resumed in accordance with normal procedure.'

Dealing with the role of the Commission and its relations with the Council, M. Couve de Murville put forward a list of ten points as a suggestion to assist subsequent discussion:

(1) The Commission should consult the member-Governments at the appropriate level before submitting proposals for Community action of particular importance to the Council.

(2) Commission proposals should not be made known to the European Parliament or the public before their submission to the Council.

(3) The executive powers granted to the Commission in any policy field should be precisely formulated, leaving no room for its discretion.

(4) Commission directives for Community policy should not

specify the detailed manner of their application by the member-states.

(5) The Council should reassert its prerogatives in diplomatic relations, particularly as regards accepting letters of credence.

(6) Approaches to the Commission by non-member-countries should be brought to the early attention of the Council.

(7) The Council should decide the nature and extent of the Community's relations with international organisations.

(8) Commission members should observe political neutrality in public statements.

(9) Community information policy should be a joint Council-Commission responsibility.

(10) The Council should exercise a closer control over the Commission's budget.

Following discussion of the French aide-memoire it was found that there were possibilities of agreement and, according to the communique, the Council adopted seven points for improving its relationship with the Commission. These were:

(1) It was desirable that the Commission, before adopting a proposal of particular importance, should, through the Permanent Representatives, make appropriate contacts with the Governments of the member-states, without this procedure affecting the right of initiative which the Commission derived from the Treaty.

(2) Proposals and all other official acts which the Commission addressed to the Council and the member-states should only be made public after the latter had formally taken cognizance of them and had the texts in their possession.

The *Official Gazette* should be arranged so that legislative acts having a binding force were published distinctly as such.

(3) The credentials of Head of Mission of non-member States accredited to the Community should be presented to the President of the Council and the President of the Commission, meeting together for this purpose.

(4) The Council and the Commission would inform each other rapidly and fully of any approaches relating to fundamental questions made to either institution by non-member States.

(5) Within the scope of the application of Article 162, the Council and the Commission would consult together on the advisability of, the procedure for, and the nature of any links which the Commission might establish, under Article 229 of the Treaty, with international organisations.

(6) Co-operation between the Council and the Commission on the Community's information policy, which had been examined by the Council on 24 September 1963, would be strengthened so that the programme of the Press and Information Service should be drawn up and carried out jointly, in accordance with procedures to be defined later and which might include an *ad hoc* body.

(7) Within the framework of the financial regulations for drawing up and putting into effect the Communities' budgets, the Council and the Commission would define methods of increasing the efficiency of control over the acceptance, authorisation, and execution of the Communities' expenditures.

It was provided that these points would be discussed between the Council of Ministers and the Commission under Article 162 of the Treaty.

At the last sitting on 29 January 1966 M. Couve de Murville put forward a tentative programme of work comprising, on the one hand, certain outstanding problems such as the budget, agricultural finance regulation, and the second alignment towards a common Customs tariff, and on the other hand the entry into force of the Treaty on the merger of the Executives and decisions on the composition of the new single Commission. During the discussion, reservations were expressed by other members on the principle of such a time-table, no decision being taken.

At a press conference after the end of the Council meeting on 29 January, Signor Colombo and M. Spaak made statements which indicated that the most drastic effects of the crisis within the Community had been overcome, and that the way had been opened for a resumption of French co-operation.

Signor Colombo said: 'We can say that the European Community is starting work again, and that is what is most important from the political point of view. We have reached some agreement, come to some understanding, and have defined certain practices, but the Treaty, with its rules and institutions remains intact. And it is according to these rules and through these institutions that the life of the Community will start again. We can only express the hope that crises like that which we have lived through in the second half of 1965 and the opening weeks of 1966 will not recur. . . .'

M. Spaak declared: 'One cannot say that all the difficulties have been overcome by any means, but we have succeeded in what we had to do. . . . As for majority voting, we are obliged to recognise that we are not entirely in agreement. But what is essential is that we recognise that the disagreement which continues does not hinder

Agriculture

France from coming back to Brussels, nor, therefore, the Community from resuming its activities.'

The E.E.C. Commission itself issued the following communique on 2 February 1966:

'The Commission is pleased that, after the Council meeting in Luxembourg, the Community can now resume its normal activities, both internal and external. There is a great deal of work to be done in the coming months, and many decisions must be taken, to make real progress towards economic union. The Commission is ready to hold consultations with the Council, in due course, in a spirit of co-operation and in accordance with Article 162 of the Treaty in order to make even closer the collaboration between itself and the Council.'

THE FINAL BREAKTHROUGH

After intense and closely argued negotiations extending over five months, from 28 February until dawn on 24 July 1966, the Ministers of Agriculture of the six E.E.C. member-countries, who were joined in the closing stages by the Foreign Ministers, agreed on the final details of the Community's common agricultural policy. Thereby culminating six years of difficult discussions.

The crisis in the E.E.C. had seriously retarded the implementation of the programme agreed in December 1964 but more rapid progress was made following the Luxembourg meetings of the Council of Ministers and the resumption of active participation by France in E.E.C. affairs.

At the first meeting of the Council of Ministers after the decision of France to return to the conference table all member-countries agreed that the target date for achieving a common agricultural policy would be 1 July 1967. This implied the fixing of common prices for all farm products, a free circulation of goods within the E.E.C., and the establishment of a common external tariff.

Six further meetings of the Council of Ministers took place between 7 March and 5 May, in an effort to agree on the proposals of the E.E.C. Commission for common price levels for milk, other dairy produce, beef and veal, sugar, rice, oilseeds and olive oil, which were presented to the Council by the Commission for consideration on 7 March 1966.

The Commission proposed the following prices as from the date of implementation of the establishment of a common price level and for the ensuing 12 months (in units of account, each unit being equivalent to one U.S. dollar):

	$ per 100 kg.
Milk (3·7 per cent fat content)—Target price	9·50
Butter—Intervention price	176·25
Threshold price	191·25
Cattle (on hoof, medium quality)—Guide price	66·25
Calves (on hoof, medium quality)—Guide price	89·50
Rice—Basic target price	18·12
Intervention price—France	12·30
Intervention price—Italy	12·00
Threshold price	17·78
Sugar—Common target price for white sugar	21·94
Intervention price for white sugar	20·84
Minimum price for sugar beet (per ton)	16·50
Oilseeds—Common norm price	18·60
Intervention price	17·40
Olive oil—Common norm price	111·00

The *target price* is the basic price determined in the Community region with the least adequate domestic supplies, i.e. that needing the largest imports; basic target prices apply to foodstuffs produced in only some member-countries, and common target prices to foodstuffs produced in all member-countries.

The *intervention price*, which should be as close as possible to the target price, is the one guaranteed to the producer.

The *threshold price*, fixed as a minimum import price, is the target price less the transport cost from the point of entry and that used for calculating the levy on imported supplies.

The *guide price*, applied to cattle, beef and veal, is a varying price according to standards, with minimum and maximum limits, and forms the basis for the calculation of Customs duties.

The *common norm price* is the measure used for calculating deficiency payments for certain products.

It was pointed out that the effect of applying common prices would render superfluous any levies or other duties on trade between member-countries and would achieve complete free trade in agricultural goods on the same date as for industrial goods. In making its proposals the Commission said that it took into account the relationship between the price of grain—already fixed—and those of other foodstuffs, the foreseeable trends of consumption and supply, and the need to encourage certain forms of food production, e.g. beef rather than milk, and also beef in preference to veal because of the world shortage of beef. The Commission estimated that the foreseeable effect of the shift from national price levels to common prices on the cost-of-living index would be as follows:

	per cent
Belgium	+0·4
Germany	-0·2
France	+0·67
Italy	-0·4
Netherlands	+1·0

As no comprehensive agreement on all the points involved in a common agricultural policy could be reached by the beginning of May the Ministers agreed at its meeting that it would be impossible to achieve the target date of 1 July 1967. The reason for the postponement was primarily that France declared that she could not accept the final removal of tariffs on industrial goods until the common agricultural market was completed. West Germany and the Netherlands thereupon proposed that 1 January 1968 should be the target date, but France then suggested that the end of 1968 would be early enough for the removal of industrial tariffs, pointing out that this would still be in advance of dates laid down in the Treaty of Rome for achieving a common market.

It was finally agreed at the meeting of Ministers that 1 July 1968 would be the date for the bringing into operation of the full common market in respect of both agricultural and industrial goods—i.e. eighteen months earlier than envisaged in the Treaty of Rome.

In addition, the following other important decisions for achieving the common agricultural policy were taken at this meeting, subject to agreement on all outstanding matters.

The free movement of agricultural produce would be achieved between 1 November 1966 and 1 July 1968, as follows:

(a) On 1 November 1966—establishing a common organisation of the market for olive oil and entry into force of the common price for this product.

(b) On 1 January 1967—implementing supplementary provisions for the common organisation of the market in fruit and vegetables and the application of quality standards within producing member-countries.

(c) On 1 July 1967—establishing common organisations of markets for sugar and oil and fats (except olive oil) and entry into force of common prices for oilseeds.

(d) On 1 September 1967—entry into force of the common price for rice.

(e) On 1 April 1968—entry into force of common prices for milk and milk products, beef and veal.

(f) By July 1968 entry into force of the common price for sugar.

(g) The Commission should make proposals by the end of 1966 for a common market organisation for tobacco and by 1 March 1967 for beverage wines (as opposed to quality wines).

Agreement was also reached on financing the European Agricultural Guidance and Guarantee Fund. For the two years 1965–66 and 1966–67 the cost of the common agricultural policy would be met entirely by percentage contributions from the member-countries to the Fund. From 1 July 1967 onwards 90 per cent of the levies on imports of foodstuffs would be handed over by the member-governments to the European Fund. This would, in fact, cover some 45 per cent of the Fund's expenditure and the remainder of the cost would be paid from the national exchequers of the member countries in the following proportions:

	1965–66 (per cent)	1966–67 (per cent)	1967 onwards (per cent)
Belgium	7·95	7·95	8·1
W. Germany	32·58	29·26	31·2
France	32·58	29·26	32·0
Italy	18·00	22·00	20·3
Luxembourg	0·22	0·22	0·2
Netherlands	9·58	9·74	8·2

The determination of these national ratios formed the subject of difficult negotiations, since the total annual expenditure on common agricultural policy was estimated to run at $1,400,000,000 and a change of even 0·1 per cent represented approximately $850,000 to be provided by a member-country.

The Council agreed to certain lump-sum payments to Italy and Belgium to compensate for the fact that common marketing organisations for certain products had not come into effect according to earlier commitments.

Italy would receive $45,000,000 for the year 1965–66 to be used for improving efficiency in the olive-oil and fruit and vegetable sectors, and a further $15,000,000 (also to be used for similar ends) for the year 1966–67 to compensate for the delay in bringing in a common regulation for tobacco.

Belgium would receive up to $4,000,000 a year for 1965–66, 1966–67, and 1967–68 to compensate for the delay in achieving a common market organisation for sugar.

A ceiling of $285,000,000 per annum was placed on the annual expenditure of the Guidance Section of the Agricultural Fund dealing with the modernisation of agriculture—the maximum which the Fund could contribute to any given project being fixed at 25 per cent

Agriculture

of the total cost, with up to 40 per cent in special circumstances. This measure was intended primarily for the benefit of Italy and Luxembourg.

For the year 1965 the Commission had approved expenditure of $17,100,000 on ninety-seven agricultural projects, out of 132 requests submitted for finance under the Guidance Section of the Agricultural Fund.

Of this total, $8,900,000 represented expenditure on improving productive facilities—mainly hydraulic works (including drainage), re-afforestation, building silos and cattlesheds, and providing plant to produce animal foodstuffs, and $8,200,000 on improving distribution facilities, particularly in the fruit and vegetables, dairy products, grain, and meat sectors.

The 1965 expenditure (in $ millions on approved projects) was as follows:

	Projects	Production	Distribution	Total
Belgium	6	—	0·75	0·75
France	21	1·71	1·98	3·69
W. Germany	21	3·0	1·97	4·97
Italy	40	3·16	2·71	5·87
Netherlands	8	0·8	0·78	1·58
Luxembourg	1	0·28	—	0.28

After two further Council meetings in June and early July final agreement on the outstanding problems of the common agricultural policy was reached at the end of a meeting held between 21–24 July and was formalised on July 26.

During the meeting the Commission put further proposals to the Ministers (i) concerning the establishment of common agricultural principles for the three remaining product groups—fruit and vegetables, sugar, fats and oils; and (ii) for fixing common prices for milk and dairy products, beef and veal, sugar, rice, oilseeds, and olive oil.

The agreement covered the following points, in addition to ratifying the provisional decisions of 11 May.

Fruit and Vegetables The new regulations for the fruit and vegetables sector completed the existing provisions for free trade in horticultural produce by permitting support buying and export subsidies. To reach this agreement major concessions were required from both the Netherlands and Italy. None of the member-countries had a market organisation for this sector, but the Netherlands had a well-established system of growers' organisations which had set up their own form of Market support. Italy, having paid to the E.E.C. her share of expenditure on goods produced of relatively little interest to her, was anxious to secure a settlement which would benefit her vitally important fruit and vegetable trade. The Netherlands, on the other hand, was reluctant to establish and help finance a system which would threaten the position built up by her growers, particularly in Community Markets.

The compromise reached involved establishing rules for a three-year trial period along the following lines:

(i) A basic price would be fixed for each major product by taking the average price for the previous three years.

(ii) Producers' organisations, the formation of which would be encouraged by direct grants, would be allowed to buy up produce when prices dropped by 15 per cent or more below this level, i.e. in a 'pre-crisis' situation.

(iii) Government intervention would take place during 1967–69 in 'crisis' situations, buying up produce when gluts caused prices to fall below 70 per cent of the basic price and being reimbursed for such purchases from the Agricultural Fund.

(iv) From 1970 onwards i.e. after the trial period, lower ceilings would be set for support buying by Governments, viz. 40–45 per cent of the basic price for cauliflowers and tomatoes; 50–55 per cent for apples and pears; 60–70 per cent for all other products, including table grapes, citrus fruits and peaches.

(v) Community financing for the fruit and vegetable sector would be limited to $60,000,000 per annum in 1967–69, of which $40,000,000 would be a guarantee for Italy, the remainder being distributed if necessary among the other five member-countries. If action to guarantee prices in Italy should require less than this total, the balance would be spent on improving agricultural structures in the fruit and vegetable sector.

Sugar Basic principles were agreed for a common market organisation, but details would be worked out at a later date. An overall quota was set for the amount of Community sugar-beet output for which there would be a guaranteed price. This total—to remain in operation until 1975—was agreed at 6,480,000 metric tons, shared between member-countries as follows (in metric tons): France, 2,400,000; West Germany, 1,750,000; Italy, 1,230,000; Netherlands, 550,000; Belgium-Luxembourg, 550,000.

Any production in excess of individual quotas by up to 35 per cent above the basic totals would qualify only for a much lower guaranteed sale price ($10 a ton, against $17). All Community countries except Italy meet their own sugar requirements from domestic beet production.

Olive Oil and Oilseeds Common market rules and price levels were fixed; import levies, analogous to those to be applied to grain imports, were imposed to protect Community producers; and direct grants to olive oil producers were agreed France and Italy produce 70–80 per cent of Community consumption of olive oil, but only 5–10 per cent of the consumption of other fats and oils (sunflower and rapeseed oils) comes from Community sources, mainly France and Germany.

Common Prices for Individual Products. The common prices agreed by the Council of Ministers were as follows:

	$ per 100 kg.
Milk—Target prices for milk of 3·7 per cent fat content:	
ex-farm	9·75
delivered dairy	10·30
Beef—Guide price for fully grown cattle	66·25
Guide price for calves	89·50
Sugar—Minimum price for beet	
(produced within quotas)	17·00
Minimum price (up to 135 per cent of quota)	10·00
Target price—white sugar	22·35
Intervention price—white sugar	21·23
Rice—Target price	18·12
Intervention price—France	12·30
Intervention price—Italy	12·00
Threshold price for greatest deficiency area	17·78
Oilseeds—Target price	20·25
Basic intervention price	19·25
Lowest intervention price	17·65
Olive Oil—Target price	115·00

The Ministers' agreement when a complete agricultural common market has been achieved will affect 10,000,000 farmers and 180,000,000 consumers.

The effect on British farmers is best summarised in an extract from N.F.U. pamphlet on what E.E.C. Agricultural Policy would mean to Britain.

'The immediate effect on British producers of the unconditional adoption of the common agricultural policy can be summarised as follows: there would be a sharp rise in the net returns to producers of wheat and barley and probably some increase in those for fat cattle; together these account for about a quarter of farm sales. For most other commodities average net receipts would be likely to decline.

'By comparison with some other commodities, cereals producers would have a degree of stability arising from the mandatory obligation of the Community authorities to support prices at the intervention levels. However, for soft wheat, the price level is higher than the Commission would have desired, the level being fixed by the

Council on a political basis. As the Community is already in surplus in soft wheat, it would be rash to assume that, if the surpluses were such that the Community were faced with heavy expenditure for the subsidisation of exports, means would not be found to check the inevitable expansion in wheat production.

'For beef and veal, the guide prices merely express price levels which are thought to be desirable for average quality cattle; if, in spite of the elaborate provisions at the frontier, market prices fall below the guide price level, support buying may take place but this is not mandatory. The regulation was put into operation during a period of acute meat shortage in the Community; for some time national guide prices were well maintained, but with the rebuilding of the European cattle herd, the market has weakened considerably in recent months.

'For pigmeat and eggs, the only stabilising factor at present is frontier protection; since the Community has reached or is approaching self-sufficiency in these products, there is little hope of stable prices. Already, the Community authorities are concerned at the prospect for egg producers and there has been a pig cycle on a Community scale.

'For milk it seems doubtful whether the Community support arrangements are such that the desired ex-farm target price for producers will be achieved. The adoption of the milk regulation—and of the higher feed costs implied by the cereal regulation—would probably mean a reduced net income for British producers, whose output today accounts for about 23 per cent of total farm sales.

'For sugar-beet, it is difficult to make any assessment since the size of the sugar-beet quota qualifying for Community support and the arrangement which would be made for cane-sugar supplies from the Commonwealth are unknown.

'It is clear from the analysis of the fruit and vegetables regulation that, without adequate safeguards to take account of production and climatic conditions of the United Kingdom the situation for many products would be extremely difficult.'

CHAPTER 6

Sales and Turnover Taxation in the Common Market

In a variety of forms, the tax on business turnover plays an important part in the fiscal systems of most western countries. In Austria, West Germany, the Netherlands and Luxembourg the tax is assessed on turnover. Italy taxes commercial transactions. Belgium uses a *taxe de transmission* when goods change hands. Britain uses a purchase tax on a limited range of goods. Switzerland taxes the turnover of the wholesaler. The United States have a sales tax levied at the point of sale as well as a tax on sales by makers of certain products. France depends upon a tax on value-added (T.V.A.).

Sales, turnover, purchase tax or T.V.A., whichever it is called, originated in most countries to provide revenue during or after the 1914–18 war.

Purchase tax was introduced in Britain in 1940 and has been used ever since for the dual purpose of raising revenue and for deflating the demand for goods on various occasions where an inflationary situation appeared to require an application of the economic brakes on selected consumer goods.

The tax on civil and commercial payments in France which began with the law of 31 December 1917 can be regarded as the first example of the contemporary system of taxing commercial transactions. It was called *Taxe sur les paiements, 1917–1920*, and was borne at the last stage of the sale of merchandise to the consumer.

The *Taxe sur les paiements, 1917–1920* was replaced in June 1920 by a turnover tax levied on each stage from production to distribution and on services of all kinds.

The French law of 31 December 1936 replaced the earlier turnover tax with a single global tax on production which was retained until 1954 when T.V.A. (*Taxe sur la valeur ajoutée* or value-added tax) was adopted.

The share of this form of taxation in the national budgets is shown in the following table which gives the total yield of central government and local taxation in 1962 expressed as a percentage of gross

84   *The Structure and Development of the Common Market*

national product at factor cost, i.e. at the estimated value of the national output of goods and services valued at prices exclusive of subsidies and indirect taxes.

TABLE I

Taxation as a percentage of Gross National Product at factor cost, 1962

	Total Taxation	Direct Taxes	Social Security Contribution	Indirect Taxes
	%	%	%	%
France	41·1	6·9	14·6	19·6
West Germany	41·0	15·6	11·6	13·8
Netherlands	34·8	14·3	9·4	11·1
Italy	33·8	7·2	11·0	15·6
United States	30·9	15·5	4·7	10·7
Belgium	30·6	9·1	7·4	14·1
United Kingdom	34·3	13·8	4·8	15·7

Source: Report of the Committee on Turnover Taxation.

Direct taxes include taxes on personal income, on business profits and on wealth. Indirect taxes include a wide range of taxes paid by suppliers of goods and services who, it is assumed, will pass the tax forward in prices so that it is borne 'indirectly' by those who use the goods and services as part of their expenditure.

Table II shows in greater detail the comparisons of the tax revenue for the United Kingdom, West Germany and France, in 1962. It shows the much greater extent to which West Germany and France rely on turnover and sales taxes. Almost one-sixth of all taxation in West Germany is derived from this form of tax, and between one-quarter and one-fifth of all taxation in France. As the table makes clear, this is not because the United Kingdom raises a smaller share of its total revenue in the form of indirect taxation; it is because the structure of indirect taxation in the United Kingdom is different. The purchase tax yields only one-fifteenth of the total of central and local taxation and the Exchequer relies much more heavily on receipts from the duties charged on tobacco and alcoholic drink. In West Germany and France indirect taxation is less selective applying to a wider range of goods and services.

With the end of the transitional period for the abolition of customs duties at the frontiers of the Common Market countries for trade with one another, the next stage towards achieving the balanced

Sales and Turnover Taxation in the Common Market 85

development of the Community is the harmonisation of taxation in the member states; and the first form of taxation to be harmonised is the indirect taxation represented by the different kinds of sales and turnover taxes. Unless this harmonisation is achieved, it is rightly held that turnover taxation distorts competition through the impact of the varying systems on costs and prices in the different countries and that the provision for compensation at the frontiers impedes the free movement of goods which has been partly achieved by the removal of customs duties.

The principal form of indirect taxation on commercial transactions in Europe, omitting the hybrid systems in operation in Italy, the Netherlands and Belgium, are (I) Purchase Tax in the United Kingdom, (II) the Cascade Tax in West Germany and (III) the French *Taxe sur la valeur ajoutée* (Value-Added Tax) commonly abbreviated as T.V.A.

I. Purchase Tax in the United Kingdom.

Purchase Tax is a single stage sales tax which is normally charged at the wholesale stage of distribution. It applies to a specified schedule of consumer goods and does not apply to services. It has three levels: 11 per cent (yielding 31 per cent of the total) on clothing, footwear and certain domestic goods) to $16\frac{1}{2}$ per cent (yielding 10 per cent of the total) on confectionery and soft drinks and $27\frac{1}{2}$ per cent (yielding 59 per cent of the total) mainly on domestic appliances, photographic radio and television equipment, clocks, jewellery, motor cars and proprietary medicines.

Manufacturers of taxable goods must be registered. Wholesalers can also be registered. Registration means that a registered seller and a registered buyer can trade with each other without attracting tax. Tax is payable when the goods pass to an unregistered buyer (e.g. a retailer) or when the goods are otherwise put to taxable use.

The transfer of goods tax-free between registered businesses is deemed to take place 'under representation', a procedure which resembles the French T.V.A. system when goods pass from seller to buyer 'under suspension of tax'.

A registered business may import goods under representation, in accordance with its certificate. This clears the goods free of purchase tax through the Customs control at the port of entry. They are taken into the importer's untaxed stock and will attract tax in due course when they pass into the hands of an unregistered buyer either as a straight re-sale or as part of the price if they are used in a manufacturing or assembling operation.

TABLE II
The composition of the Tax Revenue in the United Kingdom, West Germ<!-- cut -->
and France

	Tax Yield in U.K.		
		as % of:	
	£ million	Total Taxation	G.N.P. at factor cost
Direct taxes			
Falling on individuals, traders and partnerships.	2,500	29·2	10·0
Falling on Companies, including profits tax in U.K. (£378m)	955	11·2	3·8
Social Security Contributions	1,197	14·0	4·8
Payroll Taxes	(1)		
Indirect taxes,			
Turnover, Sales Tax. Purchase Tax in U.K.	571 (2)	6·7	2·3
Tobacco	879	10·3	3·5
Alcoholic drinks	467	5·5	1·9
Hydrocarbon oils	547	6·4	2·2
Other indirect taxes (including local rates in U.K. (915m.)	1,438	16·7	5·8
Total Indirect taxes	3,902	45·6	15·7
Total Tax yield	8,554	100·0	34·3

(1) Since these tables were compiled U.K. has adopted S.E.T. expected to yield £175<!-- cut -->
in a complete year.
(2) 1966/67 £670 million.
Source: Report of the Committee on Turnover Taxation, H.M.S.O.

A registered business is free of tax liability on goods exported in whatever form from its untaxed stocks, possession of the normal commercial documents being accepted as evidence of the export transaction.

Purchase Tax is, in all cases, a one-stage transaction. The registered manufacturer or the registered wholesaler is responsible for paying Purchase Tax on all his transactions in taxable goods. It is collected quarterly in arrears, from about 65,000 registered holders of purchase tax certificates and has an incidence of 16 per cent to 17 per cent on the value of the tax-exclusive turnover of taxable goods.

II. *The Cascade Tax in West Germany.*

The existing turnover tax in West Germany, called the Cascade Tax is cumulative on a wide range of goods and services. The number of

Sales and Turnover Taxation in the Common Market

Yield in West Germany			Tax Yield in France		
	as % of			as % of	
	Total Taxation	G.N.P. at factor cost	£ million	Total Taxation	G.N.P. at factor cost
26·8	11·0		972	10·8	4·4
11·2	4·6		550	6·1	2·5
28·2	11·6		3,206	35·5	14·6
0·8	0·3		401	4·5	1·8
16·1	6·6		2,052	22·7	9·4
3·5	1·4		191	2·1	0·9
1·8	0·7		138	1·5	0·6
3·1	1·3		498	5·5	2·3
8·5	3·5		1,012	11·3	4·6
33·0	13·5		3,891	43·1	17·8
100·0	41·0		9,020	100·0	41·1

While the tax yield under each heading varies in each country from year to year the per-
[cent]age of the different categories to the total taxation remains fairly constant.

businesses subject to this tax is about 1·7 million and the total yield in 1962 was about £1,715 million, more than three times the yield of Purchase Tax in the United Kingdom. The tax is charged in full (4 per cent) at each stage by reference to the whole value of the taxable goods or services supplied at that stage.

After the introduction of the tax in West Germany in 1918 and throughout the inter-war period, the rates of tax remained low (in the region of 2 per cent). As these rates have increased so the defects of the tax have become more widely recognised. The defects all spring from the multiple application of the tax. This means that the tax gives an arbitrary encouragement to vertical integration and penalises specialisation, because a firm which reduces the proportion of materials or components which it buys from outside suppliers will carry less tax in its total production costs. For the same reason the tax is said to have given an artificial inducement to dispense with the services of the independent wholesaler. The multiple application means that the tax penalises investment, because a firm which purchases new capital equipment from outside suppliers has to bear the tax in the cost of its purchases. And because the tax element in costs is variable, it is impossible to calculate precisely either the amount of tax which should be remitted on exports, or the amount of tax which should be imposed on imports in order that they may compete with domestic production on equal terms.

Some of these criticisms have been met in West Germany by modifications of the tax. For example, sales by vertically integrated firms in the textile industry have been taxed at a higher rate than sales by specialist firms; and sales by wholesalers who do not process the goods they handle have been subjected to tax at the specially low rate of 1 per cent.

The difficulty of calculating export rebates and countervailing import duties, to match the amount of tax which has accumulated in the domestic cost structure, has led the German authorities to prescribe broad average rates of rebates and of countervailing duty for various classes of goods. The amount of the export rebate depends on whether the goods are exported by the producer directly or through an export merchant (who will have bought them tax-paid). It has occasionally been suggested that the export rebates contain an element of subsidy. It may happen that the amount rebated, being an average, sometimes exceeds the tax which the exported goods have borne, but the West German authorities have deliberately pitched their averages on the low side to avoid giving ground for such complaint. In fact, West German exporters complain that the rebates have provided them with inadequate compensation for the tax their goods have borne.

In February 1963 the West German Government announced a proposal to replace existing cascade tax by a value-added tax. These proposals are likely to be absorbed in the proposals of the European Economic Community for a common T.V.A. tax throughout the Common Market.

III. *T.V.A. in France.*

France derives about 25 per cent of all her taxation revenue from her T.V.A. system. The combined yield of these taxes in 1962 was over £2,000 million.

T.V.A. itself is a State tax, as are two of the other constituents of the system, the *Taxe sur les prestations de services* (T.P.S.) and the

Sales and Turnover Taxation in the Common Market

Taxe Unique (on meat and wines). In addition however the system includes the *Taxe Locale* of 2·75 per cent on sales made direct to consumers; on certain wholesale transactions in which the taxpayer has the option to pay the Taxe Locale on the selling price rather than T.V.A. on his profit margin; on the transactions of artisans; on the transactions of certain co-operative buying groups; and, at the higher rate of 8·5 per cent on goods consumed on the premises or involved in the supply of furnished accommodation and on certain other services. The price of furnished accommodation itself is also taxed.

The essential characteristic of T.V.A. is that it is a comprehensive tax designed to tax consumers' expenditure, and that it achieves this object by way of fractional payments levied at each stage in the chain of production and distribution in such a way that in respect of all transactions that fall within the system deduction is allowed for tax which has already been paid at an earlier stage up to the final sale to the consumer who then bears the burden of all T.V.A. which has been paid as the goods have progressed from raw material to retail counter.

The rates of T.V.A. in France are expressed as percentages of the tax-inclusive selling price. Thus, at a T.V.A. of 20 per cent, the tax on goods sold at a tax-inclusive price of 100 is 20, equal to a rate of 25 per cent on the tax-exclusive value of 80 (which is the way United Kingdom Purchase Tax would be expressed).

By far the largest proportion of goods bear T.V.A. at the rate of 20 per cent. Other rates are 6 per cent on edible oils, sugar, jam, chocolate and allied products; 10 per cent on coal and electricity, sawn timber, soap, margarine and processed foodstuffs; 23 per cent on cameras, films and watches; 25 per cent on radio, television and certain luxury goods, as well as spirits and mineral waters.

Imports are taxed at the point of entry into France and the tax paid in imports is allowable as a deduction at subsequent stages just as if the goods have been bought in the home market and the tax paid by a French supplier.

Exports are relieved of T.V.A. The procedure mainly used is one by which the exporter, if he is a manufacturer, buys his materials or, if he is a merchant his goods, for resale 'under suspension of tax'. The goods pass tax-free from seller to buyer, whether they are for use in manufacture or for re-sale as finished products, in the same manner as under United Kingdom purchase tax, so long as the goods can be identified as destined for eventual export.

There are provisions for the exporter to claim purchases under suspension of tax up to the value of his exports during the preceding

G

year and the larger proportion of France's export trade is carried on in this way. If the goods do not come under this arrangement, goods bought for re-sale as exports, and capital equipment, materials and components bought for making exports give rise to a deduction in the purchaser's tax account in the same way as similar purchases made to supply the home market—except of course, that the final exporter is relieved from tax, whereas the final customer in the home market pays all the tax that has been paid in the earlier stages.

There is a long list of modifications and exceptions to the general application of T.V.A. both where the tax concerns goods and where it applies to services. The total number of businesses which pay one or other of the three taxes (T.V.A., T.P.S. and Taxe Locale) is very large, estimated at well over 2 m.

The *Taxe sur les Prestations de Services* (T.P.S.) is levied at the rate of 8·5 per cent on business or professional activities which do not involve purchase or sale of goods, such as the hiring of goods, the operations of banking, travel agencies, and a wide range of similar transactions in which payment is made for services rendered rather than goods supplied.

HARMONISATION IN THE COMMON MARKET

One of the objectives of the Community is to create a common market having all the characteristics of a single domestic market. The problem of the complete abolition of fiscal boundaries between the member States involves a wide range of taxation systems.

The harmonisation of turnover and sales taxation is to be undertaken in two stages. Firstly, the tax structures are to be brought into line in all the member-states. Secondly, when this has been done, the harmonisation of tax levels is to follow.

Fiscal boundaries include many other forms of taxation. Excise duties play an important part in the taxation policies of the Common Market countries, as they do the United Kingdom. There are a few items such as cigarette lighters in France; electric lamps in Italy; sugar in West Germany which present little difficulty. Of far greater complexity are the wide differences of taxes on tobacco, alcohol and petrol.

The European Economic Community have decided that the harmonised sales and turnover tax system is to be based on the Value-Added Tax. The date they have fixed to achieve harmonisation of the structures to bring all the countries into a common T.V.A. system is 1 July 1970.

Sales and Turnover Taxation in the Common Market

The arguments for adopting T.V.A. as the common system of turnover taxation in the Common Market have been stated by the Commission of the European Economic Community as follows:

(1)   T.V.A. is competitively neutral. At equal prices the same kind of goods carry the same amount of tax.

(2)   The fiscal burden is not affected by the number of intermediate stages or intermediaries involved in the production and marketing of the goods. Integrated businesses are, in spite of their apparent suppression of one or several stages, put on the same footing as non-integrated businesses.

(3)   T.V.A. encourages productivity and modernisation, tax already paid on investment goods being deductible.

(4)   T.V.A. encourages specialisation, since an increase in the number of stages to achieve greater specialisation does not lead to an increase in the tax burden.

(5)   T.V.A. permits the application of a precise tax refund on exportation and a precise basis of taxation on importation and so eliminates discrimination between home produced and foreign goods.

(6)   It adapts to the pursuit of the economic and social objectives of the Community, in particular because it allows the application of reduced rates at any stage.

The characteristics of T.V.A. as a method of imposing a general tax on the use of goods and services by the final consumer lies firstly in the fact that it is charged at each stage in production and distribution on the value that has been added to the product, by processing costs and profit in the case of manufacture or by profit in the case of re-sale and secondly that tax paid at earlier stages is deductible at each stage so that it is only at the final stage, that of the final consumption, that the tax becomes an actual fiscal charge which is no longer deductible.

The common system of value-added taxation is designed to extend to the retail trade just as does the French T.V.A. but member-states will be free to apply the system only to stages up to and including the wholesale trade and to levy, where necessary, a supplementary tax of their own on retail sales. Such permissive application of T.V.A. is being adopted by Italy for a transitional period pending the time when fiscal frontiers are abolished.

In parenthesis, it is of some interest that a value-added tax at any given rate is tantamount to a tax on the full price of the product because the tax is applicable on every item from the crude raw material onwards. As the crude raw material in its original state has been provided free by nature everything that is done to it is value added.

Example I

(1) Stage	(2) Value added at that stage	(3) Total value at end of this stage	(4) Tax on sale	(5) Deduction of tax borne at previous stage	(6) Tax 10 per cent T.V.A. payable at this stage
Manufacturer produces fibre and sells to	5s. 0d.	5s. 0d.	6d.		6d.
Processor who crimps and weaves into fabric and sells to	5s. 0d.	10s. 0d.	1s. 0d.	6d.	6d.
Garment manufacturer who makes a shirt and sells to	10s. 0d.	20s. 0d.	2s. 0d.	1s. 0d.	1s. 0d.
Retailer who adds his gross margin	10s. 0d.	30s. 0d.	3s. 0d.	2s. 0d.	1s. 0d.
					3s. 0d.

Example II

On 75,000 shirts

(1) Stage	(2) Value added +	(3) Prior Tax paid
1. Manufacturer produces fibre for 75,000 shirts. During the same accounting period he buys a new machine at £500 plus £50 tax (at 10 per cent)	18,250 500 +	50 (tax)
	18,750 +	50 (tax)
2. Processor weaves material for 75,000 shirts. Buys dye and machinery at £200 plus £20 tax (at 10 per cent).	18,550 + 200 +	1,875 (tax) 20 (tax)
	18,750 +	1,895 (tax)
3. Garment manufacturer makes 75,000 shirts. Buys buttons and thread at £500 plus £25 tax (at 5 per cent) and dye at £100 plus £10 tax (at 10 per cent).	36,900 + 500 + 100 +	3,750 (tax) 25 (tax) 10 (tax)
	37,500 +	3,785 (tax)
4. Retailer sells 75,000 shirts. Buys new van at £500 plus £100 tax (at 20 per cent).	37,000 + 500 +	7,500 (tax) 100 (tax)
	37,500 +	7,600 (tax)

Sales and Turnover Taxation in the Common Market

Examples must inevitably entail the simplification of the problem; firstly because too many stages are generally involved to make the example representative of what happens in practice and secondly because one has to select a point of time in a process which is continuous.

Example I illustrates the impact of the value-added tax on one nylon shirt, in a highly simplified form with costings, margins and profits all imaginary.

Moreover, it is assumed that the manufacturer who produces the fibre starts from the extraction of the natural crude material which he uses, and is therefore at the first stage of adding value to that crude material.

Example II elaborates the process because it introduces an element of bought-in materials on which tax has been paid and is therefore deductible at the next stages and an element of the purchase of capital equipment. Of course, the purchase by the processor of £200 worth of machinery would not in practice be allied specifically to the manufacture of these 75,000 shirts. It would take place during a given accounting period during which these particular shirts are probably

value of	(5) Tax on sale	(6) Prior tax paid now deducted	(7) T.V.A. payable
	1,875		
	50		
50 + 50 (tax)	1,925	50	£ 1,875
	3,750	1,875	
	20	20	
0 + 1,895 (tax)	3,770	1,895	£ 1,875
	7,500	3,750	
	35	35	
+ 3,785 (tax)	7,535	3,785	£3,750
	11,250	7,500	
	100	100	
0 + 7,600 (tax)	11,350	7,600	£ 3,750
		Total tax paid =	£11,250
		= 3s. 0d. per shirt	

made and sold. Nevertheless, allowing for the simplification, this is a fair example of the operation of T.V.A. through a series of manufacturing and selling stages from the processor of the crude materials to the consumers who finally buys the shirts.

The following diagram (Example III) illustrates the way in which the value-added is determined by the deduction of tax previously paid. As the value added is the difference between purchases and sales, and the tax previously paid on purchases is deducted for the tax due on sales, the taxation of the value added is calculated by means of the deduction of previous tax.

It is not necessary to wait for the sale of an individual article to deduct the tax paid on purchases. The total value of purchases or taxes previously paid and the total value of sales or tax on sales must be determined for a tax period and settlement made at the end of that period.

The earlier tax on purchases which is deductible includes all tax shown in the accounts which is borne, for example, by goods or raw materials, services, investment goods or general expenses. As tax paid earlier is deductible at the end of each tax period and tax on sales is due at the same time the corresponding goods, including longer term stocks and investment goods, are carried in the accounts at net prices. All earlier fiscal elements are thus eliminated and taxation of the disposal of goods starts afresh at each stage.

THE EFFECT OF REDUCED RATES IN T.V.A.

The deduction of tax already paid is also possible when reduced rates apply to certain transactions. However, it should be noted that when the normal rate is applied to the following stage, there is a compensatory effect since the goods are taxed again as if they had never benefited from a fiscal concession. As the following example shows, the tax payable decreases or, as in the diagram (Example IV), disappears at the stage where the reduced rate is applied, but the compensatory effect at the following stage leads to a corresponding increase in the amount of tax payable and, at the same time, the tax burden increases again to the level of the normal rate. (Tax payable at the third stage = O, at the fourth stage = 18).

The compensatory effect can, however, be avoided if the reduced rate is applied up to the last stage. This is shown in the diagram (Example V).

If the application of reduced rates would result in the amount of tax on sales being less than the tax already paid, a refund should be made. If, as in the next diagram (Example VI), the rate is 10 per cent

Sales and Turnover Taxation in the Common Market

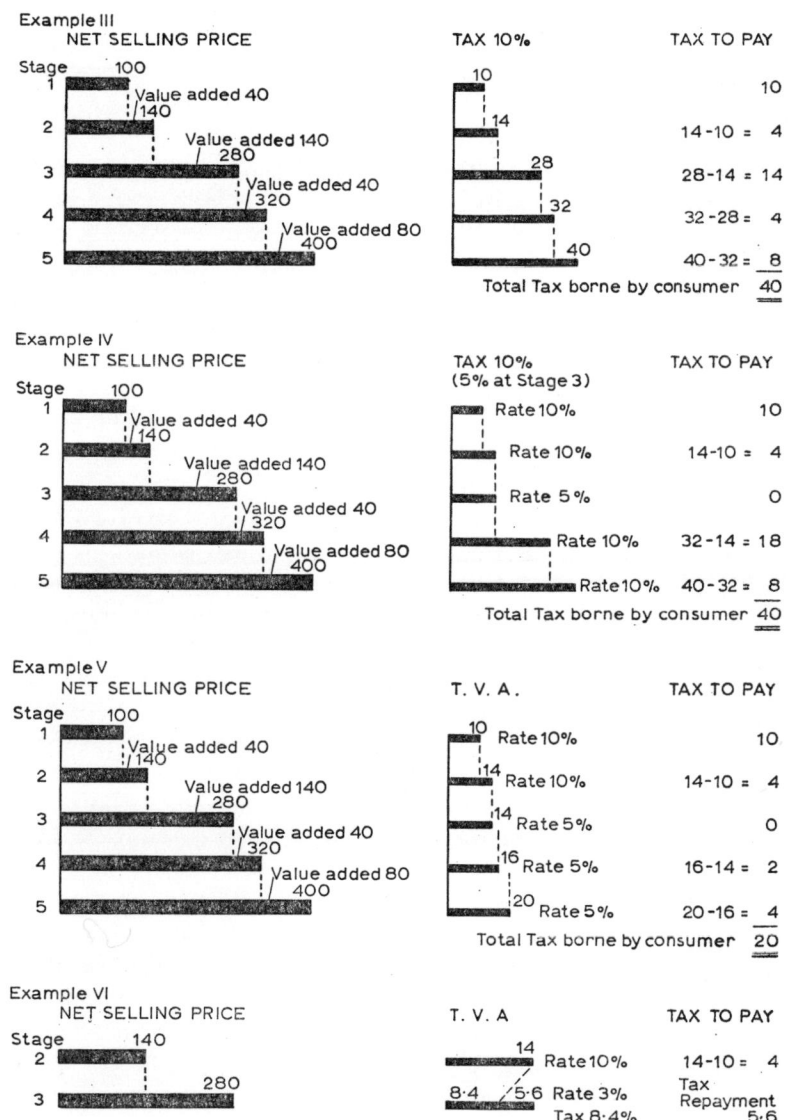

at the second stage and only 3 per cent at the third stage, the tax chargeable by application of the 3 per cent rate is not sufficient to allow the whole of the previous taxes to be deducted. This is the reason why the reduced rate must be fixed in such a way that it should normally be possible to offset all of the tax already paid. The need for refunds will thus be avoided.

THE EFFECT OF EXEMPTIONS IN T.V.A.

If, by excluding them from the field of application of T.V.A., certain branches of business activity were exempted, the firms concerned would be technically unable to deduct the taxes previously paid. Certain disadvantages would inevitably result from this.

While the tax might ultimately fall on the final consumer, it can only do so with a considerable margin of error because the fiscal charges become included permanently in the prices when they are not deductible. They become cascade taxes.

The tables on the opposite page show how non-deductibility causes an increase in the price at the succeeding stage. In these tables (A) supposes the regular application of T.V.A. at all stages and (B) supposes the exclusion of the second stage from the application of T.V.A.

There is therefore a strong argument for using reduced tax rates rather than tax exemption to avoid the compensatory effect of exemption being reflected in accumulation of tax and increases in price.

The British Purchase Tax system is reputed to be the envy of most European countries because it is collected at a single stage. The difference between T.V.A. and Purchase Tax lies largely in their history. T.V.A. was evolved in order to transform a generalised production tax which has previously fallen on investment and certain other business costs (as well as on consumer goods) into a tax falling on consumer goods only. Purchase Tax from its inception was designed as a tax on consumer goods.

The multi-stage design of T.V.A. involves a much larger and more complicated structure for administration and collection than Purchase Tax, as can be seen by the fact that the collection of the three elements of T.V.A. in France (T.V.A., T.P.S. and Taxe Locale) involves two million firms (which might be reduced to one million by a *Taxe sur le chiffre d' affaires* (T.C.A.) as has been suggested in France) whereas Purchase Tax involves only 65,000 firms. The average tax per T.V.A. taxpayer in France is about £1,000 compared with £10,000 per Purchase Taxpayer in the United Kingdom.

It is the fractional method of payment which has set the pattern of T.V.A. as the method of taxing consumers for all time. No tax ad-

TABLE A

	I Production from raw materials	II Processing	III Manufacture
Purchase price	—	100(a)	140
Added value	100	40	140
Tax base	100	140	280
Rate	10%	10%	10%
Tax		14	28
Calculation of selling price	100 + 10	140 + 14	280 + 28
Selling price	110	154	308

(a) When the goods are subject to T.V.A., the previous taxes are deducted.

TABLE B

	I Production from raw materials	II Processing	III Manufacture
Purchase price	—	110(a)	150
Added value	100	40	140
Tax base	100	—	290
Rate	10%	0%	10%
Tax	10	0	29
Calculation of selling price	100 + 10	150 + 0	290 + 29
Selling price	110	150	319(b)

(a) When the goods are not subject to T.V.A., taxes already paid are not deducted.
(b) The price increase by comparison with Table A is 319−308 = 11, including the non-deductible tax at the first stage (+ 10) and the tax charged on the latter at the third stage (= 1).

ministration could face the problem of compressing the collection of one quarter of its total tax revenue into 10 per cent of the proportion of the population who pay it now. Purchase Tax may have to change to T.V.A. T.V.A. will never change to Purchase Tax.

There is, however, one important point common to both systems. In themselves, neither T.V.A. nor Purchase Tax stimulates or impedes exports. It is sometimes held that T.V.A. favours exports. Earlier French taxes from which T.V.A. evolved created certain difficulties for export. The removal of these difficulties caused some misunderstanding of the situation.

Almost all French exports are carried on under suspension of tax at all stages; just in the same way as British exports never enter into the Purchase Tax system.

The tax base for T.V.A. includes the delivery of goods and services and the eventual standard rate of T.V.A. will be the same for the delivery of goods as for the performance of services.

The Community lists the following as services subject to T.V.A.

(1) The assignment of patents, trade marks and similar rights and the granting of licences concerning those rights.

(2) Work done to tangible goods and on behalf of a taxpayer, which constitute repairs, cleaning etc. but not any form of manufacture.

(3) Architectural and similar services connected with construction.

(4) Advertising.

(5) Transport and storage.

(6) Leasing of movable tangible goods to a payer of T.V.A.

(7) Employment Agencies.

(8) Banking transactions on behalf of a taxpayer.

(9) Services of consultants, engineer and similar technical, economic and scientific services.

(10) The fulfilment of an obligation not to exercise a professional activity enumerated in this list.

(11) The services of brokers, independent intermediaries, agents and others in connection with transactions involving goods or services.

When harmonisation of Turnover Taxation has been achieved there will remain the problem of Excise Duties, some of which are of no particular importance either as part of the budgets of the member-states or as influences on trade and competition. Others, of some importance, are regarded as capable of being brought into the future common T.V.A. system of the Community. A third category of Excise Duties, that which concerns alcohol, petroleum products and tobacco will prove the most difficult but even these will yield in the end to inclusion in the common system of T.V.A. and to adjustments affecting monopolies in the member states to conform to the letter and spirit of the Treaty. These problems were all known when the Treaty was drafted.

The next stage, after the harmonisation of indirect taxation, is the harmonisation of direct taxes. Complete co-ordination is probably impossible because direct taxes are an inseparable part of the economic and social life of each country.

The aim of the Community is, therefore, to harmonise the effects of the tax laws rather than the laws themselves, so as to remove all incentives for enterprises to enter into mergers, to move their fac-

Sales and Turnover Taxation in the Common Market 99

tories or headquarters or to invest or otherwise formulate their trading policy in so far as their policy might be influenced solely by tax considerations or advantages.

In company taxation, this broad front of co-ordination affects a range of taxes on distributed and undistributed profits, on allowances for depreciation, on the valuation of stocks, on the taxation of dividends and the problems of the international company.

A balance will be sought between restriction on movements which could distort competition on the one hand and a sufficient degree of flexibility on the other hand to allow the development of plans which are economically desirable; in particular where investment could assist to solve the problem of areas with continuing difficulties for creating new industries and employment.

The Report of the Committee on Turnover Taxation, Comd. 2,300, published as a Blue Book by H.M.S.O. known as the Richardson Report gives a very full evaluation of the principal systems in Europe and, in accordance with the terms of reference of the Committee reaches certain conclusions particularly on the comparison of T.V.A. with Purchase Tax.

CHAPTER 7

Competition—Cartels and Exclusive Dealing Agreements

The Treaty of Rome imposed on the member-countries of the Common Market a task of unprecedented complexity. It decreed that the Six should unify their economies behind a protectionist tariff wall under conditions which if they are not to be described as *planification* on a European scale must be regarded as wiping out the last vestiges of *laissez-faire*.

Its consistent level of external tariffs makes it difficult to compare them in degree with either the United States, with their range of high and low levels, or the United Kingdom with its varying levels and system of free entry for goods from the Commonwealth.

One example of this protectionist policy is Aluminium, on which there is an import duty of 10 per cent. Taken as a whole, the Common Market is a net importer of aluminium. The import duty of 10 per cent is designed to protect the French aluminium industry against the products of lower-cost producers, although under the provision of the Treaty, Germany, the largest net importer has been given a limited tariff-free quota.

Having made sure that no part of the Common Market has any advantage over another, in the price of its foodstuffs, in the cost of its raw materials, and eventually in wages (by means of the free movement of workers), in social charges, in taxation, in transport and all the other elements of the economy, the Treaty lays down Rules which are described as the 'Equalisation of Competition'. In practice all these measures can only have one meaning—there shall be free competition for all in the Common Market so long as all are equal.

It is impossible not to spare a thought for Adam Smith.

A market so large, so effectively protected and so completely equalised is a producer's dream. In theory it affords all the opportunity for economies of scale for both production and distribution. In practice it is open to every conceivable activity for market sharing and monopoly.

Competition—Cartels and Exclusive Dealing Agreements

Monopoly in our modern civilisation has been countered in different ways in different countries. The United States use their anti-trust laws; Britain has her Monopolies and Restrictive Practices legislation and the abolition of Retail Price Maintenance.

The Treaty approaches the problem from three directions. In order to ensure the complete fusion of the markets of the Six, it proscribes all agreements between enterprises or associations of enterprises which have as their object or result the prevention, restriction or distortion of competition. It controls aids granted by member-states unless justified by particular economic or regional considerations. It limits the powers of the member-states to enact fiscal provisions which could distort competition in their trade with other Common Market countries.

In some ways, the articles of the Treaty are less stringent than the Sherman Act and the Clayton Act in the United States. Monopolies and mergers are not effectively subject to legal scrutiny unless they aim at or result in the abuse of a dominant trade position. Then they fall within the provision for the banning of agreements between enterprises or associates of enterprises which have as their object or result the prevention, restriction or distortion of competition within the Common Market in Articles 85 and 86 of the Treaty. These are more far-reaching than any country in the world has attempted to enact. They cite in particular, as incompatible with the Common Market.

(a) the direct or indirect fixing of purchase or selling prices or other trading conditions.

(b) the limitation or control of production, markets, technical development or investment.

(c) market-sharing or the sharing of sources of supply.

(d) the application to parties to transactions of unequal terms in respect of equivalent supplies thereby placing them at a competitive disadvantage.

(e) the subjecting of a contract to conditions which have no connection with the subject of the contract.

(f) any agreement which allows one or more enterprises to take improper advantage of a dominant position in the Common Market.

For the purposes of the present work, it is desirable to examine closely the effect of the Rules Governing Competition upon the kind of trade practices that are normally encountered by management in industry. The present chapter covers the activities of the European Economic Community in this field with particular reference to the efforts which have been made to interpret the Rules and to implement the Treaty's chapter which defines them.

The actions of the Commission of the European Economic Community have been concentrated in the early stages upon a general category of so-called exclusive dealing agreements between businesses rather upon cartels of a more general nature.

It has always been accepted as normal trade practice for a manufacturer in one country to confer the selling rights for his productions in a part or the whole of a second country on a distributor in the second country confines his activities in the particular production to the territory for which he has been granted the sole selling rights; and refrains from selling the product back to traders either in the country of its origin or to traders in any third or additional territory. Occasionally this practice is reinforced by agreements which involve patents or trade marks. All this is the normal basis for sole distribution rights with which everyone in business has become familiar over the years.

The restrictions are designed mainly to enable a manufacturer to protect his distributor from interference from third parties which might arise, *inter alia*, from price differentials between one area of distribution and another, and to allow the distributor to reap the fruits of his activities.

Articles 85 and 86 of the Treaty strike at the roots of these practices on the grounds that the Six are now economically one and that the national frontiers which have been abolished between the Common Market countries must not be replaced by artificial frontiers maintained or enacted by commercial agreements which could prevent the free flow of goods in all directions within the Common Market and whether those goods are produced inside the Common Market or are imported from countries outside.

Article 85 (1) of the Treaty lays down that certain practices in the form of agreements between enterprises which are likely to prevent, restrict or distort competition in the Common Market are incompatible with the Common Market and are prohibited.

Article 85 (3) then enumerates certain classes of agreements to which Article 85 (1) does not apply.

The considerations laid down for obtaining a declaration that the prohibition of Article 85 (1) is inapplicable are that agreements must fulfil *both* of two positive and two negative requirements. The positive requirements are:

(1) The agreement must contribute to the improvement of production or distribution of the products or must promote technical or economic progress (e.g. agreements for rationalisation or standardisation).

Competition—Cartels and Exclusive Dealing Agreements

(2) The agreement must provide, at the same time, to users an equitable share of the benefits which result from such contribution, (e.g. that a reduction in price or an improvement in quality or in service had directly resulted).

The two negative requirements are:
(1) The agreement must not impose upon the parties any restrictive which is not essential to these objectives.
(2) The agreement must not enable the parties to eliminate competition in a substantial proportion of the goods covered.

Article 86 sets out certain 'improper practices' connected with contracts in which improper advantage is taken of a dominant industrial position in the Common Market.

To enable them to implement the provisions of Articles 85 and 86 of the Treaty, the Commission under the authority of the Council of the Community issued their first Regulation—Regulation No. 17 of 6 February 1962. This regulation sets the pattern for the whole process involved in carrying out the provisions of Articles 85 and 86. In it, the Commission elaborated the considerations which demanded the uniform and balanced application of Articles 85 and 86, claiming that it was necessary to establish a system which ensured that competition would not be distorted in the Common Market. The preamble to the Regulation underlined the need for effective supervision and made it, in principle, obligatory for all enterprises wishing to invoke the exclusion effect contained in Article 85 (3) to register all their 'agreements, decisions and concerted practices' with the Commission.

Thus, the Commission approached the problem by the unusual method of declaring virtually illegal any 'agreement, decision or concerted practice' within a wide area of commercial arrangements which are quite normal practice in trade (without being in any way monopolistic) and by making it incumbent on the parties to such arrangements to submit the agreement to the Commission to get it cleared.

Regulation No. 17 gave two methods for clearing agreements which appeared likely to be caught by Articles 85 and 86 of the Treaty:
(1) 'Negative Clearance' which, if it was granted, ensured that the agreement would be immune from attack by the Commission for being incompatible with the Treaty.
(2) A form of registration called 'Notification' which, if it is accepted by the Commission, ensures that the agreement will stand as of legal validity within the Common Market and should, other things being equal, be so regarded in the courts of the individual member countries, as well as being immune from attack by the Commission.

Regulation No. 27 of 10 May 1962 set out the precise procedure for the registration of agreements.

It became evident very soon after the issue of Regulations Nos. 17 and 27 that the Commission had extended its net too wide. Their Regulation No. 153 of 24 December 1962 went part of the way towards putting things right. This new regulation laid down two revised principles excluding certain agreements from being caught by Article 85 (1).

These exclusions concerned:

(1) Contracts with Commercial Agents, i.e. agreements between principals and agents by which the agent does not engage in activities proper to an independent trader; does not buy and sell the principals' goods on his own account; does not ever own the goods and does not (apart from the occasional 'del credere' guarantee) assume any risk resulting from the transactions.

In practice this exception covers the long-established function of the manufacturers' representative or agent working on a commission basis. The agent may be a sole agent in so far as he is the only representative of the principal in a given territory, and is paid commission on all the business that comes from that territory; but the restrictions which this relationship represents are held not to create any restraint or distortion of commission. Such contracts with Commercial Agents do not have to be submitted to the Commission.

(2) Patent Licence Contracts, in which obligations are imposed on certain forms of exploitation of an invention provided by the patent laws of the member countries, even though such obligations involve limitations

(a) of time, (e.g. a licence shorter than the life of the patent) (b) of space, (e.g. a licence granted for a part of the Common Market or to one place of exploitation or to a specific factory) and (c) of persons, (e.g. prohibitions against the licensee assigning his licence or granting sub-licences).

In general terms, this means that a patentee may, without finding his agreements caught by Article 85 (1), grant licences in which the period and area of exploitation within the Common Market are defined and exclusive, but not exceeding the period of the validity of the patent. Regulation No. 153 states that, providing the contract falls within a range of obligations of which the foregoing is a brief summary, there is no need to register such contracts or agreements with the Commission.

In the same Regulation (No. 153) the Commission provided for a simplified method for the registration of certain exclusive dealing

Competition—Cartels and Exclusive Dealing Agreements

agreements. The clause in question added a paragraph to Regulation No. 17.

The use of this simplified form of notification was, under Regulation No. 153, limited to agreements between two parties by which one party gives an undertaking to the other party to supply certain products only to the latter for the purpose of re-sale within a defined part of the territory of the Common Market; or one party gives an undertaking to the other party to buy certain specified products only from him for the purpose of trade in those products. In the notification of such agreements it was necessary to certify that reciprocal exclusive concessions for the distribution of competing products made by the grantor and the grantee had not been set up and that the grant of the exclusive concession did not limit the power of intermediaries to obtain the products from another grantee or other intermediary within the Common Market or for the grantee to sell equally to customers outside the contractual territories; and that the agreement did not include any obligation on the grantee to observe a minimum re-sale price fixed by the grantor.

The general principles covered by the simplified form of registration laid down in Regulation No. 153 have been consolidated in Regulation No. 66/67/CEE issued on 25 March 1967 which gives a block exemption from Article 85 (1) to a wide range of exclusive dealing agreements of a purely bilateral character until 31 December 1972.

Regulation No. 66/67/CEE lays down that, up to 31 December 1972, the ban on exclusive dealing agreements, Article 85 (1) of the Treaty will not apply where the agreements apply to two parties and where

(a) One undertakes, with regard to the other, to supply certain products to the other alone with a view to their resale within a specified part of the Common Market territory, or

(b) one undertakes, with regard to the other, to purchase from the other alone certain products with a view to their resale, or

(c) sole supply and purchase commitments, with a view to resale, of the type envisaged in the two preceding sub-paragraphs, have been entered into by the two undertakings.

Providing that there is no restriction on the sole concessions other than

(a) the obligation not to manufacture or distribute, during the period of the contract or until the end of one year after its expiry, products competing with the products covered by the contract;

(b) the obligation not to advertise products covered by the contract, not to establish a branch and not to maintain a warehouse for distribution, outside the territory covered by the contract.

But the concessions enumerated above do not apply where

(a) manufacturers of competing products entrust each other reciprocally with the sole distribution of those products;

(b) the contracting parties restrict intermediaries' or users' possibility of obtaining the products covered by the contract from other resellers with the Common Market, in particular where the contracting parties

(i) exercise industrial property rights with a view to interfering with the supplying to resellers or users in other parts of the Common Market of products covered by the contract, properly marked and put into circulation, or with the sale of the said products by those resellers or users in the territories covered by the contract;

(ii) exercise other rights or adopt measures with a view to interfering with the supplying to resellers or users of products covered by the contract elsewhere in the Common Market, or with the sale of the said products by those resellers or users in the territory covered by the contract.

The Commission of the European Economic Community, after examining the agreements which were submitted to them when the first Regulation was published, have come to recognise that a large proportion of the arrangements that are made between a manufacturer on the one hand and a distributor on the other have not the implications of restricting, distorting or preventing competition in such a way as to undermine the unity of the Community. They are, in fact, normal, common sense and workable trade practices.

The phases by which they have reached their conclusions have been complicated and tortuous. The philosophical analysis of what makes industry tick makes strange reading to the ordinary man, but under the conditions of the study and drafting of the regulations, this was perhaps inevitable.

The E.E.C. Commission has given considerable publicity to the cases which they selected from thousands of agreements submitted to them which they decided were caught by Article 85 (1) and on which they have taken action.

The first case resulted in the specific prohibition of an agreement between the Grundig Sales Company in West Germany and the Consten Company in France. The purpose of the agreement was to make Consten the sole distributor of Grundig products in France for which purpose Grundig had imposed a ban on all their dealers in other countries so that French purchasers could buy Grundig products only from Consten. In addition, Grundig and Consten had signed a supplementary agreement on the use of a special trade mark ('Gint') the purpose of which was to hinder the importation by firms other than Consten of Grundig products into France.

Consten sought to uphold its claim to exclusive dealership by taking action against a rival importer, Unef, of Paris, which was importing Grundig products from German wholesalers. Consten contended that Unef had not respected the established sales organisation and were introducing unfair competition. This case came before the Paris Courts and was adjourned pending a decision by the Commission on the compatibility of the exclusive distribution agreement between Grundig and Consten with the cartel rules of the Treaty.

The Commission decided that the agreement in question offended against the ban in Article 85 (1) of the Treaty and that it could not be approved under the provisions of Article 85 (3). In addition, the Commission forbade Grundig to obstruct rival imports of their products into France. The Commission held that the agreement in question constituted a restraint of competition, because the freedom of business activity of the parties to the agreement was restricted and that of firms outside the agreement was impaired. Customers for Grundig products were denied the possibility of making their purchases from other suppliers.

The Commission argued that, in the class of goods concerned, competition even at retail level is essential. The sales arrangement between Grundig and Consten was 'liable to affect trade between member-states.' The agreement was signed between two firms established in different member-states and regulated trade between those member-states in such a way that such trade was wholly in the hands of Grundig and Consten. Here was clearly a case where two commercial undertakings had set up for their own purposes trade frontiers which coincided with the national frontiers and had thereby rendered integration of the national markets into a common market more difficult. It was considered that the protection which the agreement gave Consten and consequently the obstruction of rival imports into France went beyond any restraint of competition which might conceivably be necessary for the improvement of production and distribution.

The two companies involved in this case exercised their right to challenge the legality of the decision by the Commission and they appealed to the Court of Justice of the Community. Except for a technicality that the inclusion of certain provisions in the agreement were irrelevant in the case submitted to the Court, the Court upheld the Commission's interpretation of the Regulations and the exclusive dealing agreement between the two firms remains 'incompatible with the Common Market' and illegal in terms of the Treaty.

The E.E.C. Commission has also made public its decisions to give 'Negative Clearance' to a number of so-called Exclusive Dealing Agreements.

One of such agreements was between an American firm and its distributor in Belgium, which was nothing more than a straightforward contract between a manufacturer of motor car accessories in the United States and its distributor. The contract had no limitations of marketing area, no restrictions on the suppliers not to sell direct if they wished to do so and none on the distributor not to deal in competing products.

Another such agreement concerned the grant by a French manufacturer of synthetic fibres of exclusive distribution rights to a Swiss importer with a restriction on the Swiss firm not to re-export to the Common Market. The Swiss firm would be hard put to do this anyway, because the product would bear double customs burden, and it was stated by the Commission that the contract involved no perceptible restraint of competition affecting trade in the Common Market.

A third agreement concerned the relations between a French company and a British company engaged in manufacturing and selling hairdressing preparations. In this case, the only restrictions consisted in that, the French firm having sold certain trade mark interests outside the Common Market, but retained those interests for operations within the Common Market, the British firm was not expected to compete with the French firm in the Common Market area.

A fourth agreement is one between a group of paint manufacturers under the general trade name Transocean.

These and similar cases appear to be of the nature of test cases. Such a view is borne out by the phraseology in one of the paragraphs of the preamble to Regulation No. 17. This says 'considering the such agreements, decisions and concerted practices are probably very numerous and cannot therefore all be examined at the same time and that a number of them have special features which may make them less of a threat to the development of the Common Market'.

The kinds of agreement exempted in the later regulations are the obvious exemptions. The concept of Article 85 and 86 is so wide that the Commission were bound to regard almost every agreement between manufacturer and distributor as a potential menace to the

Competition—Cartels and Exclusive Dealing Agreements

Common Market, and to start from there to sort out the wheat from the chaff.

The Regulations made by the E.E.C. Commission to implement the provisions of Articles 85 and 86 of the Treaty apply, within the Common Market to all exclusive dealing agreements whether the parties to the agreement are domiciled in the Common Market or whether one or all parties are domiciled in countries outside the Common Market. Of course, the jurisdiction of the Commission and the Court of Justice is restricted to the Common Market and agreements where one or all parties were outside could only be attacked in so far as they had some vulnerable spot inside the area. One party to an agreement, inside the Common Market playing a secondary part and following the instructions of the other party outside the Common Market might well be exposed to action by the Commission in respect of any practice which they considered was perceptibly affecting competition within the Common Market area.

Membership of the Common Market brings all parties to agreements within these supranational powers of the Community. It is part of the price of the Treaty.

CHAPTER 8

Industrial Property—
Patents and Trade Marks

The term 'Industrial Property' is used in this chapter in its proper context of patents, trade marks and design. International law on patents is a field of activity in which, strictly speaking, a layman in such matters can only comment with some reserve. Nevertheless, it cannot be avoided altogether if one is to do justice in an examination of the provisions of the Treaty of Rome to the changes which are taking place in the Common Market, and which must vitally affect industry in Britain in its production, licensing, and marketing plans for Europe in the future.

* * *

Industrial Property in the European Economic Community comes within the provisions of the Treaty under two headings. Firstly, under the general theme of the Common Market that conditions now existing or measures to be taken in the future in member-states and by industry in those countries must not constitute anything by which one State is artificially favoured or handicapped in relation to another State. This is part of the concept of the Rules of Competition. Secondly, in order to achieve this ideal concept of equality, there must be an eventual approximation of the laws of the individual member-states. This concept is provided for, partly in Article 36, but mainly in Article 100. It is important to note, however, that the Treaty does not change existing individual national systems of Industrial Property protection.

Article 100 of the Treaty of Rome falls under the chapter dealing with the Approximation of Laws and reads as follows:

The council, acting by means of a unanimous vote on a proposal of the Commission, shall issue directives for the approximation of such legislative and administrative provisions of the Member States as have a direct incidence on the establishment or functioning of the Common Market.

The Assembly and the Economic and Social Committee shall be

Industrial Property—Patents and Trade Marks 111

consulted concerning any directives whose implementation in one or more of the Member States would involve amendment of legislative provisions.

Three conclusions can be drawn in the interpretation of Article 100. They are:

(1) A free flow of goods in the whole of the Common Market must be achieved.

(2) There must be uniformity in conditions of competition; for example, uniformity would not exist in such conditions as the case of an inventor who is free to exploit a patent in country A, while the same patent is protected for X in country B and for Y in country C.

(3) Therefore, uniformity in the exercise of economic activity must be unimpeded by differences in the scope of protection given by, or in the obligations to exploit, an invention or trade mark.

In late 1959, the governments of the European Economic Community countries decided, in conjunction with the E.E.C. Commission, to set up three groups to study and prepare a programme for the harmonisation and unification of the Industrial Property laws in the Common Market countries, one group for each of the three categories of Industrial Property—patents, trade marks and design—and a further group to co-ordinate the findings of the three specialised groups. All this with particular regard for the concept of equality expressed and implied in the Treaty in relation to Industrial Property.

It was established at the outset that the kind of European Patent Law that must emerge from the process of unification should co-exist with the existing national patent laws of the member countries, but, on the other hand, that all rights under a European patent should be autonomous and to that degree independent of national patent laws.

The co-ordinating committee on Industrial Property set up by the member-states of the Community and the E.E.C. Commission produced in 1962 their 'Draft Convention relating to a European Patent Law.'

Under the provisions of the Draft Convention relating to a European Patent any State which is a party to the Paris Convention for the Protection of Industrial Property (1883, last revised at Lisbon 1958) may ask to accede to the Convention, which will then apply to the territories of the Contracting States which the latter designate on signing or ratifying their accession. There are also provisions for a form of association by special agreement involving reciprocal rights and obligations.

The principle is that the Convention will create a European Patent valid in all the Contracting States, with a European Patent Office and Courts with power to deal with European Industrial Property matters which will fall under its jurisdiction. The latter will consist, *inter alia*, of an Examining Division and Boards of Cancellation and Appeal. The procedure which it is proposed to lay down will be the same whatever the nationality of the patentee.

An application for a provisional patent will be lodged, either directly, or through the national Patent Office of the country of the applicant, with the European Patent Office, which will make a preliminary examination to establish the basic criteria of patentability, i.e. novelty, industrial use, and resulting from inventive activity.

If this first application is rejected it will be open to the applicant to revise it to meet any objections.

If it is accepted, either at the first or at a later submission, it will remain effective for a maximum period of 5 years. Before the expiry of this period specific application must be lodged for an examination of the claims. This examination will be carried out by the International Patents Institute at The Hague. Application for this examination can be made either by the original applicant or it can be made by third parties whose interests may be involved.

If no request is made to the European Patent Office within 5 years for examination and publication, the provisional patent will automatically expire as from the date of the application.

If a request is made, either by the original applicant or by a third party, the International Patents Institute at The Hague will proceed to a full examination and will publish its findings with, however, arrangements for revisions to meet the objections and reference back on these revisions to the third party if the application for examination has come from that source.

Thus, a provisional patent will, for up to 5 years, be open to objections from third parties who may institute requests for examination and publication by The Hague so as to hasten a decision if the interest of the third parties are affected; and failing such request it will be incumbent upon the original applicant to request examination and publication of his specification if it is his intention to proceed with the patent. It is expected that the examination and publication will take place 18 months after request.

If, after taking into consideration objections by third parties, the subject matter of the patent is found to be good, the European Patent Office will confirm the provisional patent and grant a full patent.

It is worth noting in this context that full publication will take place before the grant of a final patent but that none of the procedure of

Industrial Property—Patents and Trade Marks 113

examination and publication can begin in the absence of a specific request from the original applicant or from interested third parties.

If the applicant, for some reason, intends to abandon his intention of seeking a patent, he may save expense by omitting to request examination during the five years, but a third party might still apply for examination, if he so wished, in order to clarify his interest before the expiry of the Provisional Application.

As stated earlier in this chapter, the Convention will not change the individual national systems of patent protection, and it will still be possible to take out patents in any one country where the need for protection is limited to that country, even though the application be made by a foreign national.

The duration of a European Patent is proposed at 20 years from the publication of the provisional patent. There will be compulsory licensing provisions effective in the entire territory of the Convention, or these may only be applied in one particular interested State.

Proceedings for infringement will be enforceable only through the courts of the Contracting States. A Board of Cancellation will deal with cancellation of Patents and Patent Licences with retro-active effect on certain defined grounds. Pending the signing of a Convention, measures are proposed for a '*dépôt commun*' so that rights to a European Patent can be established in the transitional period.

All decisions of the Examining Board and the Board of Cancellation will be subject to appeal to the Board constituted for that purpose.

On Trade Marks, the procedure is not yet so clearly defined because of wider differences in the member states of the Common Market on the basis on which Trade Mark rights can be established. On the whole the trend is towards the German system with the right of a claimant to prior rights to be advised so that he can oppose the registration of the trade mark.

* * *

The reactions to the proposals of the European Economic Community to set up a European Patent were widespread. In 1961 the Board of Trade appointed a group whose primary task was to formulate views on the proposals of the Common Market in regard to a common patent system. At that time little information was available concerning the Common Market proposals and meantime the Council of Europe had also decided to give its attention to the problems of unification of patent laws in Europe.

In 1963, the Council of Europe produced their ideas in the form of a Convention known as the Strasbourg Convention, which was signed by all the member States of the Council of Europe. It has not yet been ratified by the United Kingdom, but in a White Paper, presented to Parliament in December 1965, the Board of Trade Patent Liaison Group reported on the legislative changes which would be involved in the ratification of the Strasbourg Convention on the unification of certain points of substantive law on patents. This report dealt with a wide range of technical points on such matters as double patenting, on methods of calculation, on methods of office management, on medical and similar treatment, etc. The report of this group states that, subject to a number of reservations, there is nothing in the Strasbourg Convention which would prevent the United Kingdom formulating a new definition of Invention, which would be necessary to meet the needs of a common European patent.

The European Patent is but one of the developments in Europe which are setting the pattern for future relationships between the countries and for devising means for their working together for which there are no precedents.

CHAPTER 9

Social Security in the Common Market

The obligations regarding workers and Social Security imposed by the Treaty setting up the European Coal and Steel Community on the High Authority (the executive body of the E.C.S.C.) and those imposed by the Treaty setting up the European Economic Community on the Commission (the executive body of the E.E.C.) are different one from the other.

The member states of the E.C.S.C. are bound to renounce all restrictions based on nationality in the employment of workers in their coal and steel industries and their Social Security Convention co-ordinates their Social Security schemes and extends their benefits to all migrant workers.

On the other hand, Article 118 of the Treaty of Rome stipulates that it shall be the aim of the Commission to promote close collaboration between member states in the social field, particularly in matters relating to employment, labour legislation and working conditions, occupational training, Social Security and protection against occupational disease and accidents.

Some of the earliest regulations issued by the countries of the E.E.C. under the Treaty laid down rules for ensuring equal treatment for workers moving from one country to another so that insured persons taking up employment in another country should retain the rights they had already acquired at the time of moving from one country to another.

An agreement drafted by the Council of Europe in Strasbourg on the 16 April 1964 to establish a European Code of Social Security extending two agreements of the 11 December 1953 called the European Interim Agreements on Social Security Schemes relating to Old Age, Invalidity and Survivors and on Social Security other than schemes for Old Age, Invalidity and Survivors was designed to secure reciprocal treatment for workers from one country moving to another. Very little of this agreement has been ratified or implemented. In any case reciprocity in matters of Social Security is not, of course, the

115

same process as unification which is the ultimate aim of the member-countries of the Common Market.

The Treaty formula for approaching a common system of Social Security throughout the European Economic Community was obviously designed to have regard for the wide differences in the national systems of the member-countries and, of course, for the strongly political bias in each country for its own system.

Moreover, Social Security plays a large part in the budget of all the European countries inside and outside the Common Market and in the level of taxation.

There could be no greater challenge to the minds of men than the task of bringing all the different systems together.

There is no exact definition of the phrase 'Social Security'. It applies generally to a heterogeneous range of state and institutional activities designed in the main to secure the population, whether by insurance or direct state contributions against sickness, disability, unemployment, old age, poverty, the burden of the large family and many of the ills and problems to which man and his dependents are subject in the sophisticated society of the modern state, and for which organised assistance is their right.

Ever since the 18th and markedly during the 19th century, fragmentary pieces of legislation were enacted in Europe to aid certain categories of indigent members of the community and workers in the coal mining industry in recognition of the obligations of the community towards its under-privileged members and those who suffered sickness and injury in their work.

The need was recognised in different ways and at different times in the six future member countries of the European Economic Community.

The problem created by the ever-widening scope of the industrial revolution speeded the movement to recognise some form of collective responsibility for the increasing mass of industrial workers. As far back as 1854 the Prussian Government introduced legislation for the protection of certain categories of workers notably apprentices, miners and railway workers. In 1881 Bismarck announced a plan to add to existing safeguards specific measures for the betterment of the necessitous members of the community.

The plan was put in action by a law on sickness insurance in 1883, on industrial accident insurance in 1884, on disability and old age in 1889. These measures were consolidated into a disability and old age insurance system for employees and for widows and orphans in 1911. The financial burden of these insurance systems was shared between employer and employee with state subsidies where necessary.

The system introduced in Germany in 1911 had a considerable influence on the first scheme which was introduced in Britain by Lloyd George in 1911 just as later schemes in Europe were influenced by the Beveridge Plan 30 years later in Britain.

The problem of harmonising the various systems of Social Security in the Six countries of the European Economic Community is extremely complex; it will be even more so if and when those systems have to be reconciled with the interpretation of Social Security in Britain and in the Scandinavian countries.

The essential difficulty lies in the fact that each country's system of Social Security is inextricably bound up with a different philosophy of what Social Security means and what it has to achieve. Each system has been developed empirically from complicated historical, political, economic and demographic origins.

As different trees root and grow in different climates and different layers of the earth's surface, so the diverse systems have grown to meet the varying needs of the different populations.

Each system has the same broad objectives but its growth has been rapid and many retain their early basis of operation through friendly societies or other co-operative organisations with strongly regional or craft characteristics. Reform has followed reform rapidly in systems which have barely had time to take root.

All the member countries of the Common Market are moving towards unification of their own fragmented systems. These movements and the changes which they involve give to the whole field of Social Security a degree of instability which renders comparison difficult and unification a long process only to be achieved by gradual stages.

Article 117 of the Rome Treaty requires that the member-states promote the improvement and working conditions of labour so as to permit the equalisation of such conditions in an upward direction.

Articles 117 and 118 state the essential need. How is it to be put into effect in the area of Social Security?

In the first instance, it is easier to harmonise those elements in the different systems which present the least divergences, and a start has been made with the interchange of information based on national experience; in the handling of Social Security for migrant workers in the Community and in consultation between the member-states to ensure that such changes as are contemplated in the national systems will tend to make harmonisation easier in the future.

Behind the essential sociological and demographic considerations, there exist all the basic common criteria.

Freedom of movement of workers within the Community as it grows demands equality of all Social Security measures. The issue cannot be forced. Rather will the solution be found in the gradual changes in national legislation on Social Security which tend to be of such a nature as to fit the pattern for the future.

All the other measures which the Common Market countries take to make them one Community will lead to the evolution of measures to unify their complex systems of Social Security. The freedom of movement of persons and capital is amongst its cardinal purposes. Time is needed and a common purpose. The Community has both. Unification of Social Security is essential to the realisation of the immediate aims of the Community.

This description outlines the different systems without attempting to do more than pick out the salient features of each system so that the reader may judge the extent of changes which will be needed to move towards harmonising them all.

Firstly, which members of the population come under Social Security provisions?

I. Dependant workers; wage and salary-earners

In general terms, this category of worker enjoys wider protection in the countries of the Community than workers who earn their livelihood in other ways. It was the wage-earner who originally needed the most help and it was upon him that most of the early systems were concentrated. Independently of considerations of history, economics and politics a system which covers groups of workers whose contributions can be deducted at the source of their wages is much easier to administer.

France In France, under the law of 4 October 1945, all wage-earners employed by another person or enterprise fall under a single plan for social insurance, workmen's compensation, health insurance, family allowance etc., whatever the level of their remuneration or their terms of service; but the deductions can only be made in respect of their earnings up to the equivalent of about £1,000 per annum, except for unemployment insurance where the ceiling is at a higher level.

Sickness, Maternity, Invalidity, Old Age and Survivors insurance is levied at the rate of 20·25 per cent on the wages of which 14·25 per cent is payable by the employer and 6 per cent by the employee.

Contributions for Family Allowance require 13·5 per cent of the

Social Security in the Common Market

wages, all paid by the employer. Accidents at work and occupational illness rates depend on the trade and the risks of that trade. Unemployment requires 0·25 per cent of which 0·2 per cent is paid by the employer and 0·05 per cent by the employee. Taken together these add up to about 35 per cent of which about 28 per cent is paid by the employer and 7 per cent by the employee.

Of the total wage cost of the employed person in France it is estimated that the cost to the employer is 72 per cent in direct wages and 28 per cent in social charges.

West Germany In West Germany, Social Security Insurance is compulsory only up to certain wage levels. These levels have been increased over the past few years. They stand at present at the equivalent of about £750 for sickness, £1,400 for pension insurance, miners and unemployment, with additions for dependants.

Contributions for sickness and maternity are at the average rate of about 10 per cent on wages, invalidity, old age, pension and survivors takes 14 per cent, unemployment takes 1·3 per cent. Accidents at work and occupational disease vary again according to the trade and are regulated by collective agreements.

In total, these contributions add up to about 26 per cent of wages of which half is paid by the employer and half by the employee.

Of the total wage cost of the employed person in Germany, it is estimated that the cost to the employer is 84 per cent in direct wages and 16 per cent in social charges.

Italy In Italy, insurance for invalidity, old age, survivors, sickness and maternity, accidents at work, social sickness and tuberculosis and unemployment is compulsory for all employed persons. Except for insurance contributions for family allowances, there is no limit on the wage level on which contributions are levied.

Contributions for sickness and maternity benefits are at the rate of 14 per cent on wages of which almost the entire amount falls on the employer; invalidity, old age and survivors is at the rate of 19·15 per cent payable as to about two thirds by the employer and one third by the employee. Family allowances take 17·5 per cent, unemployment insurance over 2·3 per cent, all payable by the employer and accidents at work average 3·9 per cent according to trade and trade agreements.

In total, the contributions in Italy amount to about 57 per cent on wages divided as to 50 per cent falling on the employer and 7 per cent on the employee.

In terms of total wage cost of the employed person in Italy, it is estimated that the cost to the employer is 68 per cent in direct wages and 32 per cent in social charges.

The Netherlands In the Netherlands, Social Security provisions embrace all employed persons, regardless of the nature of their employment but limited to those earning less than £800 per annum (£560 for old age-invalidity-survivors). The table of contributions is complicated by differentiating between the percentages paid for cash benefits and for benefits in kind. Sickness and maternity benefits take 9·5 per cent of wages, shared as to 6 per cent by the employer and 3·5 per cent by the employee. Invalidity takes 1·5 per cent payable entirely by the employer. Old age-survivors takes 8 per cent almost entirely payable by the employee. Family allowances account for 5 per cent payable by the employer and unemployment 1 per cent shared equally.

Together the contributions add up to about 25 per cent on wages of which about half falls upon the employer and half upon the employee.

Of the total wage cost of the employed worker in the Netherlands it is estimated that the cost to the employer is 86 per cent in direct wages and 14 per cent in social charges.

Belgium In Belgium, Social Security provisions embrace all employed persons, whatever the nature of their employment or the level of their remuneration.

Sickness and maternity benefit takes 7·8 per cent of wages, covering cash benefits and benefits in kind, shared equally by employer and employee, disablement takes 11 per cent shared as to 6 per cent by the employer and 5 per cent by the employee. The contributions for accidents at work and occupational illness varies according to agreements in the different industries. Family allowances take 13·5 per cent all paid by the employer; unemployment 2 per cent, shared equally.

Contributions are not paid on the excess of wages over about £1,000.

Together the contributions add up to about 33 per cent on wages divided as to about half and half between employer and employee.

In terms of total wage costs of the employed person in Belgium, it is estimated that the cost to the employer is 82 per cent in direct wages and 18 per cent in social charges.

Luxembourg In Luxembourg, Social Security contributions are compulsory for all employed persons.

Sickness and maternity benefits take 6 per cent of wages, shared as to 2 per cent by the employer and 4 per cent by the employee. Invalidity-old age-survivors takes 12 per cent, shared equally. Family allowance 4·29 per cent paid by the employer. Insurance for accidents

Social Security in the Common Market

at work and occupational illness depends on the trade.

In total, the Social Security contributions are 23 per cent on wages of which about 13 per cent is paid by the employer and 10 per cent by the employee.

Of the total wage cost of the employed worker in Luxembourg it is estimated that the cost to the employer is 83 per cent in direct wages and 17 per cent in social charges.

Thus out of the six members of the Common Market, only two, West Germany and the Netherlands, retain a wage or salary limit over which Social Security contributions are not compulsory. Apart from these two exceptions, the systems are similar in principle and different only in the levels of contributions and of benefits.

In almost all the countries, contributions are not payable on the amount of the wages over a specified upper limit.

BENEFITS

Benefits in cash In the Common Market countries sickness and other benefits in cash are almost invariably geared to the wage or income of the insured person, ranging from 50 per cent to 80 per cent without hospitalisation and from 20 per cent to 50 per cent with hospitilisation and depending on the size of family. The duration of payment of benefits in cash ranges from 78 weeks in 3 years in West Germany to a maximum of one year in other countries. Inside and outside these limits there are numerous special criteria and conditions.

Benefits in kind In view of the particular nature of benefits in kind which characterise the National Health Service in the United Kingdom, it is important to note the methods for providing these benefits in the Common Market countries.

In West Germany, Belgium, France, Luxembourg and the Netherlands, there is virtually a free choice of doctor and the patient pays the doctors fees and claims reimbursement. In West Germany and the Netherlands the insured person recovers the full amount. In Belgium the insured person (with certain exceptions) recovers 75 per cent, in France 80 per cent. In Italy, there are limited provisions for the insured person to pay part of the doctors' fees. In Luxembourg the proportion varies from one insurance fund to another, except for industrial workers who recover the full amount.

The fees for dental care are for the most part recovered in full by insured persons in all the Common Market countries.

For medicines, in general terms, in Germany the patient pays the equivalent of 1/– per prescription for the first 11 days of illness. In Belgium 25 per cent. In France 10 per cent to 30 per cent. In Italy

The Principal Social Security Contributions in the Common Market Countrie[s]

	W. GERMANY		BELGIUM	
	Contributions % of wages Ceiling		Contributions % of wages Ceiling	
Sickness, Maternity	8–11% (Average 9·66%)	7,920 DM (1,980 A.M.E.)	5%(a) +2·8% (b)	(a) 141,90[0] (2,838 A.M.E
	W. 50%		W. 50%	
	E. 50%		E. 50%	(b) 103,20[0] (2,064 A.M.[E])
Invalidity	14%			
Old Age—Survivors	W. 50% E. 50%	13,200 DM. (3,300 A.M.E.)	11% W. 5% E. 6%	—
Accidents at work Occupational Illness	Group rates fixed according to risks in different occupations. Contributions are fixed by trade bodies on an average basis. Ceiling 36,000 DM or higher.		Mainly by contri- butions to Emplo[yers'] Associations' Fu[nd] for Accidents. 0·25% for all em- ployers are varia[ble] contributions acc[ord]- ing to risks, for o[ccu]- pational illness.	
Family Allowances	Paid from Federal Budget	—	E. 10·25%	141,9[00] (2,83[8] A.M[.E])
Unemployment	1·3% W. 50% E. 50%	—	2% W. 50% E. 50%	103,2[00] (2,05[?] A.M[.E])
Notes: W. Worker (Employee) E. Employer	A.M.E. Unit = 4 DM For unemployment small concerns (less than DM 90,000) are exempt.		A.M.E. Unit = [?] (a) benefits in ca[sh] (b) benefits in ki[nd]	

There are minor variations to the tables applicable to certain classes of workers in B[elgium,] Italy and Luxembourg.

Social Security in the Common Market 123

NCE	ITALY	LUXEMBOURG		NETHERLANDS	
ributions wages ng	Contributions % of wages Ceiling	Contributions % of wages Ceiling		Contributions % of wages Ceiling	
% 11,400 NF (2,367 A.M.E.)	14·03% W. 0·15% — E. 13·88%	6% W. 4% E. 2%	138,700 FL. or 380 FL per day. (2,774 A.M.E.)	5%(a) +4·5% (b) W. 2·5% + 1% E. 2·5% + 3·5%	8,451 fl. (2,334 A.M.E.)
% 25%	19·15%	12%	—	E. 1·5%	8,451fl. (2,334 A.M.E.)
	W. 6·35% — E. 12·80%	W. 50% E. 50%	—	W. 6·8% Old Age 1·3% Survivors (E. 0·60%)	10,900 fl. (3,011 A.M.E.)
rates ling to risks. butions based al salaries, with ng of 11,400 NF A.M.E.) per	3-5% according to risks. Average 3·9% on total wages.	Group rates according to risks calculated on total salaries.		Fixed by Government (average 1·4% m. wages up to 8,451 fl.	
11,400 NF (2,307 A.M.E.)	E. 17·5% —	E. 4·29% (a)	—	E. 5%	10,900 fl. (3,011 A.M.E.)
0·25% W. 0·05% E. 0·20%	E. 2·3%	—	—	0·4%(a) +0·6%(b) W. 50% E. 50%	8,451 fl. (2,334 A.M.E.)
. Unit = 4·94 NF ity falls amily allow-	A.M.E. Unit = 625 Lires	A.M.E. Unit = 50 FL. (a) 2·80% for commercial concerns. Unemployment from public funds.		A.M.E. Unit = 3·62 fl. (a) benefits in cash (b) benefits in kind	

practically nil. In Luxembourg up to 25 per cent. In the Netherlands nil.

All the Common Market countries provide for a state of invalidity. Entitlement to benefits in cash and in kind to invalidity depends mostly upon the inability of the insured person by reason of illness or infirmity to earn more than one third to one half of the normal rate of pay for the job.

The costs of Social Security in the Common Market countries as shared between the contribution of the insured persons, the contribution of employers and public funds are roughly as follows:

	Workers Contributions	Employers Contributions	Contributions for public funds	Other benefits	
	%	%	%	%	%
West Germany	24·2	41·0	26·8	8·0	100
Belgium	17·1	39·9	34·5	8·5	100
France	16·0	63·2	17·2	3·6	100
Italy	18·4	47·8	23·3	10·5	100
Netherlands	40·0	39·3	12·7	8·0	100

II. Workers in occupations other than dependant wage-earners

There is no unemployment insurance or benefit for self-employed persons in any of the Common Market countries.

The following table shows how the other services are covered in each country by *compulsory* contributions.

	West Germany	Belgium	France	Italy	Luxembourg	Netherlands
Sickness.	*			*	*	
Maternity.	*			*	*	
Invalidity.	*		*	*	*	
Old Age.	*	**	**	*	*	**
Survivors.	*	**	**	*	*	**
Accidents at work and occupational illness.	*	*			*	
Family Allowance.	**	**	**		*	**(i)

** all categories of independent self-employed persons including the liberal professions, heads of commercial enterprises, agricultural and similar and artizans.
*limited to one or more specified categories of self-employed persons.
(i) depends on salary or wage level.

Thus in the Common Market, except Italy, self-employed persons benefit from family allowances. In all the countries there are provisions for voluntary membership for all services available to employed workers.

For old age, there is general coverage in Belgium, France and Luxembourg (except for the liberal professions) and in the Netherlands where the entire population is covered.

Social Security in the Common Market

For sickness, protection is wider in Luxembourg and in Italy than in the four other countries. In France sickness insurance has been extended to self-employed agriculturists.

Within the general category of self-employed persons there are several sub-divisions made up of artisans, people working in commerce and industry, members of the liberal professions and the self-employed in agriculture.

(a) *Artisans* The word is interpreted as craftsmen who sell the products of their own craftsmanship, but not the products made by others.

In *West Germany*, they participate in invalidity-old age-death insurance if they are registered with the appropriate guild or association. They are insured for accidents and occupational illness if their trade or professional body so provides in its statutes. They are entitled to family allowances and can contribute voluntarily to sickness insurance.

In *Belgium*, they contribute and are entitled to old age and family allowance insurance and they can be voluntary contributors to sickness, maternity, invalidity and in certain cases they can insure for occupational illness.

In *France*, Artisans are only entitled to old age and family allowance insurance and, for survivors, to a reversion of pension and death benefits. Other risks have to be covered by voluntary insurance.

In *Italy*, independent non-wage earning Artisans and members of their families working for them are entitled to benefits in kind for sickness and some rights in invalidity and old age.

In *Luxembourg*, there are special provisions for the insurance of independent non-wage earning workers.

In the *Netherlands*, these classes of persons are covered for old age, widows and orphans, and family allowances up to a limit of earnings as well as for family allowances (if they do not earn more than about £1,500) for the third and subsequent child.

(b) *Self-employed persons in business.*

In general terms, this category of self-employed person enjoys more favourable conditions in Social Security than the artisan.

In *West Germany*, they are entitled to family allowance. If their guild or association so provides in its statutes, they contribute for benefit for insurance against accidents at work and occupational illness. Voluntary schemes only are available for sickness and maternity for themselves and their families, although such insurance is compulsory for certain heads of businesses.

In *Belgium*, this category have rights only to old age pension and

Social Security services for their families. They can join voluntary schemes for sickness insurance. Widows and orphans have the right to pensions.

In *France*, self-employed persons in business have rights only to old age pension with reversion to widow, and family allowance. Under certain conditions, they can insure their families for sickness, maternity, old age and death benefits and accidents at work.

In *Italy*, Social Security for the self-employed in business is limited to owners of small businesses. These and members of their families who work for them as well as their commercial agents and representatives, are entitled to Social Security in respect of services in kind for sickness. Agents working on commission are also insured for old age invalidity.

In *Luxembourg*, self-employed persons in business participate in sickness and maternity, pensions for invalidity and old age, family allowance and birth payments. They can participate voluntarily in insurance for accidents at work and occupational illness.

In the *Netherlands*, the whole population participate in old age pension insurance, the heads of a business included. These can draw family allowance with three children and an income of less than the equivalent of £350 per annum. Voluntary participation is available for sick benefits in kind; and for medical care if the income is less than the equivalent of £800 plus £25 for each child.

Thus the method of fixing the contributions for self-employed persons varies greatly from one country to another.

In France in certain sectors of Social Security, there are fixed annual rates and in other sectors rates which vary according to the remuneration or the level of the benefits which the person chooses, subject to a minimum contribution.

In the other countries, contributions depend mainly upon the income of the insured self-employed person, with the State contributing the balance. The level of contribution mostly carries a ceiling and insurance beyond that is not subject to assessment for contribution.

(c) *Self-employed persons in Agriculture.*

Self-employed persons in Agriculture (Agriculturists or Cultivators) are subject to special regimes in the Common Market countries.

In *West Germany*, this category excludes persons whose agricultural activities are subsidiary to their other interests and who do not depend for their livelihood upon their agricultural activities, and the classification is based upon the extent of those activities.

Those who fall within the category of cultivators participate in old age-assistance-insurance for themselves and their widow or widower;

and accidents at work. They can, under specified conditions, become voluntary members of old age pension and sickness insurance in which event their dependents can receive sick benefits in cash for illness and maternity; widows receive benefits from the old age-assistance scheme and pension after the death of the insured person.

In *France*, agriculturists are recognised as self-employed if their income is above a certain minimum level. If not, they are regarded as wage-earners and fall under the Social Security regime for sickness-invalidity, old age, widows pension and family allowance.

In *Italy*, bona fide self-employed agriculturists fall under compulsory insurance for sickness and maternity benefits in kind, for old age, death, accidents at work and occupational illness. They are excluded from family allowance.

In *Luxembourg*, agriculturists are later to be included in benefits in kind and cash for sickness and maternity. They are entitled to retirement pension and are the only class of self-employed persons under compulsory insurance for accidents at work and occupational illness. They are entitled to family allowance similar to other categories of workers. Survivors are entitled to certain Social Security services.

(d) *Members of the Liberal Professions.*

In *West Germany*, the legislation of the Lander makes it compulsory for certain groups of the liberal professions to join insurance schemes for retirement pensions. They can also voluntarily take part in state insurance for sickness and old age pensions. Certain independent professions (midwives, nurses, musicians, actors, etc.) are regarded as employed persons for sickness benefits and pensions.

In *Belgium*, the position of persons in the liberal professions is similar to that of Artisans.

In *France*, too, they are treated in the same way as other independent self-employed persons for family allowance and old age. Only doctors and pharmacists are entitled to invalidity benefits in cash.

In *Italy*, members of the liberal professions have no rights to family allowance, but they are entitled to certain benefits in kind for sickness, invalidity and old age.

In *Luxembourg*, they are included in benefits in cash and certain benefits in kind for sickness, maternity and family allowance. Their families are entitled to insurance for sickness and maternity.

Each of the Common Market countries is engaged in revising its Social Security services in more or less degree.

Belgium is concerned with establishing a uniform basis for old age insurance for the entire population and in re-classifying the categories of occupation with particular regard for encouraging the setting up of new industrial enterprises and in co-ordinating the different administratives branches.

France is concerned with the reform of the system of family allowance and unification of those concerned with old age.

Italy, too, is moving toward functional unification and simplification.

The Netherlands are engaged upon the reform of Social Security services so that benefits can be related to lost earnings and the degree of incapacity. It has been suggested that the ceiling on earnings should be abolished and there are moves to make family allowance available to all.

In an area so complex as Social Security, harmonisation is a vague term which can be interpreted in many ways and the Treaty confines its definition of the requirements for improving Social Security more to a statement of intent rather than to any fixed purpose. The intergovernmental Committees working within the Community have made progress largely because their method is one of exploration and consultation which allows time for a basis of collaboration to evolve from widely different systems.

Because the Common Market is an *economic* union it implies that workers must be able to move over national boundaries without difficulties. It is therefore essential that a degree of harmonisation of payments and benefits wherever they are paid or received should be achieved.

CHAPTER 10

Mobility of People and Capital

Lionello Levi Sandri, vice-president of the E.E.C. Commission and Commission member with special responsibility for Social Affairs has said that the Common Market's social policy does not lend itself to systematic treatment but the 'upward harmonisation' of living and working conditions is a fundamental principle of the Treaty. An *economic* union implies freedom of movement for labour and such aspects of social policy as achieving equal pay for men and women, the alignment of social security benefits and payments, the equating of relative values of national professional qualifications, the process of allowing freedom of establishment and freedom to supply services together with retraining schemes are essential contributions in attempting to achieve the aims of the Treaty.

In fulfilment of the principle of equal remuneration for equal work between men and women as laid down in Article 119 of the Treaty, the Commission sent a formal recommendation to member-countries on 20 July 1960 summarising its interpretation of the Article and suggested ways of applying it from 30 June 1961—the date laid down in the Treaty. It was also proposed, and it was subsequently approved by the Council that the maximum differences should be reduced by 15 per cent by 30 June 1962 and to 10 per cent by 30 June 1963 and that all discrimination should be eliminated by 31 December 1964. However the translation of this policy from principle to practice has met with some obstacles. The target date of December 1964 was not met but women's average earnings are now much nearer the average for men than they were in 1957.

* * *

It is essential to differentiate between 'mobility' of labour and 'migration' of labour. At a Conference on Regional Economies held in Brussels in 1961, Robert Marjolin, vice-president of the Commission said that migration of labour from region to region or country to country is sometimes necessary but such movements are generally accompanied by sociological, psychological and political difficulties and he stressed that wherever possible the aim should be for industry to move to the worker. When the worker moves to the work it generally means movement from rural areas to congested central areas. The large investments and contributions by the European Investment Bank and European Development Fund, in Southern Italy are an indication of the E.E.C.'s concern in this matter.

However in an economic union the *right* to freedom of movement is there. A worker should be able to move to another country to work or he can look for another job in his own town. Great stress has been laid on E.E.C. retraining schemes to help greater mobility between jobs in the same region rather than for greater mobility between regions.

The first move towards intra-community movement of workers came from a decision of the Council on 12 June 1961 to implement the first regulations. These came into force on 1 September 1961. The regulations provided that any vacancies on the national labour market could be filled within three weeks by the domestic administration from its own nationals but that after this period offers of employment would be transmitted to the other member-countries. Workers accepting this offer and moving to another Community country would be able to renew their labour permits there for the same occupation after one year of regular employment; for any other occupation for which they were qualified, after three years; and for any kind of paid work, after four years. Automatic granting of labour permits would apply in the case of occupations for which there was a labour shortage, while workers specifically applied for by an employer would be granted a permit without reference to the domestic labour market if supported by family reasons or the needs of the firm concerned. Since that first regulation came into force free movement has been virtually achieved although in exceptional circumstances a fortnight's period of priority for local labour can be introduced if unemployment is unduly high in certain areas or skills. With a working population of over 75,000,000 it will be seen from the table on the following page that, in fact, migration has been small.

The Treaty also provides for freedom of establishment of firms, branches, agencies and for individuals such as doctors, dentists, architects etc. and also the freedom to supply such services as building, banking, insurance, wholesale and retail distribution and the exercise of the liberal professions anywhere in the Community by the end of the transition period. A first directive was adopted by the Council of Ministers on 25 October 1961. The programme envisaged

Mobility of People and Capital

INTRA-COMMUNITY MOVEMENT OF WORKERS SINCE THE ENTRY INTO FORCE OF REGULATIONS

Figures relate to first work permits issued to workers of the member-state moving from one Community country to another.

	E.E.C. total	Italian Contribution to E.E.C. total
1961	292,494	233,249
1962	281,549	221,173
1963	231,701	177,572
1964	240,390	180,137
1965	317,927	254,185
1966	260,619	216,357

the abolition of discrimination based on nationality hitherto restricting access to numerous activities, as follows:

by end-1963 for the textile, footwear, paper, basic chemicals, metal-working industries, wholesale trade, banking and dealings in property;

by end-1965 for retail distribution, department stores and the food industry;

by end-1967 for pharmacies (chemists), veterinary surgeons, insurance agents and transport;

by end-1969 for education, film production and publicity material.

As far as the members of the medical profession are concerned, while the principle of the acceptance of equivalence of qualifications has been established, the Treaty does not over-ride all the different national laws relating to the practice of medicine. The unofficial, but very effective Permanent Committee of the doctors of the Community is recognised as the spokesman for the medical profession in the Community and is engaged in the task of evolving a basis for implementing the principle and practice of the free movement of doctors.

The member-countries are not pledged to adopt identical legislation and regulations but must ensure that nationals of other member-countries enjoy equal rights with their own citizens.

* * *

Details of the aims of the European Social Fund are given in the chapter on the Treaty of Rome p. 28. The main aims of the Fund are to help finance vocational retraining, resettlement and other aids, in order to ensure the re-employment of workers who have to change their jobs. By the end of 1966 the Fund had contributed $40,400,000, being half the cost, to retrain and resettle 508,000 workers, of whom

310,000 were Italian, 103,000 Germany, 80,000 French and the remainder from the Benelux countries.

FREEDOM OF MOVEMENT OF CAPITAL

Without free movement of capital it is unlikely that there would be real freedom of movement of labour or freedom of establishment of services. The first directive for the implementation of Article 67 of the Treaty on freedom of movement of capital was approved by the Council of Ministers in May 1960 and came into force in June 1960. It established:

(1) unconditional freedom of capital movements connected with the freeing of trade goods, of services, and of the movement of persons, and also with the free exercise of the right of establishment;

(2) unconditional and irreversible freedom for sale and purchase of stocks and shares quoted on the Community's stock exchanges;

(3) conditional freedom with regard to the issuing and placing of stocks and shares on capital markets, and for the purchase of unquoted stocks and shares. Any member-country might, however, maintain or reimpose existing restrictions if their abolition was likely to hinder the achievement of its economic policy objectives.

Under this directive West Germany, Belgium and Luxembourg were not required to take any further liberalisation measures since their foreign currency legislation already went beyond the obligations imposed by the Directive.

By 1967 some liberalisation of capital movements between member-countries had been achieved and attention has been paid to removing exchange controls to give investors and borrowers access to the Community's capital market.

CHAPTER 11

A Common Transport Policy

Comparatively slow progress has been made on a Common Transport policy. The Treaty laid down the guide lines and these are given on page 23. A memorandum on a Common Transport Policy on the lines of Article 79 (1) was submitted by the Commission to the Council of Ministers on 28 April 1961. After the Ministers of Transport of the Six had agreed on 28 November 1961, to consult each other about any future legislative or administrative changes in the transport policy of their own countries, the Council of Ministers asked the Commission in February 1962, to present detailed proposals for a common transport policy for roads, railways, and inland waterways by May of that year.

The Commission's programme was based on the principles of (i) equality of treatment; (ii) financial independence; (iii) freedom of action for transport enterprises; (iv) free choice by the user of the means of transport; and (v) co-ordination of investment, the Commission's proposals included the following aspects:
Access to the Market The Commission's proposals for intra-Community traffic aimed at the rapid elimination of discrimination on grounds of nationality, easing of quotas on carriers, and the supervision of transport capacity. Regulations governing the admission to the market by member-states would be brought into line simultaneously. The Commission proposed that present bilateral quotas be gradually replaced by a Community quota open to carriers in the Six irrespective of nationality; this change would be spread over five years beginning in 1964 and be completed by 1969 by the introduction of a Community procedure for managing the quota. The programme also proposed a gradual procedure for admitting non-resident carriers to domestic road and inland waterways services.
Transport Rate Policy The Commission proposed for all types of transport a system of scales of charges subject to prior publication. Each transport undertaking would be free to determine its own tariffs with certain limits to be laid down by the public authorities con-

cerned. From 1 July 1964, member-states would apply rate scales on the basis of the common principles though using their own procedure. From 1966 national systems would be harmonised so as to establish a common tariff system throughout the Community by 1969.

Various measures of harmonisation were proposed, including (a) the abolition of double taxation; (b) the harmonisation of the Rules governing duty-free entry of fuel in the tanks of motor vehicles; (c) the alignment of the basis of assessment of vehicle tax between member-states; (d) harmonisation of taxes on fuel; and (e) equal fiscal treatment of rail, road, and waterways transport.

The next landmark in transport policy was when the Council of Ministers agreed on 22 June 1965, a framework for a Community transport system which would regulate competition in all sectors by the progressive introduction of fixed-rate limits in two separate stages.

During the first stage—1966 to 1969—only commercial transport between member-countries would be subject to E.E.C. regulations. Upper and lower tariff limits would be published for certain classes of road and rail traffic, though contracts could be made outside these rates under certain circumstances provided the details were published. This contrasts with the British system, where private hauliers may charge what the traffic will bear. Non-binding reference limits would be fixed for water transport, but contracts made outside these limits would also be published.

In the second stage—1969 to 1972—the reference limit system would be extended to certain categories of national and international traffic of heavy goods (the Council had still to decide on a definition) and also on other forms of national transport. By 1970, therefore, almost all road transportation and a significant part of rail goods traffic in the Common Market would be covered by a strict system of rate control, while a more flexible system would apply to all waterborne traffic and the remaining section of railway traffic, though probably to only a small part of road haulage.

A final tariff structure has yet to be agreed.

CHAPTER 12

The European Coal and Steel Community

The European Coal and Steel Community (E.C.S.C.) set up in 1952, was the pioneer of European integration. It applied the Community method to the coal and steel industries as a first step towards integration of the economy as a whole.

From the start the European Coal and Steel Community passed through a period of rapid growth. Steel output more than doubled from 42 million metric tons in 1952 to 85 million metric tons in 1966. The action of the High Authority and the operation of the Community aided this development by bringing price stability, easing distribution of coal during the boom, providing new markets for iron-ore and steel through a more rational trade pattern, and stimulating competition. Since 1965, faced with the danger of excess supply the High Authority has intervened to restrain over-production of steel and to limit additions to capacity.

The coal industry, after expanding initially in conditions of acute shortage, found that a growing share of the energy market was being won by oil and other new sources of energy: in 1965 coal provided only 38 per cent of total energy consumption, compared with 53 per cent in 1960 and 73 per cent in 1950. In this situation the High Authority's task is to ensure the orderly retreat of coal at a pace which avoids social or economic disruption. Uneconomic pits are being closed and others regrouped and modernised. Average productivity in the Community rose from 1·4 tons per manshift underground in 1953 to 2·6 tons in 1966.

Since coal output first began to fall in 1957, the number of workers employed in the Community's coal industry dropped by over 400,000 to 650,000 in 1966. The E.C.S.C. Treaty's retraining and re-employment provisions have greatly eased the impact of this major change; an amendment to the E.C.S.C. Treaty in March 1960 extended and widened the High Authority's powers to apply such measures. The High Authority is also promoting industrial redevelopment in the areas until now mainly dependent on coalmining for their livelihood. A plan for cutting back Belgian coal capacity by one third between 1960 and 1964 was carried out under High Authority supervision. In 1965 a High Authority decision authorised subsidies by member governments to ease the problems involved in mine closures and to speed up modernisation. In February 1967 the Six agreed on a system of subsidies for coking coal to enable Community production to compete with imported supplies.

The High Authority has direct powers to control restrictive trading practices. All company mergers in the coal and steel sector require the approval of the High Authority, which is given only if the resulting unit will not hold a dominant position in its sector of the market; any firm or group which already has a dominant market position is subject to strict High Authority control. Cartels and other trade agreements are illegal unless explicitly authorised.

The High Authority carries out an industrial policy for coal and steel by means of:

(1)   short and long-term Community-wide forecasts for supply and demand.
(2)   investment guidance and co-ordination, notably through loans to firms.
(3)   joint research programs, aided by High Authority funds.
(4)   Community help for regional development.

Regular short-term forecasts supply detailed information on market developments in coal and steel, while medium and long-term forecasts, known as General Objectives, guide industry on modernisation, production and investment needs. Additional guidance on priorities is provided by the 'opinions' which the High Authority issues, in line with the General Objectives, on major investment projects, which firms are required to submit to it. It also aids certain key projects directly by relending the proceeds of loans which it raises on advantageous terms in the world's capital markets.

From 1954 to September 1966 the High Authority raised nearly $650 million in loans ($736 million if loan guarantees are included) and relent $580 million to part-finance new industrial projects worth in total more than twice this amount and representing well over 10 per cent of all investment in coal and steel in the Community during this period.

The High Authority also makes grants for pure and applied research projects related to coal and steel production, full details of which are supplied to all interested bodies in the Community. This aid, totalling $50 million for sixty-five projects by 1966, makes larger individual projects possible and cuts down duplication of effort.

The European Coal and Steel Community

Lastly, the High Authority provides loans to help regional development in areas affected by decline or changes in the coal, steel or iron-ore industries. It has lent $30 million to help build new factories creating employment for 9,000 workers and has earmarked a further $56 million for this purpose from 1966 onwards. The transition from coal or steel to new industrial activities is further softened by aid in retraining and re-employing workers.

The Community Executives believe that the coal problem can only be solved as part of a general Community policy for energy, including oil, gas, atomic power and hydro-electricity. With energy costs a basic factor in any industrial economy, a common energy policy is also vital to the completion of the common market.

Energy policy was not included as such in the Community treaties, since the E.C.S.C. the Common Market and Euratom each cover separate sectors of this field.

However, a special inter-Executive working group has been set up under the chairmanship of the High Authority, and this led to the signature in April 1964 of a Protocol of Agreement on Energy. This lays down the objectives of a common energy policy which must reconcile cheapness with an adequate guarantee for security of supply. At present, most Community-produced energy—for example, coal—is relatively expensive compared with imports, which in 1965 provided 46 per cent of Community power supplies. New Community sources of energy—natural gas and atomic power—should begin to provide significant amounts of cheaper energy in the mid-1970's, but imports will meanwhile continue to rise, and will eventually supply at least half the Community's requirements.

The first European labour card, enabling skilled coal and steel workers to move freely within the Community, was issued on 1 September 1957. On 7 December 1957 an agreement on Social Security for Migrant Workers was concluded, and was subsequently extended by the E.E.C. to all workers.

From 1955 to 1966 the High Authority approved re-adaptation projects involving 270,000 workers—including roughly 220,000 coal miners—and expenditure of $81 million. The governments concerned contributed a like sum. Re-adaptation initially eased the consequences of increased competition in the common market, and now ensures that the brunt of structural and technical change in the coal and steel industries is not borne by the workers. It is playing a major part in the long-term re-organisation of the E.C.S.C. industries.

Re-adaptation provides for tiding-over allowances between jobs (maximum period two years; 90–100 per cent of previous earnings for first four months). The making up of pay in the new job to 100 per cent of old wages (for up to two years). The payment of removal and transfer costs and the free training for a new job.

HEALTH, SAFETY, SOCIAL SURVEYS

The High Authority has allocated $26 million as grants for research into industrial medicine and safety. Work on such problems as silicosis, pneumoconiosis, industrial noise, air pollution, and rehabilitation after accidents has been co-ordinated throughout the Community and stimulated where necessary. The High Authority has also carried out surveys of real wages, household budgets, employment, labour mobility, and housing conditions, which have provided the first Community-wide comparative data on which trade unions and employers can base their studies and claims.

After negotiations which began in Paris in June 1950, and had lasted for nine months, the draft of a treaty setting up a 'European Coal and Steel Community' (Communauté Européenne du Charbon et de l'Acier) under a supra-national authority was initialled on 19 March, 1951, by representatives of France, West Germany, Italy, Belgium, the Netherlands, and Luxembourg, the Treaty itself being signed in Paris on 18 April 1951, by the Foreign Ministers of the six participating countries.

The six-nation conference for the pooling of the coal and steel resources of Western Europe under a supra-national authority, based on the proposals out-lined on 9 May 1950, by M. Robert Schuman, the French Foreign Minister, opened at the Quai d'Orsay on 20 June 1950, after the French Government's invitation to such a conference had been accepted by the Governments of West Germany, Italy, and the Benelux countries. The French delegation was led by M. Jean Monnet, Commissioner-General for Planning and Reconstruction, who, with M. Schuman himself, had played a major part in drawing up the 'Schuman Plan'; the West German delegation by Professor Walter Hallstein, Secretary-General for Foreign Affairs; the Italian delegation by Professor Paolo Taviani, a member of the Italian Parliament, who had been actively associated in the formulation of the Schuman plan; the Belgian delegation by M. Max Suetens, Ambassador in Paris; the Netherlands delegation by Dr. Dirk Spierenburg, of the Ministry of Economic Affairs; and the Luxembourg delegation by M. Albert Wehrer, Minister in Paris.

The conference was opened by M. Schuman, who stressed that 'no system such as that to which we look forward has ever been tried in practice', and that sovereign States had never before 'entrusted or

The European Coal and Steel Community

even contemplated the delegation of a fraction of their sovereignty to an independent, supranational organisation' such as it was proposed to set up. He continued: 'We shall have to draw up a draft treaty which will define the main lines of this common authority, its powers, its machinery, the means of appealing against its decisions and of bringing its responsibilities into play. We shall have to consider—without, however, including them in the treaty—the technical details which will be embodied in agreements to be drawn up later, after the treaty itself has been ratified. Without losing sight of the special needs of our own countries, we must be aware that national interests nowadays consist precisely in finding, beyond national boundaries, the means of achieving a more rational economic structure, cheaper and greater production, and greater and more accessible markets'.

After emphasising that the French plan was not designed to conflict with or over-ride other plans for the integration of the European economy, such as those formulated by Dr. Strikker in the O.E.E.C., M. Schuman drew attention to the fact that a special characteristic of the French proposals, over and above their economic implications, was their political value, arising from the French Government's desire 'to associate in a joint and permanent work of peace two nations which for centuries have clashed in bloody conflict'.

Expressing regret that the British Government had not seen its way to participate in the Paris conference, M. Schuman declared: 'We had earnestly wished that Britain might be present at our discussions. We cannot conceive of Europe without her. We know, and find comfort in the thought, that the British Government wishes our work well. Certain differences which prevented it from taking part, at least at the present stage, appeared in the course of explanations which were both frank and friendly. We continue to hope that the doubts and scruples, which a somewhat doctrinaire outlook was unable to overcome, will finally give way before more positive achievements. The French Government will act in accordance with the wishes of all the participating countries in keeping the British Government informed of the progress of negotiations, and will give it the possibility, if not of joining in our work—and this we continue to hope for—at least of bringing to our attention its own comments and observations, which might open the prospect of future co-operation.'

After initial exchanges of views between the delegations, the French Government issued on 27 June 1950, a series of draft proposals aimed at 'facilitating the formulation and the working out in common of a treaty to give effect to the French proposal of 9 May (i.e. M. Schuman's plan for the integration of coal and steel resources under a supra-national authority). The conference was thereupon adjourned for a short period to enable these proposals to be studied by the various Governments, but re-assembled in Paris in 3 July 1950 when it was agreed to set up five expert 'working parties' to study the following specific problems raised by the French draft: (1) institutional questions such as the proposed supra-national authority, democratic control of that body, and methods of arbitration in the event of disputes; (2) commercial policy; (3) definition of the terms 'coal' and 'steel' as envisaged under M. Schuman's proposals; (4) questions of production and prices; and (5) problems relating to wages and conditions of labour.

The five working parties completed their studies of specific aspects of the Schuman Plan on 10 August 1950 when the Quai d'Orsay announced that the preliminary phase of the negotiations had been completed and that the final phase of the conference would commence after a month's adjournment. The negotiations were resumed some three weeks later, and thereafter continued at intervals, with several adjournments, for another six months, during which period close contact was maintained with the national Governments with regard to the detailed provisions of the draft treaty.

On 19 March 1951 the draft of the treaty creating a 'European Coal and Steel Community' was signed at the Quai d'Orsay by the leaders of the French, West German, Italian, Belgian, Netherlands, and Luxembourg delegations. At the same time the text of the draft treaty was officially made public, together with an agreement covering the transitional period (fixed at five years) between the signing of the treaty and its application.

In a speech after the signing ceremony, M. Monnet laid special emphasis on three aspects of the treaty which, he declared, would transform the economy of Western Europe: (1) the supra-national character of the European Coal and Steel Community; (2) the creation of a single market of 150,000,000 consumers and the pooling of the coal and steel resources of six nations; (3) 'the elimination of restrictive cartel practices and of excessive concentrations of economic power'. He also emphasised that, for the first time, six countries had come together 'not to seek a provisional compromise among national interests but to take a concerted view of their common interests', a development which represented 'a fundamental change in the nature of the relations among the countries of Europe, from the national form which has opposed and divided them to the supra-national form which reconciles and unites them'. Speeches in support

The European Coal and Steel Community

were made by the leaders of the other delegations, Professor Hallstein (West Germany) declaring that the treaty was an important step towards the achievement of a United Europe.

After the initialling of the treaty, the Governments of West Germany, Italy, Belgium, the Netherlands, and Luxembourg were invited by the French Government to send their Foreign Ministers to a further conference in Paris with the aim of reaching agreement on outstanding questions relating to the various organs of the European Coal and Steel Community which had not been settled in the draft treaty, e.g. the number of members of the High Authority, the Common Assembly, the Council of Ministers, the method in which those members would be chosen, and their voting powers. Accordingly, a conference of Foreign Ministers opened at the Quai d'Orsay on 12 April under the chairmanship of M. Robert Schuman (France), West Germany being represented by Dr. Konrad Adenauer (Federal Chancellor and Foreign Minister), Italy by Count Carlo Sforza, Belgium by Mr. Paul Van Zeeland, the Netherlands by Dr. Dirk Stikker, and Luxembourg by M. Joseph Bech. The conference was also attended by the Belgian Minister of Foreign Trade (M. Meurice), the Netherlands Minister for Economic Affairs (Professor van den Brink), and the leaders of the national delegation which had drawn up the treaty, including M. Monnet and Professor Hallstein.

The conference ended on 18 April when the six Foreign Ministers, together with M. Meurice and Professor van den Brink, signed a Joint Delegation formally setting up the European Coal and Steel Community, the name under which the 'Schuman Plan' organisation will be officially known. The treaty, which was for 50 years, provided for the institution of a common market by the abolition of import and export duties, subsidies, and other restrictive practices on the movement of coal and steel between the participating countries, and the establishment of a High Authority, an Assembly, a Council, and a Court of Justice as the administrative institutions of the Community.

A summary of the main provisions of the Treaty constituting the European Coal and Steel Community is given below.

PREAMBLE

'The President of the German Federal Republic, H.R.H. the Prince Royal of Belgium, the President of the French Republic, the President of the Italian Republic, H.R.H. the Grand Duchess of Luxembourg, and H.M. the Queen of the Netherlands;

'Considering that world peace may be safeguarded only by creative efforts equal to the dangers which menace it;

'Convinced that the contribution which an organised and vital Europe can bring to civilisation is indispensable to the maintenance of peaceful relations;

'Conscious of the fact that Europe can be built only by concrete actions which create a real solidarity and by the establishment of common bases for economic development;

'Desirous of assisting through the expansion of their basic production in raising the standard of living and in furthering the works of peace;

'Resolved to substitute for historic rivalries a fusion of their essential interests; to establish, by creating an economic community, the foundation of a broad and independent community among peoples long divided by bloody conflicts; and to lay the bases of institutions capable of giving direction to their future common destiny;

'Have decided to create a European Coal and Steel Community and . . . have designated. . . plenipotentiaries. . . and have agreed to the following provisions';

THE EUROPEAN COAL AND STEEL COMMUNITY

Art. 1 'By the present Treaty the High Contracting Parties institute among themselves a European Coal and Steel Community, based on a common market, common objectives, and common institutions.'

Art. 2 'The mission of the European Coal and Steel Community is to contribute to economic expansion, the development of employment and the improvement of the standard of living in the participating countries through the institution, in harmony with the general economy of the member-states, of a common market as defined in Art. 4.

The Community must progressively establish conditions which will in themselves assure the most rational distribution of production at the highest possible level of productivity, while safeguarding the continuity of employment and avoiding the creating of fundamental and persistent disturbances in the economies of the member-states.'

Art. 3 Within the framework of their respective powers and responsibilities, the institutions of the Community should: '(a) see that the common market is regularly supplied, taking account of the needs of third countries; (b) assure to all consumers in comparable positions within the common market equal access to the sources of production; (c) seek the establishment of the lowest prices which are possible without requiring any corresponding rise either in the prices charged by the same enterprises in other transactions or in the price-level as a whole in another period, while at the same time permitting

The European Coal and Steel Community

necessary amortisation and providing normal possibilities of remuneration for capital invested; (d) see that conditions are maintained which will encourage enterprises to expand and improve their ability to produce and to promote a policy of rational development of natural resources, avoiding inconsiderate exhaustion of such resources; (e) promote the improvement of the living and working conditions of the labour force in each of the industries under its jurisdiction so as to make possible the equalisation of such conditions in an upward direction; (f) further the development of international trade and see that equitable limits are observed in prices charged on external markets; (g) promote the regular expansion and the modernisation of production, as well as the improvement of its quality, under conditions which preclude any protection against competing industries, except where justified by illegitimate action on the part of such industries or in their favour'.

Art. 4 The following were recognised to be incompatible with the common market for coal and steel, and were therefore 'abolished and prohibited' within the Community: (a) import and export duties, or charges with an equivalent effect, and quantitative restrictions on the movement of coal and steel; (b) measures or practices discriminating among producers, buyers, or consumers, specifically as concerned prices, delivery terms and transportation rates, as well as measures or practices which hampered the buyer in the free choice of his supplier; (c) subsidies or state assistance, or special charges imposed by the state, in any form whatsoever; (d) restrictive practices tending towards the division of markets or the exploitation of the consumer.

Art. 5 The Community would accomplish its mission with 'limited direct intervention', and to this end it would: 'enlighten and facilitate the action of the interested parties' by collecting information, organising consultations, and defining general objectives; place financial means at the disposal of enterprises for their investments and participate in the expenses of re-adaptation; assure the establishment, maintenance, and observance of normal conditions of competition, and take direct action with respect to production and the operation of the market only when circumstances made it absolutely necessary, publish the justifications for its action and take the necessary measures to ensure observance of the rules set forth in the Treaty. The institutions of the Community should carry out these activities with 'as little administrative machinery as possible' and in close co-operation with the interested parties.

Art. 6 Provided that the Community should have 'juridical personality' and that it should enjoy, in its international relationships, 'the juridical capacity necessary to the exercise of its functions and the attainment of its ends'.

ECONOMIC AND SOCIAL PROVISIONS

General Provisions (*Arts*. 46–48) The High Authority might at any time consult the Governments, the various interested parties (enterprises, workers, consumers, and dealers) and their associations, as well as any experts, and should by these means:

(1) Carry on a permanent study of markets and price tendencies;

(2) Periodically draw up non-compulsory programme forecasts dealing with production, consumption, exports, and imports;

(3) Periodically work out general programmes with respect to modernisation, the long-term orientation of manufacturing, and the expansion of productive capacity;

(4) At the request of the interested Governments, participate in the study of the possibilities of re-employment, either in existing industries or through the creation of new activities, of workers set free by the evolution of the market or by technical transformations;

(5) Gather all information necessary to the appraisal of the possibilities of improving the living and working conditions of the labour force in the industries under its jurisdiction, and of the risks which menaced such living conditions.

The High Authority would not divulge information which by its nature was considered a professional secret, and in particular information pertaining to the commercial relations or the breakdown of the costs of production of enterprises. With this reservation, it should publish such data as might be useful to Governments or to any other interested parties. The High Authority might impose fines and daily penalty payments upon those enterprises which evaded their obligations resulting from decisions made in application of these provisions, or which knowingly furnished false information.

The right of enterprises to form associations was not affected by the Treaty, but membership of such associations must be voluntary; these associations could engage in any activity which was not contrary to the provisions of the Treaty or to the decisions or recommendations of the High Authority.

Financial Provisions (*Arts*. 49–53) The High Authority was empowered to procure the funds necessary to the accomplishment of its mission (a) by placing levies on the production of coal and steel (b) by borrowing, whilst it might also receive grants. The levies were intended to cover administrative expenses, the non-reimbursable assistance provided for re-adaptation (see below), and expenditures to en_ courage technical and economic research, but the funds obtained by borrowing might be used by the High Authority only to grant loans. The levies would be assessed annually on the various products according to their average value, but the rate of levy might not exceed 1 per cent unless previously authorised by a two-thirds majority of the Council.

Investment and Financial Assistance (Arts. 54–56) The High Authority might facilitate the carrying out of investment programmes by granting loans to enterprises or by giving its guarantee to loans which they might obtain elsewhere. With the concurrence of the Council acting by unanimous vote, the High Authority might assist by the same means in financing works and installations which contributed directly and principally to increase production, lower production costs, or facilitate marketing of products subject to its jurisdiction. In order to encourage co-ordinated development of investments, however, the High Authority might require enterprises to submit individual programmes in advance.

If the High Authority found that the financing of a programme or the operation of the installations which entailed would require subsidies, assistance, protection, or discrimination contrary to the Treaty, it could prohibit the enterprise concerned from resorting to resources other than its own funds to put such programme into effect.

The High Authority would encourage technical and economic research concerning the production and the development of consumption of coal and steel, as well as labour safety in these industries, and to this end would establish appropriate contacts among existing research organisations. After consultation with the Consultative Committee, the High Authority might initiate and facilitate the development of such research work either by encouraging joint financing by the interested enterprises or by earmarking for that purpose any grants it might receive.

If the introduction of technical processes or new equipment within the framework of the general programmes of the High Authority should lead to an exceptional reduction in labour requirements in the coal and steel industries, creating special difficulties in one or more areas for the re-employment of the workers released, the High Authority, on the request of the interested Governments, (a) would consult the Consultative Committee; (b) might facilitate the financing of such programmes as it might approve for the creation, either in the industries subject to its jurisdiction or, with the concurrence of the Council, in any other industry, of 'new and economically sound' activities capable of assuring productive employment to the workers thus released; and (c) would grant non-reimbursable assistance to contribute to: (i) the payment of grants to workers to tide them over until they could obtain new employment, (ii) the granting of allowances to the workers for reinstallation expenses (iii) the financing of technical training for workers who were led to change their employment. The High Authority would grant non-reimbursable assistance, however, only on the condition that the interested state paid a special contribution at least equal to such assistance, unless a two-thirds majority of the Council authorised an exception to this rule.

Production (Arts. 57–59) In the field of production the High Authority would give preference to the indirect means of action at its disposal (such as co-operation with Governments) to regularise or influence general consumption, particularly that of the public services, or intervention on prices and commercial policy as provided for in the Treaty.

In case of decline in demand and if the High Authority deemed that the Community was faced with a 'period of manifest crisis' and that the action provided for above was not sufficient to cope with the situation, it should, with the concurrence of the Council, establish a system of production quotas on an equitable basis. It might, in particular, regulate the rate of operation of enterprises by appropriate levies on tonnages exceeding a reference level defined by a general decision, the amounts thus obtained being earmarked for the support of those enterprises whose production rate had dropped below the level envisaged, especially with a view to ensuring for them as far as possible the maintenance of employment.

The system of quotas would be terminated automatically on a proposal made to the Council by the High Authority after consultation with the Consultative Committee, or by the Government of one of the member-states, except in the case of a contrary decision of the Council; such a decision must be taken by unanimous vote if the proposal originated with the High Authority, or by simple majority if it originated with a Government. The High Authority might impose upon enterprises violating the decisions taken by it in application of the present articles, fines not to exceed the sum equal to the value of the irregular production.

If, on the other hand, the High Authority found that the Community was faced with a serious shortage of certain or all of the products subject to its jurisdiction, it should establish consumption priorities and determine the allocation of the coal and steel resources of the Community among the industries subject to its jurisdiction, exports, and other consumption. On the basis of the consumption priorities thus determined, the High Authority should, after consulting the enterprises concerned, establish manufacturing programmes which the enterprises would be required to execute. If the quantities actually exported by a member-state were less than the scheduled quantities which were included in the basis for total allocations to the state in question, the High Authority would, to the extent necessary, redistribute among the member-states the additional availabilities for consumption thus created whenever a new allocation was made. It might in addition, with the concurrence of the Council, decide on the establishment in all member-states of restrictions on exports to third countries and might impose upon enterprises which violated the above decisions, fines not exceeding twice the value of the manufactures or deliveries prescribed and not executed or diverted from their proper use.

Prices (*Arts*. 60–64) Pricing practices contrary to the provisions of Arts. 2–4 were prohibited, particularly (a) unfair competitive practices (especially purely temporary or purely local reductions the purpose of which was to acquire a monopoly position within the common market), and (b) 'discriminatory practices involving the application by a seller within the single market of unequal conditions to compatable transactions especially according to the nationality of the buyer'. For the above purposes:

(a) The price scales and conditions of sales to be applied by enterprises within the single market would be made public to the extent and in the form prescribed by the High Authority after consultation with the Consultative Committee; if the High Authority considered that an enterprise had chosen an abnormal base point for its price quotations, in particular one which made it possible to evade the provisions listed in (b) below, it would make the appropriate recommendations to that enterprise;

(b) The prices charged by an enterprise within the common market, calculated on the base of the point chosen for the enterprise's price scale, must not as a result of the methods of quotation: (i) be higher than the price indicated by the price scale in question for a comparable transaction, or (ii) be less than this price by a margin greater than either the margin which would make it possible to align the offer in question on that price scale, set up on the basis of another point, which procured for the buyer the lowest price at the place of delivery, or a limit fixed by the High Authority for each category of products, taking into account the origin and destination of such products.

The High Authority might also fix for one or more products subject to its jurisdiction maximum and minimum prices within the common market, and maximum or minimum export prices. If the High Authority considered that such an action was appropriate 'in order to prevent the price of coal from being established at the level of the production costs of the most costly mine whose production was temporarily required to assure the accomplishment of the aims of Art. 3,' it might authorise compensations (a) among enterprises of the same coal basin to which the same price scales were applicable; (b) after consulting the Council, among enterprises situated in different coal basins.

The High Authority might impose upon enterprises which violated these price provisions, or the decisions taken in application thereof, fines not exceeding twice the value of the irregular sales.

Agreements and Concentrations (*Arts.* 65–66) All agreements among enterprises, all decisions of associations of enterprises, and all concerted practices which would tend, directly or indirectly, to prevent, restrict, or impede the normal operation of competition within the common market were forbidden, especially those intended (a) to fix or influence prices; (b) to restrict or control production, technical development, or investments; (c) to allocate markets, products, customers, or sources of supply.

However, the High Authority would authorise enterprises to agree among themselves to specialise in the production of, or to engage in in joint buying or selling of, specified products if it considered (a) that such specialisation, or such joint buying or selling, would contribute to a substantial improvement in the production or marketing of the products in question; (b) that the agreement in question was essential to achieve such effects, and did not impose any restrictions not necessary for that purpose; (c) that it was not susceptible of giving the interested enterprises the power to influence prices, or to control or limit the production or marketing of an appreciable part of the products in question within the Common Market, or of protecting them from effective competition by other enterprises within the Common Market.

Any transaction which would have in itself the direct or indirect effect of bringing about a concentration should first be submitted to the High Authority, which would only grant the authorisation if it found that the transaction in question would not give to the interested persons or enterprises the power (a) to influence prices, to control or restrain production or marketing, or to impair the maintenance of effective competition in a substantial part of the market for such products, or (b) to evade the rules of competition resulting from the application of the Treaty, particularly by establishing an artificially privileged position involving a material advantage in access to supplies or markets.

If a concentration should occur the High Authority would order the separation of the enterprises or assets wrongly concentrated, or the cessation of common control, as well as any other action which it deemed appropriate to re-establish the independent operation of the enterprises or assets in question and to restore normal conditions of competition. If the interested parties failed to fulfil their obligations the High Authority itself would take measures of execution and might impose fines.

Impairment of the Conditions of Competition (Art. 67) Any action of a member-state which might have noticeable repercussions on the conditions of competition in the coal and steel industries would be brought by the interested Government to the attention of the High Authority. If such an action was liable to provoke a serious disequilibrium by increasing the differentials in costs of production otherwise than through variations in productivity, the High Authority, after consulting the Consultative Committee and the Council, might take the following measures:

(a) If the action of the state concerned produced harmful effects for coal or steel enterprises coming under its jurisdiction, the High Authority might authorise that state to grant to such enterprises assistance, the amount conditions, and duration of which would be determined in agreement with the High Authority;

(b) If the action of that state produced harmful effects for coal or steel enterprises subject to the jurisdiction of other member-states, the High Authority might address a recommendation to the state in question 'with a view to remedying such effects by such measures as that state may deem most compatible with its own economic equilibrium'.

Wages and Movement of Labour (Arts. 68-69) The methods of fixing wages and social benefits in force in the various member-states should not, as regards the coal and steel industries, be affected by the application of the Treaty, subject to the following provisions:

(a) If the High Authority found that abnormally low prices practised by one or several enterprises were the result of wages fixed by those enterprises at an abnormally low level in comparison with the actual wage level in the same region, it should make the necessary recommendations to the interested enterprises after consulting the Consultative Committee;

(b) If the High Authority found that a lowering of wages was leading to a drop in the standard of living of the labour force, and at the same time was being used as a means of permanent economic adjustment by enterprises or as a weapon of competition among enterprises, it should address to the enterprise or Government concerned a recommendation intended to assure the labour force of compensatory benefits to be paid for by the enterprise in question. This provision should not apply, however, to (i) overall measures taken by a member-state to re-establish its external equilibrium; (ii) wage decreases resulting from the application of the sliding scale legally or contractually established; (iii) wage decreases brought about by a decrease in the cost of living (iv) wage decreases to correct abnormal increases previously granted under exceptional circumstances no longer in existence.

If an enterprise failed to conform to a recommendation made to it in the above connection, the High Authority might impose on it fines and daily penalty payments not exceeding twice the amount of the savings in labour costs unjustifiably effected.

The member-states further agreed to prohibit any discrimination in remuneration and working conditions between national workers and immigrant workers (without prejudice to special measures concerning frontier workers), and would work out among themselves any necessary arrangements so that social security measures did not stand in the way of the movement of labour.

Transport (Art. 70) It was recognised that the establishment of the E.C.S.C. required the application of such transport rates for coal and steel as would 'make possible comparable price conditions to consumers in comparable positions'. Discriminations in transport rates, and conditions of any kind based on the country of origin or of destination of the products in question, were strictly forbidden for traffic among member-states whilst the application of special internal tariff measures in the interest of one or several coal- or steel-producing enterprises would be subject to the prior agreement of the High Authority.

Commercial Policy (Arts. 71–75) Unless otherwise stipulated in the Treaty, the competence of the Governments of the member-states with respect to commercial policy would not be affected by the Treaty.

Minimum rates, below which the member-states were bound not to lower their customs duties on coal and steel with regard to third countries, and maximum rates, above which they were bound not to raise such duties, might be fixed by unanimous decisions of the Council upon the proposal of the High Authority; between the limits thus fixed, each Government could set its own tariffs according to its national procedure.

The administration of import and export licensing in relations with third Powers should be the responsibility of the Government on whose territory was located the point of origin for exports or the point of destination for imports, but the High Authority would be empowered to supervise the administration and control of such licensing where coal and steel were concerned.

The High Authority was also empowered to take all measures in conformity with the Treaty in the following circumstances: (a) if it was established that countries which were not members of the Community, or enterprises situated in such countries, were engaged in dumping operations or other practices condemned by the Havana Charter; (b) if a difference between the offers made by enterprises outside the jurisdiction of the Community and those made by enterprises within its jurisdiction was due exclusively to the fact that those of the former were based on competitive conditions contrary to the provisions of the Treaty; (c) if coal or steel was imported into the territory of one or several of the member-states of the Community 'in relatively increased quantities and under such conditions that these imports inflict, or threaten to inflict, serious damage on production, within the E.C.S.C., or similar or directly competitive products'.

The member-states bound themselves to keep the High Authority informed of proposed commercial agreements or arrangements relating to coal, steel, or the importation of other raw materials, and of specialised equipment necessary to the production of coal and steel.

The remaining clauses of the Treaty (Arts. 76–100) provided, *inter alia*, that the Community should enjoy on the territory of the member-states the privileges and immunities necessary to the exercise of its functions; that the seat of the institutions of the Community should be fixed by common agreement; and that the fiscal year of the Community should extend from 1 July to 30 June. The Treaty would apply to the European territories of the member-states, but each bound itself to extend to the other member-states the preferential measures which it enjoyed with respect to coal and steel in the non-European territories under its jurisdiction. It was expressly stated that the establishment of the Community in no way prejudiced the régime of ownership of the enterprises subject to the provisions of the Treaty. (Arts. 76–85.)

The member-states bound themselves to take all general and specific measures which would assure the execution of their obligations under the decisions and recommendations of the institutions of the Community, and to facilitate the accomplishment of the Community's purposes. They bound themselves to refrain from any measures compatible with the existence of the E.C.S.C., and agreed, to the extent of their competence, to take all appropriate measures to assure the international payments arising out of trade in coal and steel within the E.C.S.C., and to lend assistance to each other to facilitate such payments. (Art. 86.)

The signatories also agreed 'not to avail themselves of any treaties, conventions, or agreements existing among them to submit any difference arising out of the interpretation or application of the present Treaty to a method of settlement other than those provided for therein'. (Art. 87.)

If the High Authority considered that a state was delinquent with respect to any of the obligations imposed on it by the Treaty, it would take note of the delinquency in a decision accompanied by a justification. It would allow the state in question a period of time within which to execute its obligation, whilst the state would have the right to appeal to the Court's plenary jurisdiction within two months from the notification of the decision. If the state had not taken steps for the fulfilment of its obligation within the period fixed by the High Authority, or if its appeal was rejected, the High Authority could, with the concurrence of a two-thirds majority of the Council, (a) suspend the payment of sums which the High Authority might owe to the State in question; (b) adopt measures, or authorise other States to adopt measures, so as to correct the effects of the delinquency in question. If these measures should prove inoperative, the High Authority would lay the matter before the Council. (Art. 88.)

Any dispute among member-states concerning the application of the Treaty which could not be settled by a procedure provided for in the Treaty might be submitted to the Court at the request of one of the parties to the dispute. The Court would also have jurisdiction to settle any disputes between member-states relating to the purposes of the Treaty if such a dispute was submitted to it by virtue of an agreement to arbitrate. (Art. 89.)

If an enterprise did not make within the prescribed time limit a payment for which it was liable to the High Authority, the latter might suspend settlement of sums due by it to that enterprise up to the amount of the payment in question. All decisions of the High Authority imposing financial obligations on enterprises would be executory, and would be enforced on the territory of member-states through the legal procedures in effect in those States. Enforcement of such decisions could be suspended only by a decision of the Court. (Arts. 91–92.)

The European Coal and Steel Community

The High Authority would maintain whatever relationships appeared useful with the United Nations and with the Organisation for European Economic Co-operation, and would keep those organisations regularly informed of the Community's activities. The relations of the Community with the Council of Europe would be assured under the terms of an annexed Protocol. (Arts. 93–94.)

If, following the expiration of the transition period unforeseen difficulties which were brought out by experience in applying the Treaty, or a profound change in the economic or technical conditions which affected the common coal and steel market, made necessary an adaptation of the rules concerning the exercise by the High Authority of the powers conferred upon it, appropriate modifications might be made provided that they did not modify the provisions of Arts. 2, 3 and 4 or the relationship among the powers of the High Authority and of the other institutions of the Community. These modifications would be proposed jointly by the High Authority and the Council, acting by a five-sixths majority; would then be submitted to the opinion of the Court; and after examination by the Court would be transmitted to the Assembly, which could approve them by a majority of three-quarters of the members present and voting, compromising two-thirds of the total membership. (Art. 95.)

Following the expiration of the transition period, amendments might be proposed by member-states or by the High Authority; the Council, on a two-thirds majority vote, could then approve the calling of a conference of Government representatives of the member-states to consider such amendments. (Art. 96.)

The Treaty would run for a period of 50 years from the date of its entry into force (Art. 97), and other European States might accede to it by a unanimous vote of the Council. (Art. 98.)

The Treaty would be ratified by all the member-states (instruments of ratification being deposited with the French Government), and would enter into force on the date of deposit of the last instrument of ratification. If all the instruments of ratification had not been deposited six months after the signing of the Treaty, the Governments of the States which had ratified would consult among themselves on the measures to be taken. (Art. 99.)

On 1 July 1967, the High Authority was merged into the single Commission for E.C.S.C., E.E.C. and Euratom, see page 40.

CHAPTER 13

The European Atomic Energy Community

Euratom, the European Atomic Energy Community, was set up in 1958 to help develop a civil nuclear industry in Europe and thereby help raise living standards, which are closely linked to the level of energy consumption.

Electricity consumption in Western Europe, as in all industrialised countries, is rising rapidly. In the Community it is doubling every decade, and by 1980 at least four times as much electricity will be needed as in 1960. The role of atomic energy in producing electricity will also rise rapidly. In 1965 only 1 per cent of all electricity generated was of nuclear origin; the proportion will be 3 per cent in 1968 and in the range of 20–25 per cent by 1980. Nuclear power stations coming into operation in 1968–70 will be competitive with conventional stations in many areas of the Community.

Euratom's role is to ensure that the Community undertakes the research necessary for the development of nuclear energy not only for power production, but also through the use of radio-isotopes and radio-active sources, for agricultural, industrial and medical purposes.

Euratom supplements and co-ordinates research undertaken in the Community, pools and disseminates scientific information, and promotes the training of scientists and technicians. For its first five-year research programme (1958–62) the Commission had at its disposal $215 million; for the second five year programme (1963–67) this sum was doubled, to $432 million. Euratom research takes place:

(a)   in its own research centres:

Ispra, north of Milan, Italy, where work is at present concentrated on the fields of experiment opened up by the ORGEL heavy-water reactor;

Geel, Belgium—the Central Nuclear Measurements Bureau;

Karlsruhe, Germany—the European Transuranium Institute;

Petten, Holland, a general-purpose establishment.

(b)   through 'association contracts' under which Euratom and a

The European Atomic Energy Community

partner organisation in a member country jointly finance certain large-scale research projects, Euratom assigning scientific staff to joint teams. For instance, all fast-reactor and thermonuclear-fusion research in the Community is tied into the Euratom network of association contracts.

(c) by contracting specific assignments to national centres or firms. Altogether over 700 such contracts have been executed or are under way.

(d) by joining international projects such as the European Nuclear Energy Agency (E.N.E.A.) Dragon project at Winfrith, England.

Euratom has organised a large Information and Documentation Centre and has worked out a Community policy on the ownership of patents resulting from Euratom research.

Euratom also encourages the development of the Community's nuclear industry. It has brought into being, since 1 January 1959, a common market for all nuclear materials and equipment, and a low or suspended common external tariff on imports of nuclear materials from non-member countries.

Euratom has:

(a) put into force a plan for the free movement of qualified atomic workers.

(b) drawn up with other European countries an insurance convention providing joint Community coverage—supplementary to that of O.E.C.D.—for large-scale atomic risks.

(c) earmarked $32 million to help build power plants of special importance to the Community. The installations aided in return pass on to the Euratom Commission their constructional and operational experience, which will then be made available to all requiring it.

(d) granted 'joint enterprise' status to three power-reactor projects; joint enterprises, which must be projects of outstanding importance to the Community, enjoy special fiscal and other privileges.

(e) set up a radio-isotope information bureau to provide information on the rapidly increasing uses of isotopes in industry.

To safeguard both nuclear workers and the general population, Euratom has laid down Basic Standards for health protection which have been incorporated into the laws of the Community countries. These Basic Standards, which are among the most up-to-date and comprehensive in the world, are subject to continuous revision in the light of scientific advance. In addition, the Commission maintains a constant check on the level of radio-activity in the atmosphere, water and soil, on the basis of data regularly supplied by the six countries' control posts.

Euratom is pledged to ensure that ores, raw materials and fissile matter are not diverted from their declared use. Enterprises submit to the Commission details of the equipment of their installations and regular returns on their stocks, transfers and transactions of materials. The Commission operates an international on-the-spot inspection system to check on the returns. Any enterprise breaking these regulations may be subjected to sanctions, but no significant contraventions have been detected up to now.

The Treaty of the European Atomic Energy Community (Euratom) was signed and came into force on the same day as the Treaty creating the E.E.C.

The aims of the Community were defined in the preamble as the raising of living standards in the member-countries and the promotion of trade with non-Community countries. The tasks of Euratom were defined in Article 1 of the Treaty as the creation within a short period of the technical and industrial conditions necessary to utilise nuclear discoveries, and especially to produce nuclear energy on a large scale. This result would be achieved by joint measures of the member-countries and through the activities of the institutions of the Community.

PROVISIONS FOR NUCLEAR DEVELOPMENT

These provisions of the Treaty (Articles 4–106) were divided into sections dealing respectively with the development of nuclear research, dissemination of nuclear information, protection of health, investments, Community undertakings, supplies of nuclear materials, security measures, ownership of fissile material, and external relations. Details were as follows:

Development of Research The Commission would promote and facilitate research in the member-countries by the following means:

(1) It would set up a Community Nuclear Research Centre to ensure the execution of research programmes. This Centre would also be responsible, *inter alia*, for standardising nuclear terminology and measurements, and a Central Nuclear Measurements Bureau would be established in this connexion. Schools for training specialists would be set up in conjunction with the Centre, and an institution of university rank would be created at a later stage.

(2) To supplement nuclear research by member-countries, the Commission would work out research and training programmes, not

exceeding five years, to be carried out by the Community Nuclear Research Centre. It might, however, conclude research contracts for part of these programmes with undertakings or nationals of member-countries, and also with international organisations or with nationals and undertakings of non-Community States. These programmes would require the unanimous approval of the Council of Ministers.

(3) The Commission would endeavour to co-ordinate the research conducted in the individual member-states. To this end, it would invite member-states, undertakings, and individuals to inform it of their research programmes in a specified field, and would express an opinion on these programmes. It would also attempt to prevent wasteful duplication and to direct research into less well-explored channels; would regularly consult public and private research bodies; would publish (with the agreement of the interested parties) the research programmes in operation; and might convene representatives of public and private research centres for mutual consultation and exchanges of information.

(4) The Commission might extend financial and/or technical assistance for research work as follows: (a) by a direct financial contribution repayable or otherwise; (b) by the organisation of joint financing by those concerned; (c) by supplying raw or fissile materials, either against payment or free of charge; or (d) by making available installations, equipment or experts, either against payment or free of charge.

Dissemination of Information

(1) The Commission would be obliged to pass on to interested persons and undertakings in the member-countries all the information acquired by the Community, and to issue to them at their request non-exclusive licences, provided they were in a position to exploit them effectively. A special procedure would apply to information which had to be kept secret for defence reasons (see below).

(2) The Commission would also seek (by way of agreement) to obtain information from the member-countries on all patents, patent applications, or working models covering inventions which would be useful to the Community. It would do its utmost to promote the issue of licences for such patents, etc.

(3) A compulsory notification procedure would apply to certain inventions. Under this procedure, member-countries would be required to notify the Commission, within 18 months of the lodging of such applications, of the details of any applications for patents for

'specifically nuclear objects'. In the case of applications covering objects which, while not specifically nuclear, were considered after preliminary examination to be directly connected with the development of nuclear energy, member-countries would be obliged to notify the Commission within 18 months, and to communicate full details within another two months if requested by the Commission. A special procedure would again apply to secret defence inventions.

(4) For inventions covered by the foregoing paragraph, certain compulsory powers would be available to the Commission, which could demand the issue of a licence if it considered this desirable even though no amicable agreement had been reached between the holder of the patent and the applicant for a licence. In all cases where such a licence was issued, the amount of compensation to be paid would be settled between the owner of the patent and the holder of the licence.

(5) An arbitration Committee would be set up to deal with disputes between either (a) the Commission and the owner of a patent; or (b) the owner of a patent and a licensee on the subject of compensation. The Committee's members would be appointed by the Council of Ministers on the proposal of the Court of Justice. The final decisions of the Committee would have the force of *res judicata* as between the parties involved; but, after a lapse of one year, a request might be made for the revision of a decision if fresh circumstances had arisen to justify such a step.

(6) Special confidential procedures would be adopted in the case of information which the Community had acquired from its research programme, and the disclosure of which might be considered detrimental to the defence interests of one or more member-countries. The Council of Ministers would draw up the necessary security regulations defining the various categories of secrecy and the security measures to be adopted.

(7) The Commission would evolve a system whereby member-states, undertakings or individuals could exchange progress or final reports about their research. This system would have to guarantee the confidential nature of such exchanges, but the Commission would be entitled to transmit such reports to the Community Nuclear Research Centre for information, on the understanding that the Centre would have no right of utilisation save with the consent of the originators.

Public Health The Community would establish a code of basic standards governing personal safety against dangers resulting from ionising radiation. This code would be drafted by the Commission,

The European Atomic Energy Community

and submitted to the Council of Ministers for approval, after the Commission had heard the views of a group of persons selected by the Scientific and Technical Committee from amongst scientific experts in the field of public health. In addition, an information and study centre for personal safety problems would be set up within the Community Nuclear Research Centre.

Investments To stimulate initiative by public and private undertakings in the nuclear energy field, and to promote a planned development of their investments, the Commission would publish programmes indicating the Community's production aims and the capital investments thereby implied, after hearing the views of the Social and Economic Committee.

Public and private undertakings in member-countries which were contemplating investments in the nuclear energy field would be required to inform the Commission at least three months before work began or the first contracts were concluded. Such investment projects would be published, subject to the agreement of the parties concerned and their Governments.

Community Undertakings Undertakings of outstanding importance for the development of nuclear industry in the Community might be declared Community undertakings by a decision of the Council of Ministers, taken on a proposal by the Commission. This proposal would cover the statutes and site of the undertaking. The necessary finance, and the participation of the Community as well as of non-Community countries, international institutions, or foreign nationals, in the financing or management of the undertaking.

A Community undertaking would enjoy a special status; would be a legal entity of its own with the right to own property, enter into agreements, and assume rights and obligations; but, unless otherwise stipulated, would be subject to general industrial and commercial laws and regulations.

The Council could grant Community undertakings all or some of a certain number of privileges—viz., special facilities for the purchase or expropriation of property; exemption from dues and taxes; exemption from transfer, re-transfer, and registration dues and charges; exemption from Customs duties and from economic or fiscal restrictions on scientific and technical material, or substances treated by the undertaking; and the right to hold funds and foreign currency of any kind, with freedom of transfer.

Council decisions on the creation of Community enterprises would in general be taken by a qualified majority, but the following decisions would require unanimity: (i) Financial participation by the

Community; (ii) the granting of the above-mentioned privileges; (iii) participation of non-Community States or their nationals in the financing or management of the enterprise.

Amendments to the statutes of such enterprises would have to be approved by the Council of Ministers. Disputes affecting them would be settled by the competent national courts, except for those matters reserved to the Court of Justice of the Community.

Supplies A joint policy would be pursued with regard to the supply of ores, raw materials, and special fissile matter on the basis of the principle of equal access to resources. For this purpose the Commission would set up a Commercial Agency which would be a corporate body, vested with financial independence and able to conduct its affairs according to business rules, but controlled by the Commission. The Agency (the majority of whose capital would have to be owned by the Community and the member-countries) would possess (i) an option to purchase any of the materials in question produced in member-states; and (ii) the exclusive right to conclude contracts for the purchase or sale of such materials outside the Community.

Resources within the Community All producers of ores, materials, and special fissile matter would be under an obligation to offer their products to the Agency immediately they became available, and the Agency would normally exercise its option by means of contracts with the producers. The Agency could exercise this option at any stage of production except in the following cases: (i) a producer engaged in the mining of ores as well as in the production of nuclear material need offer his product to the Agency only once, the same applying to a group of undertakings co-operating with each other in these processes; (ii) Community undertakings would supply ores, raw materials, and special fissile matter produced by them according to their statutory or contractual obligations; (iii) in the case of special fissile matter the Agency, while exercising its option, might leave the material with the producer, either to be used by the latter, or to be placed in stock, or to be placed at the disposal of undertakings associated with the producer for the execution of programmes of which the Commission had been notified.

When the Agency did not exercise its option the producer might continue to use or process the material himself, or he might be authorised by the Commission to dispose of the material outside the Community at a price not less than that of his previous offer to the Agency. In the case of special fissile material, however, only the Agency could export this to other countries, with the Commission's consent.

Resources outside the Community While the Agency would normally have the exclusive right to conclude contracts for supplies from non-Community countries, consumers would be entitled to do so if the Commission found at any time that the Agency's prices for such supplies were excessively high, or that the Agency could not deliver all or some of the required supplies within a reasonable time; the Commission's ruling would be taken on an application from the consumers concerned. Any contracts concluded by consumers would have to be notified to the Commission, which might object to them within one month if they violated the aims of the Community.

Transactions with Agency—Prices To enable the Agency to satisfy all demands, producers and users would notify it at regular intervals of their available output and requirements. The Agency would endeavour to satisfy all applications for ores, materials, or special fissile matter, but if unable to do so fully would distribute the available supplies on a proportional basis.

Prices would be regulated by the interplay of supply and demand, member-countries being forbidden to infringe this rule by national legislation. Price adjustments designed solely to give certain consumers a monopoly would likewise be prohibited. On a proposal of the Commission the Council of Ministers could fix prices by unanimous vote. The Commission would also be entitled to put forward proposals to consumers for the standardisation of prices.

Other Provisions The Commission would be entitled to make recommendations regarding prospecting and the exploitation of mines, and might participate financially in such activities. Member-states would be required to send the Commission annual reports on prospecting, reserves and mining investments.

After seven years from the entry into force of the Treaty, the Council of Ministers would either confirm or replace all provisions relating to supplies.

Security The Commission would be required to ensure (i) that ores, raw materials and special fissile matter were not diverted from their intended use as declared by their consumers; and (ii) that arrangements for their supply, and any special control measures accepted by the Community in an agreement with a non-Community State or international organisation, were observed.

To this end, the Commission would:

(a) Request declarations from all the undertakings concerned describing the basic technical characteristics of their equipment;

(b) Request statements of all transactions in order to facilitate accounting of ores, raw materials and special fissile matter;

(c) Insist, if necessary, on all surplus special fissile matter temporarily not in use being placed in deposit;

(d) Arrange for its inspectors to carry out checks and, where necessary impose sanctions ranging from a warning to the complete withdrawal of raw materials or special fissile matter.

Ownership of Special Fissile Matter All special fissile matter would be the property of the Community. Member-states, undertakings or individuals, however, would be entitled to the widest possible utilisation and consumption of the special fissile matter which had legitimately come into their possession.

On behalf of the Community, the Agency would keep a special account relating to fissile matter transactions and entitled 'Financial Account for Special Fissile Matter'. This account would not show any changes in the value of the fissile matter, which would be entirely at the risk of those having the matter in their possession, leaving neither profit nor loss to the Agency.

Common Market in Nuclear Materials A common market in nuclear materials would be set up, involving the following obligations on member-countries;

(a) to introduce, one year after the coming into force of the Treaty, a common Customs tariff for nuclear minerals and products imported from non-Community Countries;

(b) to repeal between each other, after the same one-year period, all import and export duties and taxes on such minerals, materials and products (the non-European territories of member-states being entitled, however, to continue to levy duties and taxes of a purely fiscal character);

(c) to apply the procedure laid down in the Common Market Treaty for the gradual abolition of internal tariffs and quantitative import restrictions between member-countries, and for the introduction of a uniform Customs tariff, to all other products which might be used in the nuclear industry;

(d) to admit nationals of the other member-countries, without discrimination, to all posts and occupations requiring qualifications in the nuclear sphere, as well as to participation in the construction of nuclear undertakings;

(e) to set up an insurance scheme covering risks arising from the use of atomic energy;

(f) to facilitate the transfer between member-countries of capital needed for nuclear projects, and to permit the transfer to other member-countries of payments in connection with nuclear transactions and employment in nuclear industries or research.

The European Atomic Energy Community

External Relations The Commission would be responsible for any liaison needed with the various international organisations and, subject to the Council's approval, might conclude agreements with these bodies or with non-Community countries. Member-states would be required to notify the Commission of any clauses in agreements or arrangements concluded, or to be concluded, with non-Community States which fell within the scope of the Treaty. The Commission would consider whether such clauses were compatible with the Treaty and would be entitled, if necessary, to bring any such matter before the Court of Justice.

FINANCIAL AND GENERAL PROVISIONS

The remaining principal provisions of the Treaty covered the following subjects *inter alia*:

Finance Estimates of all the Community's revenue and expenditure (apart from those of the Commercial Agency and the joint undertakings) would be drawn up for each financial year and entered either in the operational budget or the research and investment budget. The revenue and expenditure of the Agency, which would operate on commercial lines, would be estimated separately.

The receipts of the operational budget would consist mainly of the financial contributions of the member-countries, in the following proportions: France, Italy and West Germany, each 28 per cent; Belgium and the Netherlands, each 7·9 per cent; Luxembourg, 0·2 per cent. The receipts of the research and investment budget would consist of similar contributions, but with a slightly different proportionate scale, viz. France and West Germany, each 30 per cent; Italy, 23 per cent; Belgium 9·9 per cent; the Netherlands, 6·9 per cent; Luxembourg 0·2 per cent.

The above contributions might be replaced, in whole or part, by the proceeds of taxes levied by the Community in the member-countries; the introduction of such taxes would be decided by the Council of Ministers on the proposal of the Commission.

The Community would also be entitled to raise loans to finance research or investment.

The preliminary draft budgets of the various Community institutions under the aegis of the Commission would have to be submitted to the Council of Ministers not later than 30 September of each year (the financial year being 1 January–31 December). The Council would be entitled to propose amendments but would be required, in its turn, to submit the budgets to the Assembly by 21 October at the latest. If the Assembly either signified its approval or expressed no opinion within a month, the draft budgets would be deemed to be finally adopted. If the Assembly proposed amendments, the final decision would lie with the Council of Ministers.

The Council's decision would be taken by a qualified majority. For the adoption of the operational budget this would be the normal qualified majority—i.e. at least 12 out of 17 votes. For the adoption of the research and investment budget, however, the votes of the Council members would be weighted as follows:

France 30, West Germany 30, Italy 23, Belgium 9, the Netherlands 7, and Luxembourg 1. A qualified majority in this case would require at least 67 votes.

Overseas Territories Unless otherwise provided, the Treaty would apply to non-European territories under the jurisdiction of member-states.

Amendment of the Treaty The Commission or any member-state would be entitled to submit proposals for amending the Treaty to the Council of Ministers, which could then decide to convene a conference of the member-states to consider such proposals.

Admission of New Members Any European State could apply to become a member of the Community, and could be admitted by unanimous vote of the Council of Ministers. In the case of a successful application, the conditions of admission and the resultant changes in the Treaty would be set out in an agreement between the member-states and the applicant State.

An Annex to the Treaty outlined the first five-year research programme of the Community, costing $215,000,000.

REPORT OF EURATOM'S 'THREE WISE MEN'

The report of the three experts appointed on 16 November 1956 to estimate 'the amount of nuclear energy which could be produced in the near future by the six countries', and to suggest 'the means which should be employed to achieve this', was published on 7 May 1957 under the title 'A Target for Euratom'.

Following their visit to the United States the 'Three wise men' visited Britain from 25 February to 2 March 1957, for discussions with Lord Salisbury, then Lord President of the Council and the Cabinet member responsible for atomic energy; Lord Mills, the then Minister of Power; Sir Edwin Plowden, chairman of the U.K. Atomic Energy Authority; and officials of the A.E.A. and of the Central Electricity Authority. They also visited the Calder Hall and Windscale reactors and met representatives of four nuclear power plant construction companies to discuss the possibility of exports of British nuclear

The European Atomic Energy Community

power plants to the Community countries. A joint statement issued by the three experts and the A.E.A. on 1 March 1957, stated that the latter 'had declared its willingness to facilitate contacts between U.K. firms and firms within the Euratom countries interested in the building of nuclear reactors'. The Authority also expressed its willingness 'to give such assistance as lies in its power towards the training of scientists and engineers'.

The basic recommendation in the report issued by the 'Three wise men' (which is summarised below under cross-headings) was that the Community countries should install 15,000,000 kilowatts of nuclear generating capacity by the end of 1967.

Need for Nuclear Energy Dealing with the Euratom countries' growing dependence on energy imports, the report said they amounted at present to 100,000,000 tons of coal equivalent (23 per cent of their total energy requirements); would rise to 200,000,000 tons (33 per cent) by 1967; and might reach 300,000,000 tons (40 per cent) in ten years by 1977. Imports of this 'enormous' size would plan an unusually severe strain on the payments position of the six countries, since they implied expenditure rising from the present level of $2,000,000,000 to $4,000,000,000 by 1967 and $6,000,000,000 by about 1975. In addition, since most of these imports were, and would continue to be, in the form of Middle Eastern oil, there would always be a danger (which the Suez crises had amply illustrated) that supplies might be cut off for political reasons. Only nuclear energy, in the shape of big nuclear power stations producing base-load electricity, could rescue the Euratom countries from this precarious situation.

The report went on to recommend that 15,000,000 kilowatts of nuclear generating capacity should be built by 1967. This nuclear capacity, however, would not begin to make a really big contribution to the electricity systems of the six nations until 1963, since nuclear power stations took four years to build and no substantial constructions orders could be placed before the end of 1958. Nevertheless, if the plan suggested were implemented the six countries would be able to stabilise their energy imports at the estimated 1963 level—i.e. 165,000,000 tons of coal equivalent per year.

Comparison between Euratom and British Programmes Comparing the proposed Euratom programme with the existing British programme, the report noted that the Euratom target was $2\frac{1}{2}$ times the British target of 6,000,000 kilowatts of nuclear capacity by 1965. Pointing out that the ratio of population as between the six Euratom countries and Great Britain was 3 to 1, and that of electricity output 2·8 to 1, the report concluded that the Euratom target compared favourably with the British. As regards the engineering resources available for the construction of reactors, the report noted that British industry expected to be able to install 5,000,000–6,000,000 kilowatts of nuclear capacity at home by 1965 and at the same time to provide a similar amount for export. Since the total engineering capacity of the six Euratom countries was 1·6 times that of Britain, it was considered that the Euratom target was quite feasible from the point of view of engineering resources.

Co-operation with other Countries Reviewing the prospects of co-operation with the United States, Great Britain and Canada, the report stated that 'two-way traffic' could be set up between Euratom and the U.S.A. The latter country would provide fissile materials, technical knowledge, and training facilities for Euratom's scientists and technicians, while at a later stage Euratom would make available in return the practical knowledge gained by the large-scale industrial application of atomic power. The British authorities were similarly willing to provide technical training facilities and also to facilitate contacts between British firms in the nuclear construction field and their Euratom counterparts. In the case of Canada, co-operation would be possible in two spheres: (i) the supply of natural uranium, and (ii) the construction of prototypes of a heavy-water reactor which the Canadians had developed, and which promised to be particularly suitable for European requirements. The report recommended that agreements of association should be concluded between Euratom and the three countries in question immediately after the former's establishment. Close co-operation was also recommended with Austria, Switzerland and the Scandinavian countries.

Reactors The report said that while there were a dozen prototype reactors in an advanced stage of design or under construction, there were only two types ready for commercial use: the American pressurised-water/boiling-water type, using slightly enriched uranium, and the British gas-cooled type, using natural uranium. Of those types not yet in the commercial phase, Euratom should pay close attention to two—a version of the gas-cooled type, operating on slightly enriched uranium, and the above-mentioned heavy-water type developed mainly in Canada. For a speedy start to its programme, Euratom would either have to buy reactors from America and Britain or build them under licence.

Nuclear Fuels As far as could be ascertained, the nuclear fuel required to reach the target would be obtainable without much difficulty, the total cost for the ten-year period amounting to about

$2,000,000,000. As regards two related questions—the fabrication of fuel elements, and the chemical processing of spent fuel—the Community would have to rely initially on Britain and America for such services, but would later build its own plants for these purposes, once the possession of a sufficient number of reactors had made such a project economic.

On the question of enriched uranium, the report advised that a decision on the construction of a Community plant for producing such material should be deferred. It pointed out in this connection: (i) that the U.S.A. could provide the Community with the required amounts of this material at low prices; (ii) that the same material produced in Europe would cost two to three times as much; (iii) that a Euratom plant for this purpose would take several years to build and involve exceptionally heavy capital investment; and (iv) that future technological developments would almost certainly reduce, and might even extinguish, the need for this material.

Costs of Nuclear-produced Electricity The report went on to compare the costs of electricity produced by nuclear and conventional (i.e. coal- and oil-fired) stations. The conclusion reached was that there was no substantial difference between the two types, the (estimated) cost of nuclear electricity being \$0·0011–\$0·0014 per kilowatt-hour and the (known) cost of conventional electricity \$0·0011–\$0·0012 per kilowatt-hour. It was further observed that while the costs of conventional electricity were moving slowly upwards, those of nuclear power were moving slowly downwards.

Capital Investment The investment costs for nuclear stations were, broadly speaking, somewhat more than $2\frac{1}{2}$ times those for conventional plant; in the case of the Euratom target of 15,000,000 kilowatts, they would amount to \$6,000,000,000 as compared with \$2,000,000,000 for equivalent conventional capacity. Though representing at first sight an immense additional burden for the national economies of the six countries, the former amount would, in fact, be offset by the anticipated gradual decrease in expenditure on imported conventional fuels. To help electricity undertakings with the heavy initial outlay for nuclear stations, it was recommended that the Euratom Commission should consider the possibility of incentives, such as increased depreciation allowances, to cover the first and most difficult years.

Insurance against Nuclear Risks This section of the report dealt briefly with the need for a common legislative approach on insurance for nuclear plant, especially as regards the third-party liability of companies engaged in reactor construction and operation, and the liability of non-Community manufacturers with respect to the performance of their products.

The final section of the report stressed the role which Euratom would have to play 'in particular by providing the means to bridge the gap, in the initial period, between the commercial risk which firms face in building nuclear plant and the public need for the most rapid progress'.

CHAPTER 14

Agreements of Association

AGREEMENT ON ASSOCIATE MEMBERSHIP OF GREECE

An agreement was initialled in Brussels on 30 March 1961 whereby Greece became associated with the European Economic Community in a customs union, with provision for her to become a full member of the E.E.C. when her economic progress permitted. The Council of Ministers of the E.E.C. gave its final approval to the Agreement on 12 June.

The Greek request for association had been accepted in principle by the member-countries of the E.E.C. on 25 July 1959, but negotiations on details extended over the next two years, in the course of which Greek ministers and officials had numerous meetings with officials of the E.E.C. and with ministers and officials of individual countries of the Community.

The chief topics covered in these negotiations were as follows:

(1) The date at which tariff reductions by Greece *vis-à-vis* the Six should commence and the speed at which they should be effected, having regard to the state of developments of the Greek economy.

(2) The expansion of markets for Greek agricultural products (especially tobacco and citrus fruits) in the member-countries of the E.E.C. Italy expressed particular concern at the possible effects which Greek exports might have on her own exports of citrus fruits, but a compromise was finally reached whereby a ceiling was fixed on the quantity of fruits which might be exported by Greece under conditions of equal treatment with exports by E.E.C. member-countries. A compromise was also eventually reached with Italy on the level of Italian imports of Greek tobacco.

(3) Greece's trade relations with third countries, in which connexion Greece demanded the right to accord favourable treatment to products imported from third countries in order to promote the export to those countries of her own agricultural products, so long as the E.E.C. could not guarantee that Greece's output of these products

would be fully absorbed in the markets of the E.E.C. member-countries.

(4) The nature of an 'escape' clause.

(5) The granting of loans to Greece by the E.E.C. Originally the E.E.C. had proposed to make new loans dependent on the settlement of Greece's pre-war debt totalling the equivalent of £75,000,000 (with an additional £75,000,000 representing accumulated unpaid interest since 1941); of this sum, nearly 80 per cent was in sterling, 17 per cent in dollars, and the remainder in French francs.

Greece put forward the argument that only a very small portion of the debt was owned in E.E.C. member-countries, that Germany and Italy had been responsible for war devastation in Greece, and that post-war reparations had been insufficient to enable Greece to develop her economy to the point at which she could resume repayment of the debt. A statement issued by the Greek Ministry of Finance on 24 August 1960, declared that Greece had 'repeatedly expressed her eagerness for a settlement of the pre-war public debt based on the capabilities and needs of the Greek people ... in spite of the terrible trial of her economy during the war and post-war periods and the need to concentrate all her resources and capabilities on her economic development'; discussions, had, however, revealed a conflict on basic points which made agreement impossible.

Eventually, however, agreement on the unconditional granting of loans was reached and embodied in a special protocol.

The main provisions of the final agreement are summarised below:
Greek Association with the E.E.C. Under Article 238 of the Treaty of Rome Greece would not become a full member of the European Economic Community but associated herself with it on the basis of a customs union, with the prospect of her incorporation into the Community when the progress of her economy allowed her to assume fully the obligations deriving from the Rome treaty.

The object of the Association was defined as the 'continuous and balanced strengthening of trade and economic relations between the contracting parties, having particular regard to the need to secure an accelerated development of the Greek economy'.

INTERNAL TARIFFS BETWEEN GREECE AND E.E.C.

Member-countries A customs union would become fully effective after a transitional period during which Greece would receive special consideration. In principle she would reduce her tariffs over twelve years from the date of the Agreement coming into force, at the rate of 10 per cent immediately, 10 per cent at the end of each 18-month

Agreements of Association

period for the first nine years, and a further 10 per cent at the end of each of the remaining three years.

In order to assist in the development of Greek industry, however, there would be special concessions in the case of most industrial goods purchased in Greece, the transitional period for these lasting 22 years. Thus, during the first 10 years tariffs would be reduced by a total of 20 per cent, i.e. a 5 per cent reduction on the date of the Agreement coming into effect, and three reductions of 5 per cent each at intervals of $2\frac{1}{2}$ years; from the end of the tenth year until the end of the twenty-second, the remaining 80 per cent of the original tariffs would be reduced at the rate laid down for normal tariff elimination, i.e. one-tenth (or 8 per cent of the original tariff) at the end of the tenth year, one-tenth at the end of each 18-month period for the next nine years, and one-tenth at the end of each of the last three years. It was estimated that the 22-year transitional period would apply to approximately one-third of Greece's imports from the Community.

Tariff reductions which had already taken place among the six member-countries of the E.E.C., as well as any further reductions, would, upon the Agreement coming into effect, immediately and automatically apply to Greek products. Thus the tariff would immediately be reduced by 30–40 per cent for Greek industrial products and by 20–30 per cent for Greek agricultural products, all tariffs *vis-à-vis* Greece being completely eliminated by 1969 at the latest.

In order to protect newly established industries, Greece would be permitted during the 12-year transition period to impose new tariffs or to increase existing ones by a maximum of 25 per cent *ad valorem*, provided that imports from the E.E.C. of the products affected did not exceed 10 per cent of the total imports from the member-countries of the Community in 1958. These tariffs might be maintained for nine years and would then be progressively reduced, being eliminated in any case by the end of the 22-year transitional period.

External Tariffs Greece accepted the tariffs of the E.E.C.'s common external tariff scale, so that at the end of the 12 or 22-year transitional period (whichever applied to the articles in question) goods imported from third countries would be subject both in Greece and in the E.E.C. member-countries to a common external tariff.

In the case of tobacco, raisins, olives, colophony and turpentine (the five products in which Greece has a 'special and increased interest') the following special provisions in favour of Greece would apply during the first 12 years: (i) the *ad valorem* tariff of the common external tariff scale on 1 Oct. 1960 might not be modified by more than 20 per cent without the prior consent of Greece, e.g. the E.E.C.

ad valorem tariff *vis-a-vis* third countries of 30 per cent on tobacco might not be reduced below 24 per cent; (ii) the prior approval of Greece would also be sought before any special tariff quotas were granted by the E.E.C. member-countries for more than 22,000 tons out of the total of 130,000 tons of tobacco imported annually from third countries, and for more than 15 per cent of the annual E.E.C. imports from third countries of raisins, olives, colophony and turpentine.

For up to 10 per cent of her imports from third countries, Greece would be permitted to grant special tariff quotas without the prior approval of the E.E.C. provided the special tariffs would equal those currently applied for corresponding imports from E.E.C. member-countries.

Quantitative Restrictions These would be progressively eliminated between Greece and the E.E.C. In particular, the equivalent of 60 per cent of Greek private imports from E.E.C. countries in 1958 would be permanently liberalised within one year, rising to 75 per cent at the end of the fifth year and to 80 per cent at the end of the tenth year. Global quotas for E.E.C. member-countries equal to Greece's imports from those countries in the first year after the Agreement came into effect would be increased from the third to the tenth year by 10 per cent per annum on a cumulative basis; after the tenth year the rate of increase would be raised to 20 per cent for each 18-month period, all quantitative restrictions being eliminated by the end of the 22-year period. The expansion of import quotas and import liberalisation already effected or to be carried out in the future between member-countries of the E.E.C. would be extended to Greece.

Special Agricultural Provisions The Agreement aimed at harmonising the agricultural policies of the signatory countries, so that Greek agricultural products would receive equal treatment with similar products of the Six. If for any reason Greece found that such a harmonisation for a particular product ran contrary to her interests, she might decline to implement it, in which case she would be entitled to enjoy at least a most-favoured-nation status as regards her relations with the Community for that particular commodity.

All Greece's key farm products (tobacco, raisins, olives, etc., and all fruit and vegetables) would immediately enjoy equal treatment with similar products of the six member-countries of the Community. For Greek wines quotas had been fixed covering the normal maximum annual exports in recent years, within which they would enjoy equal treatment; these quotas would be increased whenever the quotas prevailing among the Six underwent an increase.

Agreements of Association 173

At the special insistence of Italy, a protocol was added providing that if the export trade of any E.E.C. member-country was adversely affected by Greek exports of citrus fruits, grapes and peaches, the E.E.C. Council of Ministers might decide that Greek exports of these products which were in excess of the amount stipulated in the protocol would not enjoy the status provided by the Agreement. The limits were set at 22,000 tons for citrus fruits, rising to 45,000 tons by the end of the fifth year; 15,000 tons for fresh grapes, rising to 31,000 tons; and 40,000 tons for peaches, rising to 83,000 tons. After the fifth year the limits would be agreed by both sides until Greek agricultural policy was completely harmonised with that of the Six. In the case of citrus fruits, the limits might be subject to revision if Greece experienced particular difficulties with her exports to third countries with which she was linked by bilateral clearing agreements.

A more rapid tariff reduction by the Six would be applied to Greek exports of raisins and tobacco, viz. the tariffs in force on 1 January 1957 would be halved immediately the Agreement came into force, and would be completely eliminated in the case of raisins within six years and in the case of tobacco by the end of 1967.

The French Monopole du Tabac would stabilise its purchase of Greek tobacco at the average level of the years 1957–59, and would increase them in the same proportion as those countries which imported tobacco freely; the Italian Tobacco Monopoly would procure from Greece at least 60 per cent of its purchases of tobacco for internal consumption (i.e. excluding tobacco destined for re-export), with a guaranteed annual minimum value of 2,800,000 dollars.

The tariff and quota status for imports of other farm products by either side would become permanent at the level in force when the Agreement came into effect. In the case of meat and dairy products, however, Greece would grant limited tariff reductions, amounting in general to 20 per cent within the first 10 years but to 40 per cent for ham, 35 per cent for cheeses, and 30 per cent for butter.

Other Provisions The Agreement also provided for the establishment of a common economic policy on the model of the Treaty of Rome, taking into account the needs and resources of Greece. The movement of workers, services, and capital would be liberalised; a common policy would be established for vocational training and the exchange of young workers; and tax legislation, currency policy, transport systems, and the rules of competition would be harmonised. The Council of the Association (see below) would determine the exact conditions for the implementation of these provisions.

Institutions The application of the Agreement would be supervised by a newly created Council of the Association, composed of members of the Council of Ministers and of the Commission of the E.E.C. and of the Greek Government. Each side would have one vote and the Council would take its decisions on the basis of unanimity; if it found itself unable to solve the differences submitted to it, it might refer them to the European Court of Justice or to arbitration. In the latter case, the E.E.C. and Greece would each appoint one arbitrator, and these two arbitrators would then co-opt a third as Umpire. The President of the European Court of Justice would act as Umpire for the first five years, and thereafter the Umpire would, in case of dispute, be appointed by the President of the International Court of Justice.

Escape Clause In the case of serious difficulties being encountered by any member of the Association, the E.E.C. member-countries would have the right of recourse to Article 226 of the Treaty of Rome, while Greece would enjoy equal status as regards the application of this Article. This right, however, would remain in force only during the transitional period of the Treaty of Rome and, in the case of the E.E.C. countries, might only be applied after prior consultation with Greece. Moreover, in such a case it would not be possible for all the E.E.C. member-countries to take joint protective measures against Greece, and the member-country in difficulties could not direct its protective measures against Greece alone, but would have to apply them against all the other E.E.C. member-countries. Up to 1969, Greece would be entitled to resort to protective measures in the event of difficulties in any sector of her economy, and might resort to such measures unilaterally after prior consultations with the E.E.C.

Loans to Greece A special protocol provided for loans to Greece of up to $125,000,000 to be used during the first five years of the Agreement. These loans would be for 25 years, and might be spent either in drachmas or foreign currencies. The Six would subsidise by up to 3 per cent per annum the rate of interest on loans representing two-thirds of the total financial support (i.e. on a maximum of approximately $83,000,000). They also agreed to consider within the first five years the provision of additional financial support, specifically through the recognition of Greece's need to apply for loans to the European Investment Bank.

   The principal developments under the Association Agreement have been that in accordance with the provisions of the Association Agreement the E.E.C. extended to Greek products the internal tariff reductions introduced within the Six on 1 January 1966 but a more favourable treatment was granted for the Greek key export products

Agreements of Association

—raisins and tobacco. Greece reduced her customs duties in November 1965 for imports from the E.E.C. by 30 per cent for most products and by 10 to 20 per cent for products subject to slower rates of dismantlement. For imports from non-E.E.C. countries Greece has started to align her tariffs on the Community's common external tariff on 1 November 1965.

At a meeting of the Council of Association held in Brussels in June 1964 it was agreed that a plan to bring the Greek and the E.E.C. agricultural policies into harmony would be in two stages:
(a) The first stage would allow Greece the levies and other mechanisms of the common agricultural policy, without, however implementing the Common Market price structure; at the same time Greek agricultural produce would receive qualified preference on the E.E.C. markets.
(b) In the second stage Greece would progressively align her agricultural prices and protection levels on those prevailing in the E.E.C. would open her markets to Community farm exports while U.S. agricultural assistance would have to be discontinued. The Ministers were unable to agree a time-table for this plan, the Greek government asked for a longer period for the first stage when 31 December 1967 was suggested as an ending date. These difficulties made it impossible to reach a decision on harmonisation within the time-limit laid down in Article 35 of the Association Agreement, i.e. 12 November 1964 and therefore the period has been extended several times.

AGREEMENT ON ASSOCIATE MEMBERSHIP OF TURKEY

An agreement and two supplementary protocols whereby Turkey became associated with the European Economic Community in a Customs union, with provision for her to become a full member of the E.E.C. when her economic progress permitted, were initialled in Brussels on 25 June 1963 and signed in Ankara on 12 September 1963. After ratification documents had been exchanged on 28 October 1964 the association agreement came into force on 1 December 1964.

The Turkish Government first applied for the association of Turkey with the E.E.C. on 31 October 1959. The Community for its part was interested in associating a country situated on the confines of Europe, but the content of association agreement had to take into consideration Turkey's need to speed up industrialisation, modernise agriculture, and improve infrastructures before planning any mutual reduction of Customs duties leading to a Customs union. The final agreement laid down that its objectives should be attained by stages, its main provisions are:

The First or Preparatory Stage

During an initial period of five years Turkey would continue her efforts to strengthen her economic and commercial position. The E,E.C. would assist these efforts in two main ways:
(1) By granting tariff quotas to ensure that Turkey could sell in the Common Market specified amounts of four agricultural products which made up 37 per cent of her total export trade. Annual tariff quotas would accordingly be opened by member-states for 12,500 tons of tobacco, 30,000 tons of dried grapes, 13,000 tons of dried figs, and 17,000 tons of hazel-nuts. After a period of two years from the entry into force of the agreement, the Council of Association would be able to increase the tariff quotas and, after three years, to take measures to promote the marketing of other products in the Community. In the first year of the Association (1965) the quota for tobacco was taken up by Turkish exporters to 76 per cent; raisins by 83·5 per cent; dried figs by 98·5 and hazel-nuts by 100 per cent. Increased quotas were arranged for 1966 and 1967.
(2) By granting loans to Turkey through the European Investment Bank. Under a Finance Protocol these loans would total $175,000,000 and would be applied to capital projects serving to increase the productivity of the Turkish economy, contributing to the attainment of the agreement's objectives, and fitting into the framework of the Turkish development plan. Loans would be made by the E.I.B. directly to the responsible Turkish organisations, but loans for normal profit-making projects would be made to the Turkish State, which would re-lend the money to the appropriate body or enterprise. The E.I.B. and the Turkish Government signed a general convention on these loans on 8 December 1964.

The Second or Transitional Stage

During this stage, which might last up to a maximum of 12 years, a Customs union between Turkey and the E.E.C. would gradually be established on the basis of mutually balanced obligations. Details of this stage have not yet been planned because they will ddpend on the situation existing when the move is made from the preparatory stage. The framework of the trade and economic arrangements was, however, laid down as follows:
(i) The Principles of the Customs union and its timing would be on the basis of Article XXIV of G.A.T.T. It would cover all trade and

would entail the adoption by Turkey of the common Customs tariff. With a few exceptions it was planned to have the union fully established in 12 years. A special system would be introduced for agricultural products in order to take into consideration the Community's agricultural policy. Detailed arrangements would be made by the Council of Association and laid down in a protocol.

(ii) During this preparatory stage Turkey would bring her economic policy into line with that of the Community, particularly as regards: (1) free movement of persons; (2) transport policy; and (3) rules of competition.

The Third or Definitive Stage

The third stage would be based on a full Customs union between Turkey and the E.E.C. including a common external tariff and with growing co-ordination and integration in all fields of economic policy. The agreement envisaged that when a full Customs union had been achieved Turkey would be eligible to apply for full membership of the European Economic Community.

Institutions The application of the Agreement would be supervised by a newly created Council of the Association composed of members of the six Governments and the Council of Ministers and Commission of the E.E.C., and of the Turkish Government. Each of the two parties would have equal voting rights and the chairmanship would alternate between Turkey and the E.E.C. every six months. During the preparatory stage the Council of Association would be the forum for periodical discussions on how the association was working, and would be competent to resolve any dispute or difficulty concerning the association or to refer such disputes or difficulties to an existing juridical authority.

Protocol on Transition from First to Second Stage

A 'Provisional Protocol' attached to the agreement stipulated that the Council of Association should examine after four years the question of whether the transition to the second stage could be implemented having regard to Turkey's economic progress, and whether agreement could be achieved on the conditions, details, and timeschedules for the implementation of the second stage. Such an agreement would have to be laid down in a supplementary protocol requiring unanimous acceptance and ratification by all the countries concerned before the transition to the second stage could come into effect. If no such protocol was signed after the first four years, the preparatory stage would be extended by up to another six to a maximum of 10 years, and the Council of Association would then have to decide about the arrangements to take effect after the tenth year.

AGREEMENT ON MEMBERSHIP OF THE ASSOCIATION OF AFRICAN STATES

The Convention of Association between the E.E.C. and the associated African States and Madagascar was signed on 20 July 1963, at Yaoundé (Cameroon), after protracted negotiations on certain of its terms, especially the total amount of financial aid to the associated countries had been successfully concluded, the figure finally agreed being $730,000,000. In view of the delay, the European Parliament had proposed on 25 March 1963, that certain adjustments in the transitional provisions would be required, including financial authority for the Commission to continue technical assistance after 1 July 1963, and the duty-free admission of certain tropical products by member-countries.

After ratification the Convention came into force on 1 June 1964, together with a parallel decision of the E.E.C. on the association arrangements between the Community and overseas dependent territories and French overseas departments.

The principal provisions of the Association Convention were as follows:

Trade

(a) Exports from the associated states to the E.E.C. member-states would benefit from the same gradual elimination of duties and expansion of quotas as the member-states were to apply amongst themselves.

(b) Pineapples, coconuts, coffee, tea, cocoa, pepper, vanilla, cloves, and nutmeg would enter member-states duty free. The common external tariff would operate for these products at reduced rates.

(c) When fixing common agricultural policy the E.E.C. would protect the interests of associated states with respect to those products which were similar to, or competed with, European products, particularly oilseed and sugar.

(d) Not later than six months after the effective date of the Convention, the associated states would extend the same tariff treatment to products originating in all member-states and would gradually abolish quantitive restrictions. They might nevertheless retain or introduce Customs duties on products imported from member-states when such duties corresponded to the requirements of their development and industrialisation or were intended to contribute to

Agreements of Association

their budgets; in the event of these measures proving inadequate because of balance-of-payments difficulties, the associated states might also retain or introduce quantitative restrictions.

(e) The E.E.C. would help finance schemes which would enable certain products of the associated states to be marketed throughout the Community at competitive prices.

Financial and Technical Co-operation The object of the Convention —to foster the economic and social development of the associated states—would, as in the earlier convention, be achieved mainly by means of the European Development Fund (E.D.F.). The Fund would, however, be assisted by the European Investment Bank (E.I.B.), which had hitherto only operated for the benefit of the E.E.C. member-states themselves.

There were four main features in the new association system:

(a) An increase in the amount of aid. In the initial period, aid from the European Development Fund to African and other dependent territories amount to $581,000,000 but under the new association system the total would be $800,000,000. Of this sum $730,000,000 would be allotted to the eighteen associated states and $70,000,000 to the dependent territories and the four French overseas departments The new total represented a 38 per cent increase in aid.

(b) Whereas previously the E.E.C. had only been able to grant aid outright, under the new convention a much wider range of financial methods was provided. Thus, the $730,000,000 to be allocated to the associated states would be distributed as follows: (i) Non-reimbursable grants by E.D.F.—$620,000,000; (ii) E.D.F. loans on special terms such as very long periods of repayment, periods of grace, and low rates of interest—$46,000,000; (iii) E.I.B. loans on ordinary terms—$64,000,000; (iv) Interest rebates subtracted from the total amount of non-reimbursable grants, thus enabling the E.D.F. to cut to 3 per cent the interest on E.I.B. loans; (v) Short-term advances to stabilise commodity prices up to a ceiling of $50,000,000 from the cash holdings of the Fund.

(c) Hitherto the E.E.C. could only finance capital investment and, on occasions, certain technical assistance schemes. Under the new Convention the scope of its aid was widened as follows: (i) Traditional type of capital investment: $500,000,000; (ii) Aids to production, including additional bonuses so that products could gradually be marketed at competitive prices, structural aids to production, and aids to diversification to remedy weaknesses in single-crop economies; (iii) Stabilisation measures to mitigate fluctuations in prices for agricultural products; (iv) Technical assistance.

(d) In the first period of association the E.E.C. was not formally entitled to intervene in the field of technical co-operation, but experience had shown that it was imperative for the E.E.C. Commission to be empowered to finance, through the E.D.F. schemes for technical co-operation connected with investments.

Right of Establishment, Services, Payments and Capital

The provisions on establishment were based on the principle of non-discrimination in the associated states against nationals and companies from the member-states, subject to reciprocity with respect to nationals and companies from the associated states in the member-states. At the same time the signatories undertook to free payments and capital movements connected with the facilities for establishment.

The Institutions Both the E.E.C. and the associated African states and Madagascar would be equally represented on the institutions of the Association, viz. (a) The Council of Association assisted by the Associated Committee; (b) The Parliamentary Conference of the Association; (c) The Court of Arbitration of the Association.

The Council of Association would consist of the members of the E.E.C. Council of Ministers, members of the E.E.C. Commission, and one member of the Government of each associated state. The Council would meet at least once a year and the chairmanship would be held in turn by a member of the E.E.C. Council and a member of the Government of an associated state.

The Association Committee would comprise one representative from each member-state, one of the Commission, and one from each associated state, the chairmanship procedure being the same as for the Council. The committee, whose aims and terms of reference would be determined by the Council, would have to ensure the continuity necessary for the smooth functioning of the Association.

The Parliamentary Conference of the Association would consist of members of the European Parliament and members of the Parliaments of the associated states.

The Court of Arbitration of the Association would deal with disputes in Association matters which could not be settled in the Council of Association. It would have five members appointed by the Council, viz., a president, two judges appointed after nomination by the E.E.C. Council, and two after nomination by the associated states. Majority rulings would be binding on the litigants to the disputes.

General Provisions The Convention would be valid for five years,

Agreements of Association 181

but might be terminated at six months' notice by the Community in respect of any associated state or by any associated state in the respect of the Community.

The Associated African States, eighteen in number, are—Burundi, Cameroon, Central African Republic, Chad, Congo (Brazzaville), Congo (Kinshasa), Dahomey, Gabon, Ivory Coast, Madagascar, Mali, Mauritania, Niger, Rwanda, Senegal, Somalia, Togo and Upper Volta.

AGREEMENT ON ASSOCIATE MEMBERSHIP OF NIGERIA

An agreement making Nigeria an associated member of the European Economic Community was signed in Lagos on 16 July 1966, by Brigadier B. O. A. Ogundipe (then Chief of Staff) on behalf of Nigeria and Dr. Joseph Luns (the Netherlands Foreign Minister) on behalf of the E.E.C. When the Association Convention with the French-speaking African states was concluded at Yaoundé on 20 July 1963, the member-states of the E.E.C. declared their readiness to negotiate in a sympathetic spirit with any other countries who so requested and whose economic structure and production was comparable with those of the Associated States. Nigeria thus became the first Commonwealth country to enter into association with the European Economic Community.

The draft agreement was divided into three main sections:

All Nigerian exports, with the exception of four commodities, would enter the E.E.C. free of duty when the agreement came into force.

The four exceptions would be groundnut oil, palm oil, cocoa beans, and plywood—all of which would be subject to a tariff quota based on the average of Nigeria's exports of these products to the Common Market in the years 1962, 1963 and 1964. The quota would increase by 3 per cent per annum, or by 6 per cent, with free entry of plywood, if Nigeria increased from 2 per cent to 5 per cent its tariff preference on certain imports from the Community. The twenty-six products involved included macaroni, spaghetti, vermouth, brandy, some agricultural machinery, radios, radiograms and household goods. These products accounted in 1963 for £3,500,000 worth of exports from the E.E.C. to Nigeria, compared with only £108,000 worth of exports by Britain.

Nigeria would be allowed to keep various restrictions on her imports from the Community because of her industrial and development needs. This provision would allow her, in particular, to impose quantitative restriction on imports from the E.E.C. if her financial stability or the economic health of any sector of her economy were to be impaired.

In the event of Nigeria applying export taxes she would not discriminate between member-countries of the E.E.C. Nigeria retained the right to establish customs unions or free trade areas with other countries.

The agreement provided that nationals and companies of every member-country would be treated on an equal footing. Reciprocity could not be granted to Nigeria until such time as the E.E.C. had a common policy on the right of establishment.

The E.E.C. and Nigeria would authorise payments and transfers for goods and services.

Nigeria would endeavour not to impose new exchange control restrictions, and the E.E.C. in turn would not put new restrictions on the flow of private capital to Nigeria.

An Association Council would be established consisting of an E.E.C. and a Nigerian representative, each representative having one vote. The Council would meet at least once a year at ministerial level and more frequently at ambassadorial level.

Its Secretariat would be headed by a Nigerian and a Community representative.

An *ad hoc* arbitration tribunal, composed of one member nominated by Nigeria, one nominated by the Community, and one nominated by the Association Council after consultation with Nigeria and the Six, would settle any disputes which might arise.

Following the publication of the draft agreement, both the United States and the British Governments officially objected to its terms, but Nigeria did not accept their point of view.

The British attitude, which coincided with the U.S. viewpoint, took the form of representations that the proposed agreement, introducing preferences for E.E.C. and Nigeria in each other's markets, would not establish a free trade area and would not therefore conform to G.A.T.T. rules. (To be accepted by G.A.T.T. an agreement not covering a free trade area would require specific waivers granted by Britain, the U.S.A. and other members affected in order to make it permissible.)

Nigeria, on the other hand, claimed that she had a strong case for defending her traditional trading interests, which had been seriously undermined by the creation of the Common Market, because her large sales to the E.E.C., and particularly to West Germany and the Netherlands, had been jeopardised by the E.E.C. preferences granted to the present African Associates. Nigeria also argued that the new

Agreements of Association

preferences would harm Britain very little, and in any case would be far less damaging than a full free trade area.

The agreement as finally signed on 16 July 1966, conformed to the draft approved a year earlier and will be valid until 31 May 1969, i.e. the same date on which the Yaoundé Convention terminates.

A Nigerian proposal to implement the agreement before ratification by the Community and its six member-countries was rejected by the E.E.C.

TRADE AGREEMENT WITH IRAN

A trade agreement between the E.E.C. and Iran was signed in Brussels on 14 October 1963, this being the first agreement of a purely commercial nature with a non-member country. Coming into force on 1 December 1963 it was of three years' duration but was extended for another year to 30 November 1967 on 27 October 1966.

The agreement provided for temporary reductions in the E.E.C.'s common external tariff for carpets, carpeting and rugs; dried grapes and apricots; and caviar—all products of special importance to Iran's economy. In addition, the agreement fixed a tariff quota for raisins imported by Community countries from Iran, the quota being equal to 15 per cent of such imports from all non-member and non-associated countries, with the duty temporarily reduced to 2 per cent.

It was agreed that a Joint Committee of representatives of the Community and Iran was to be set up to supervise the implementation of the agreement.

TRADE AGREEMENT WITH ISRAEL

A trade agreement between the E.E.C. and Israel was signed in Brussels on 4 June 1964, after prolonged negotiations.

The agreement came into force on 1 July 1964 for a period of three years, with a possible extension. It provided for (a) temporary reductions of the Community's external Customs tariff for the import of a number of Israeli products; (b) the immediate alignment on the present or reduced rates of that tariff for certain products imported from Israel by member-states whose relevant Customs duties were otherwise in excess of these rates; and (c) higher import quotas for certain Israeli products sent to France and Italy.

The temporary tariff reductions, ranging from 10 to 40 per cent, covered twenty-one agricultural and industrial products, including grapefruit, grapefruit juice, outer garments made of synthetic fibres, window glass for hothouses, and some chemical and aluminium products.

Products for which those member-countries with higher Customs duties would apply the lower rate in the common Customs tariff included oranges, fruit juices (other than grapefruit), and dried vegetables.

A joint committee of representatives of the E.E.C. and of Israel would supervise the application of the agreement. This committee would examine any agreements which the Community might conclude with other orange-producing non-member countries and which were likely to affect materially the outlets for oranges in Community markets.

AGREEMENT ON TRADE AND TECHNICAL CO-OPERATION WITH THE LEBANON

An agreement on trade and technical co-operation with the Lebanon, the first of its kind, was signed by the E.E.C. and Lebanon in Brussels on 21 May 1965.

Under the agreement—valid for three years and renewable—(a) E.E.C. member-countries and Lebanon granted each other most-favoured-nation treatment—an arrangement of particular importance to Lebanon because the latter is not a member of G.A.T.T.; (b) a joint committee would be set up to watch over trade development between Lebanon and E.E.C. countries; (c) the latter countries would co-ordinate their technical co-operation with Lebanon, send experts to Lebanon, organise technical training for Lebanese nationals in the Community, and enable studies to be carried out on the exploitation of Lebanon's natural resources and supply technical equipment; (d) the Six would facilitate the dissemination of information on investment possibilities in Lebanon.

The agreement was concluded between the Community as well as its member-countries on the one hand and Lebanon on the other, as technical assistance is a field still reserved for the national governments.

CHAPTER 15

The Development Fund and Investment Bank

The aim which the Treaty assigns for the association of the overseas countries with the European Economic Community is: ' . . . to promote the economic and social development of the overseas countries and territories, and to establish close economic relations between them and the Community as a whole . . . This association shall in the first place permit the furthering of the interests and prosperity of the inhabitants of these countries and territories in such a manner as to lead them to the economic, social and cultural development which they expect.' (Article 131.)

EUROPEAN DEVELOPMENT FUND

One of the specific means to this end is the European Development Fund for which the Treaty and the Implementing Convention on the association provide.

The European Development Fund finances economic or social development schemes in the associated overseas countries by means of outright grants. The Fund has three particular features: it is a Community Fund; its action is supplementary; and it is democratically operated.

It is a Community institution, maintained by contributions from the six member-states of the European Community which exercise no national control over the capital once contributed. It was never intended that contributions to the Fund should become, as it were, national credits offered to the associated countries in each of the national currencies concerned, and used only in that currency. Such an arrangement, which would have obliged the associated countries to use such credits in Francs, Marks, Florins or Lire only for purchases in the individual member states concerned, would have been contrary to the unity of purpose which the Fund represents.

The Fund is supplementary—one more of the many national and international agencies now concerned with spreading prosperity more equitably throughout the world. Its contributions supplement the investment efforts of the associated countries themselves and the aid they already receive bilaterally or multilaterally: they are also a part of a general policy of assistance to developing economies, in which commercial, legal, and technical aid is at least equally important.

The Fund is democratically operated because the choice, the working out and the implementation of the projects which it finances, rests with the Governments of the associated countries themselves. Development plans are not prepared elsewhere: it is the countries that benefit from the Fund which decide what projects to propose for financing, and this takes place through the agency of their own official bodies.

The European Development Fund Finances:

Social projects: improvements in equipment for public health, educational or scientific purposes, and in social services and living conditions; technical or scientific research affecting the people of the country concerned.

Economic projects for the improvement of the associated overseas countries' economy and their infrastructure. The Fund's aid forms part of the economic and social policy laid down by the responsible Governments and is implemented through the development programme of each Government, if possible in such a way as to stimulate further economic development. For example, it may be used to improve the infrastructure which makes possible private investment and enterprise; or for general and technical training, on which economic progress and social betterment very largely depend.

Priority is given to schemes that will have an almost immediate and direct effect on the standard of living.

The Fund leaves to the Governments the initiative in suggesting projects for which they want assistance. There are no conditions attaching to the grant of assistance.

Simple Rules:

The regulations of the European Development Fund are simple. As far as is possible they avoid involving the associated overseas States in procedural complexities caused by unwieldy, exacting, and bureaucratic routine.

The European Development Fund is run by a staff of forty-eight, including economists, accountants and technicians such as engineers and architects.

Development Fund and Investment Bank

Consideration of the Requests:

The formal request is submitted by the Government of the overseas associated country concerned.

It is received at the office of the Fund in Brussels. The various documents filed with the request are examined, and economists and overseas specialists are appointed to consider with the relevant technical services the set of projects concerned, and to work out arrangements for carrying them out. The Standing Committee of the Fund considers the request.

The Commission announces its decision. If an economic project is concerned, it is translated into the four official languages of the E.E.C. and referred to the Council of Ministers, which makes known its decision within a month. For social projects the Commission's decision is sufficient.

The financial agreement with the Government concerned is drawn up and signed.

Carrying out the Projects:

The country itself draws up the request for tenders. These papers are passed by the Technical Controller in the country concerned and sent to the Fund, which has them translated into the official languages of the Community and publishes notices of invitation to tender in the official gazette of the European Communities.

After a period of anything between one and four months—it depends on the scale of the project—tenders are sent in and their examination begun by the appropriate technical service of the country concerned, under the guidance of an adjudicating committee.

Once a tender firm has been accepted, the technical services draw up the contract and have it signed. The Commission is informed and takes the necessary steps to effect payment.

Payments are made in instalments as the work proceeds, to the order of the authority in the country concerned and through the bank at which the E.E.C. keeps its account. Payments are made very promptly. Provisional and final acceptance complete the process.

It is to be noted that as soon as the financial agreement has been signed, the project is carried out on the responsibility of the associated country itself, by its authorities and in its own way. The Commission intervenes only in order to assist through technical control in the drawing up of invitations to tender and in solving problems arising in the implementation of assisted projects.

Of the total of over $900,000,000 multilateral aid given by the Six the amount allocated by the first European Development Fund in the period 1958–63 was $581,000,000 and by the current (i.e. second) European Development Fund up to January 1967, $358,000,000 for 173 projects has been, or is being, distributed.

The distribution of amounts from the Second European Development Fund among associated countries and territories is as follows:

Associated African States	$
Burundi	6,192,000
Cameroon	16,487,000
Central African Republic	14,580,000
Congo (Brazzaville)	11,409,000
Congo (Kinshasa)	37,943,000
Ivory Coast	40,762,000
Dahomey	8,254,000
Gabon	2,378,000
Upper Volta	6,872,000
Madagascar	43,676,000
Mali	13,899,000
Mauritania	11,484,000
Niger	10,432,000
Rwanda	7,332,000
Senegal	29,436,000
Somalia	10,059,000
Chad	24,904,000
Togo	3,739,000
Overseas Territories and Departments	
Netherlands Antilles	6,709,000
Comoro Islands	944,000
French Somaliland	622,000
Guadeloupe	375,000
Réunion	8,102,000
New Caledonia	2,395,000
French Polynesia	869,000
Surinam	1,148,000
Aid not distributed	17,333,000

Aid from the Fund has been used for such purposes as building schools, improving medical facilities, modernisation of rural areas such as constructing wells, soil conservation and anti-erosion campaigns, improvement in transport and improvements in urban conditions.

Sixty-six per cent of the aid was allocated to modernisation of economic infrastructure and development of production and 23 per cent for social development.

THE EUROPEAN INVESTMENT BANK

The aims of the European Investment Bank as laid down in the Treaty are to promote a common investment policy within the Community

Development Fund and Investment Bank

and grant loans, on a non-profit basis, or guarantees for (1) projects in under-developed regions; (2) the modernisation, reorganisation, or extension of industries which are difficult to finance on a purely national basis; (3) new industries of joint interest to several member-countries which, because of their size or special character, would be difficult to finance by a single member-country.

By 31 December 1966 the Bank had signed contracts for $708,520,000 for 135 loans for all member and associated member-countries.

Some of the projects in which the Bank has invested have been:

(a) Development projects in regions of Apulia, Campania and Abruzzi and the modernisation of the important Mont Cenis railway line linking Paris and Genoa via Turin. The total amount provided was $50,000,000 divided between four projects in the iron and steel industries, engineering industries, clothing industries and the railway modernisation.

(b) A thermal power station built in West Berlin, financed by the bank to the extent of $2,400,000.

(c) Four loans for the construction of major roadworks: (i) a new road from Athens to Corinth in Greece $2,000,000; (ii) a new road from Corinth to Patras in Greece $6,200,000; (iii) modernisation of the road from Antirrion to Agrinion in Greece $2,600,000; (iv) a new road from Lamia to Larissa in Greece $6,200,000.

(d) Irrigation and development of the Metaponto Plain in Italy $24,000,000.

(e) Construction of a thermal power station at Salerno in Italy $15,000,000.

Several small loans have been made to Associated African States and several loans to Turkey including one for the construction of a dam on the Euphrates.

The capital structure of the Bank is given on p. 29 and in addition to the capital subscribed by member-countries the Bank has successfully raised funds in the capital markets of Europe and U.S.A. at interest rates ranging from $4\frac{1}{2}$ to $6\frac{1}{2}$ per cent.

CHAPTER 16

Economic Growth in the Common Market

The Treaty binds the member-states to consider their economic policy as a matter of common interest and to consult regularly on joint action in this field. For the specialised aspects of economic policy the Community can draw on the advice of the Monetary, Budgetary Policy and Central Bank Governors' committees. Current questions, and in particular short-term fluctuations in economic activity are handled with the aid of the *Short-term Economic Policy Committee*.

On 15 April 1964 the Council of the E.E.C. adopted a decision establishing a *Medium-term Economic Policy Committee* and two years later the Committee published a first five-year programme which was approved by the Council in February 1967 but is subject to annual revision in the light of developments.

Forecasting of economic growth for the three major countries of the Six (France, West Germany and Italy) has also been undertaken by the Organisation for Economic Co-operation and Development (O.E.C.D.). The projections made by E.E.C. are higher for West Germany than the O.E.C.D. projections and most economists predict that the annual revision for the E.E.C. forecasts will show a slowing down of growth because of the change in economic tempo in West Germany.

Forecasting is a hazardous business and it is really only a quarter of a century since there has been general acceptance of Social Accounting and even today the instruments used in building these indicators are still inadequate. However decisions for the future have to be taken and a scientific attempt to predict the future is as safe as the businessman's hunch or the politician's gamble and as time passes the instruments for forecasting are improving. This improvement will, in turn, help to make economics a more exact science.

There are many ways of measuring the economic well-being of a nation or community and none are completely accurate. Most economists agree that the best available instrument for measuring this

Economic Growth in the Common Market 191

well-being is to calculate the total output of goods produced and services rendered for each year. This social accounting of total output or aggregate supply of goods and services is called *gross national product* or simply G.N.P. It can be defined as 'the total market value of all final goods and services produced in the economy in one year'. Increases in this total from year to year represent growth rates and are generally expressed as percentages but it is necessary to treat the raw figures with some reserve because a large increase in G.N.P. together with an even larger increase of population might well mean a decrease in G.N.P. *per capita*. Also inflation has to be taken into consideration; mere increase in figures because of inflation could mean no increase in standard of living of a people and again total increase in G.N.P. might not be very evenly divided between the population. With these and other reservations G.N.P. does help us to analyse the past and predict the future and as the Medium-term Economic Policy Committee reported to the Council of Ministers...

The past determines to a great extent the future, and so past trends must be studied if the problems which will face the Community's economy in the near future are to be understood.

In 1957 the economies of the six States which signed the Treaty of Rome had emerged from the difficulties of the reconstruction period that followed the Second World War, but they were rigidly separated from one another, and several of them were still unable to ensure full employment for their manpower, to maintain the stability of their currencies, or to achieve balance in their foreign trade.

By 1965 full employment was to all intents and purposes achieved, currencies were on a firm basis and the European Economic Community had already made a decisive contribution to the liberalisation and the expansion of international trade.

Meanwhile, the countries of the Community had, largely thanks to the establishment of the Common Market, achieved a higher average rate of economic growth than that achieved by most other major industrial powers.

The contribution to these developments made by the fresh surge of competition between the economies of the six countries should be stressed: it has been a key factor in the economic progress achieved over this period. Consequently, the Committee was right in taking the view throughout its programme that increased competition is vital to the attainment of the objectives set.

Be that as it may, the danger is great that the successes thus attained and the hopes founded on them may mask certain unfavourable trends which, although they may be concealed from view, will inevitably affect the pattern of development in the years ahead.

Unemployment has virtually disappeared—at least in five of the member-countries—and, in the Community as a whole, average real incomes are rising steadily: unfortunately, this growth is accompanied by an upward price movement which is appreciably more rapid here than in the main competing countries and which is steadily eroding the ability of E.E.C. countries to compete. What is more, the factors which in the recent past have fed this inflation are likely to grow in strength in the coming years.

Europe is more prosperous than ever; this only makes more intolerable the situation of those of its inhabitants left behind in the general march forward. Moreover, regions and industries lagging behind the rest are already a burden for the Community as a whole and will be a brake on future development. In making it the duty of the Community to promote the harmonious development of economic activity throughout its territory, the Treaty sets not only an economic objective, but also a social objective, referred to in Article 117, where stress is laid on the need to improve the living and working conditions of labour so as to permit their equalisation in an upward direction.

It is true that since the inception of the Common Market some of the more extreme disparities in social conditions have been narrowed down. It remains none the less true that the incomes of the various social categories are still advancing in a manner that is far from being as harmonious as it should be: in this connexion, the prosperity already attained must be distributed more fairly. Another point is that the main obstacle to more rapid growth in the next five years, and consequently to higher living standards, will lie in the inadequate facilities for the retraining of workers. Lack of geographical mobility could also prove a problem, for where all else fails, workers may have to move to new areas to find new jobs. The task now incumbent on the authorities is not only to make good the time lost in the establishment of proper facilities for general and technical education and retraining and for receiving workers from other areas, but also to see that infrastructure in this field is abreast of requirements. An effort must be made to eliminate progressively the hardship suffered by workers who have to move to a new area to find work.

The need for such an effort is particularly marked in respect of that growing fraction of the farming community which, in its own interest must, at least in the long term and because of the requirements of general development, accept retraining and resettlement, for this group feels more keenly than others the discomfort and distress involved.

The need for geographical mobility of workers should not, however, be allowed to outweigh all other considerations, notably the need to avoid hardship caused by the uprooting of families. In order to take account of both these needs every effort must be made to set up new industries in localities where there are large pools of manpower that could be available and where the industries pay their way—from the outset or within a reasonable period.

A vigorous drive in the next five years is therefore required if current tendencies in the regional location of development activities are to be corrected. True, the creation of the Common Market, far from aggravating the present disparities between the different Member States with regard to economic development, has in fact brought trends closer together; but the fact remains that disparities between various regions in the Community have continued to get worse, since certain of them have been enjoying the full benefits of growth whilst some of the most backward, or those most directly hit by technological developments, have practically not shared in growth at all.

Regional policies would no doubt be doomed to failure if their aim were too wide a scattering of industry; no doubt, too, any harmonious regional development of policy must impose, at least initially, some burden on the community; but in the long term harmonisation along these lines is unquestionably one of the conditions governing the full employment of the factors of production.

The progress of any modern society is geared to that of the sciences and their technical applications. What science and technology mean to the economies of today is similar to what the presence of raw materials and energy sources meant to the economies of the past. Research is the most refined form of investment. On the quantity and quality of research will depend, in the long run, the capacity of the economies to develop and to compete.

It is difficult at the present time to assess accurately the scale of what has been achieved in this field by the Community and to establish what its impact on growth has been. No study is more urgent than one which would throw light on the current situation and on the trend of which it is a part.

Meanwhile, failing more reliable criteria, a comparison with the performance of other advanced industrial countries, carried out on the basis of very incomplete figures, is the only evidence available. This comparison shows beyond doubt that the Community is lagging behind. Its growing inferiority in the scientific and technological fields spells danger for the future.

In most of the traditional industries technical inferiority can, at least for a time, be offset by lower labour costs—which obviously means that competitiveness can be maintained only at the cost of sacrifices in terms of income and working conditions that could not be accepted indefinitely. But in a growing number of new advanced industries, firms can compete on international markets only if the technical quality of their products is of the highest order. The Community's failure to keep up with other countries in this field means that it is likely to be eliminated from a range of industries on which the future depends.

If the six countries are to remain, as they have probably been for a generation, the world's main importers of discoveries and principal exporters of intelligence, they will condemn themselves to a cumulative process of under-development which will soon render their decline incurable.

The Community must therefore embark at the earliest possible moment on a comprehensive capital operation—in both the private and public sectors—to develop research, and it must launch a comprehensive scheme to reorganise its industries.

Insecurity of the Balances to be achieved

The growth prospects set out in the programme depend on a variety of factors, in particular on the possibility of establishing in practice the balance between physical production and monetary demand and the balance of external trade on the lines forecast.

It is important, therefore, to examine what prospects there are of establishing the general equilibrium forecast, to enquire into the consequences of a possible failure and to consider the specific measures that would then have to be taken.

The average annual growth rate of the aggregate Community product during the last five years was, in volume (i.e. at constant prices), about 4·9 per cent. For the next five years the rate is estimated at 4·3 per cent (see table on page 201). The difference is mainly accounted for by a lower German contribution, since the other member-states believe that the growth rates achieved in the past could well be maintained in the years ahead. All the countries assume relatively stable prices.

Two factors, however, bring out the uncertainty of these assumptions; for one thing, the number of hours put in per worker is expected to decline and the rate at which the overall supply of available manpower increased will on the whole also tend to decline; secondly,

Economic Growth in the Common Market 195

the undue expansion of overall demand and notably of private consumption since 1960 has meant that growth in recent years has entailed too sharp an upward price movement, a deterioration in the balance of payments and at times an unsatisfactory trend in productive investment.

There are no grounds for hoping that the strain caused by excess demand will ease spontaneously; indeed, recent difficulties are liable to recur, given the pressure of private and collective requirements. The very fact that some degree of inflation has been tolerated in the past has engendered bad habits and so increases the dangers of the present situation and the damage that will be done tomorrow. At best, then, the overall economic equilibrium forecast for the next five years is as insecure as it has been in the recent past.

The main threat to the future stability of the economy is the excessive expansion of overall monetary demand, mainly in the form of personal demand.

It is possible that the monetary demand of households may continue throughout 1966–70 to advance at much the same rate as has ruled in the Community during the last few years. The effect of this would be that during an initial period there would be an apparent gain in real consumption on the rates shown in the projections, but such a trend would be at the expense of external equilibrium or of the progress of the other components of internal demand (productive investment or public expenditure on goods and services). It is clear that external disequilibrium could not be allowed to continue for long and that the internal adjustments which it would necessitate would affect directly the internal growth both of private consumption and of the other components of demand.

A slowdown in productive investment would also jeopardise growth potential and the outlook for the competitiveness of the economies. There would then be no certainty as to the overall growth rate of the economy during the later part of the five-year period.

On the face of it, the only way of enabling private consumption to grow more rapidly would be to slow down the expansion of public expenditure. But in fact this is not really a satisfactory solution.

At the beginning of the century, collective expenditure seldom accounted for more than 15 per cent of the gross domestic product of the major countries. Everywhere nowadays the authorities, despite the cost in the shape of taxes, spend more than one third of the gross domestic product, a proportion which rises to nearly one half in those countries which have built up their social systems most extensively. It seems unlikely that this trend will be reversed.

To imagine that this rising trend could easily be arrested would be tantamount to saying that a balance had been reached between the satisfaction of individual needs and the satisfaction of collective requirements. It has not. Less care is devoted to the health of the public than to ensuring that there is an ample quantity of food; traffic on the roads is increasing more than the availability and quality of roads and the amount of parking space; collective facilities for education, culture, learning and leisure still lag far behind the development of private acquisitions of all kinds. This being so, everybody must realise that an undue growth of private consumption would be bound to mean that people had even less in the way of hospitals, of roads, of schools. In addition, a large proportion of public expenditure determines future economic growth (transport, education, research, housing).

Consequently the standard of living and still more the quality of life itself will now, and even more in the future, depend to a great extent on a supply of collective equipment and services which can in the last resort be financed only through taxation.

Be this as it may, action to slow down the expansion of public investment could be of little benefit to private consumption—which would show an improvement of barely 1 per cent for a cut of 15 per cent to 20 per cent in public investment. All in all, then, it would be unrealistic to expect the growth of real consumption by households to be faster, over the period as a whole, than is shown in the projections.

If the progress of private consumption were to attain a higher rate early in the five-year period, the authorities would inevitably be obliged to curb its growth relatively sharply later on, and the undesirable, perhaps even painful consequences of this, notably for employment in certain industries, would by far outweigh any initial advantages. It is, therefore, evident that the expansion of private consumption must be kept within bounds during the next few years.

No one can be unaware of the difficulties involved in getting the public to accept the measures, however necessary they may be, which such constraint entails. Moreover, the very success of the entire medium-term economic policy will depend on close co-operation between workers, managements and governments, especially over an incomes policy which must aim at ensuring that the various social groups each obtain a fair share in the growing volume of production while the overall growth of consumption and expenditure is maintained within reasonable limits. Lastly, it must be stressed that the main guidelines for economic policy described below, have been specially worked out so as to minimise the sacrifices imposed on consumers by the requirements of general equilibrium and by measures designed to ensure a better future for all, and that the implementation of these guidelines will probably make a decisive contribution to harmonious economic progress in the Community between now and 1970.

A number of member-states have based their budget projections on the assumption that the level of taxation will not be raised. It is in fact unlikely that it can be left unchanged. Despite the progressive nature of certain taxes it is realised in a number of countries that to have the general level unchanged would mean budget deficits and that these would have—unless the government were prepared consciously to risk introducing an element of inflation into the economy —to be covered through domestic long-term loans.

Here, certain changes are discernible.

In the first place, the attainment of the overall growth rate written into the projections implies that there will be appreciably more rapid progress in productive investment; but as firms are short of funds of their own, they will have to borrow more from the capital markets whose capacity is already too limited. It is therefore dangerous to expect that private saving will make any substantial contribution to covering the requirements of public financing.

In addition, since the growth of collective requirements is very likely to remain more rapid than the expansion of production, it would probably not be sound administration if the central government and the local authorities were—apart from exceptional cases— to finance from funds that had to be repaid a growing volume of expenditure that brought nothing back to the budget.

Nothing in the foregoing must be taken to imply acceptance of a policy of largesse in public expenditure. On the contrary, since for the five-year period as a whole a rapid increase in public expenditure is expected, it is more important than ever to ensure that the increased taxation which will probably be necessary is fully justified by the additional advantages it will procure. Moreover, the present level and the probable increase in public budgets adds fresh urgency to the old problem of how certain items of collective expenditure can be reduced.

It is generally accepted that the operational budgets of the central government and of the local authorities are so rigid that even a policy of drastic austerity could not cut expenditure substantially. This is often true in the short term; but in the medium term, more rational organisation and management methods and a systematic review of the functions of the public authorities might well make substantial savings possible.

Again, transfer expenditure must be reconsidered from the angle of what is needed for economic progress and of what is possible in the light of social progress. Certain subsidies that enable unproductive industries to be maintained artificially amount to an irrational misuse of capital; nor is it certain that the extent to which social risks are covered is always proportionate to their gravity; some of these risks —notably those connected with the occupational and geographical mobility of manpower—are now of considerable economic and social importance.

Public finance programmes covering several years must be established. This concept raises certain problems of interpretation. Apart from the difficulty of expressing in the various Community languages a concept which involves varying administrative definitions, the fear has been expressed that any unduly stringent programming of budgetary operations might introduce an excessive degree of rigidity into the administration of public finance.

These difficulties can be overcome if agreement is reached on the objectives and limits of public finance programming. These appear to be of three kinds.

In the first place, it would be irrational to go on confining public finance policy to the narrow framework of annual budgets now that an attempt is being made to stretch general economic planning to cover several years. Being a field in which governments enjoy special privileges, public finance policy must be the centrepiece of general economic policy. Consequently, the aggregate budget appropriations for each year must be fixed in the light of what the economic projections used as basis for the medium-term programme show to be possible; the impact of new laws or regulations involving financial commitments must be examined from this same point of view; and the value of each measure must be assessed after a comprehensive study which alone can restore its real significance to the role of budgetary unity: to decide on the basis of firm information what expenditure should have priority and to make certain that the commitments authorised do not in the aggregate greatly exceed resources.

This is the first point in the proposal of public finance programmes covering several years; on this basis the programmes remain purely indicative and serve merely as background to the decisions taken by Governments and Parliaments. The institution by member-states of such a system of programmes is all the more necessary since, as we have seen, the situation of the public finances over the next five years seems likely to be highly insecure.

Moreover public finance policy—like general economic policy, of which it is an essential part—consists in determining the tasks which have priority and in taking the appropriate measures to ensure their proper execution; this often extends over several years, particularly in the case of major collective investments. The rational implementation of the political decisions taken in this way demands that the authorities responsible for executing them should from the outset be given firm assurances concerning the volume and regularity of the funds at their disposal. It is clear that guarantees of this kind cannot be provided within the framework of annual budgets.

Another point is that investment appropriations are often treated as one of the most elastic components in public expenditure and frequently suffer considerable amendment from one year to another, without reference to an overall plan and on purely short-term considerations. The result, both in budgetary administration and in the execution of expenditure—especially of public works—is a wasteful lack of continuity hindering the proper observance of agreed priorities.

There is then a good case for a second and more ambitious approach to the programming of public finance in accordance with which investment moneys would be committed for several years ahead.

But an obstacle to this approach is the recurrent need for a short-term strategic reserve, were it only to offset business fluctuations. This difficulty is a real one. There would however be no difficulty over the member-states arranging for a certain proportion of their investment expenditure, representing that part regarded as taking priority over the rest, to be earmarked in the form of an irrevocable commitment over a number of years.

In addition, the budgets of the local authorities is most member-countries account for more than half of all public investment. On both the counts given above the programming of these local budgets over several years is no less necessary than it is in central government finance—though it is important to safeguard, and often even to strengthen, the independence of the local authorities.

The right solution lies in the progressive and concerted co-ordination of the financial activity of the various public authorities. The existence at national level of a medium-term budgetary programme or plan, in the preparation of which the representatives of the local authorities have been associated, could well make a national contribution to harmonisation. In addition, the states should consider the possibility of adjusting their arrangements on subsidies to local authorities in the light of the effort made by these authorities to adapt their own financial policies to the requirements of the medium-term economic policy.

In all likelihood, the rate of increase of collective expenditure will none the less remain far higher than that of overall growth (4·3 per cent in the years to come. Public investment, in particular, is considered likely to continue expanding at twice this rate (8·7 per cent), while the rate of growth of private consumption would drop from 5·3 per cent to about 4·1 per cent.

The main conclusions to be drawn in this respect from the projections are as follows:

(i) Despite the action which the authorities are expected to take, the growth rates assumed for private consumption probably lie at the upper limit of what is compatible with a broadly balanced growth.

(ii) Even if the general policy recommendations formulated in this programme are promptly implemented, there will still be a risk that the upward movement of prices may reach the danger point.

This being so, taxation policy should be so framed as to produce the funds which will enable the authorities to cope with collective requirements and to slow down the increase in private consumption.

If the inflationary development of demand in the next five years is to be countered, greater rigour in the budget appears all the more necessary when it is remembered that too restrictive a monetary policy would rapidly lead to a slowdown in productive investment. Moreover it is, in most member-countries at least, by no means certain that a general incomes policy will meet with early success; and if success there is to be, a severe financial policy will in any case be required.

In these circumstances the increased tax burden should be so distributed that it would step up personal saving, especially saving by persons in paid employment, and so curb consumption.

The conditions necessary to secure the general equilibrium of economic growth in the Community during the next five-year period may admittedly seem harsh. It is however important that their scope should be exactly understood.

If the responsible authorities cocked a snook at these conditions and the lessons to be learnt from the medium-term projections, and if they ignored the guidelines set out in the medium-term programme, they would do a disservice to the harmonious development of the European economy.

On the other hand, if they accept conscientiously the existing constraints and the resulting priorities, they may find, thanks to improved utilisation of their traditional means of intervention, that they are able to shape medium-term, economic developments and to make possible an annual growth rate of private consumption of about 3·3 per cent per inhabitant.

Economic Growth in the Common Market

This growth rate would mean a 100 per cent improvement in the standard of living in twenty years.

Inflationary trends, inadequate regional integration, scientific and technological backwardness: these are the three sources of weakness liable to undermine the Community's medium-term economic prospects.

The first of these arises from the insecurity of the situations written

THE EXPANSION OF REAL GROSS NATIONAL PRODUCT
1950–5, 1955–60, 1960–5 and first estimates 1965–70

	% share of total O.E.C.D. output 1963	Annual average percentage rates of increase			ESTIMATES
		1950–5	1955–60	1960–5	1965–70
France	7·3	4·3	3·3	5·5	4·8
W. Germany	8·6	9·3[1]	6·3[1]	4·8[2]	3·5[2]
Italy	4·1	6·0	5·5	5·1	5·0
Belgium	1·3	—	2·5	4·5	4·0
Luxembourg	0·1	—	3·0	2·9	3·2
Netherlands	1·3	5·5	4·2	4·8	4·5
Greece	0·4	7·0	5·4	8·7	7·5
Turkey	0·6	6·3	5·2	4·3	—
United Kingdom	7·7	2·7	2·8	3·3	4·1[4]
USA	53·3	4·3	2·2	4·5	4·5
Total O.E.C.D.	100·0	5·2	3·5	4·9	4·6
Total E.E.C.	22·7	6·7	5·3	4·9	4·3
Total Efta	12·3	3·1	3·2	4·0	4·2

Source: Economic Growth 1960–70 O.E.C.D.

1 Excluding Saar and West Berlin
2 Including Saar and West Berlin
3 Although various new estimates of growth by individual countries, E.E.C. and O.E.C.D. are taking place the figures given are the only totally comparable figures available. The revised estimates tend to be downwards.
4 In July 1966 the United Kingdom government announced that the Plan target would have to be revised downwards and in his budget speech on 11 April 1967 the Chancellor of the Exchequer estimated that the growth rate would be approximately 3 per cent per annum.

into the projections, both in the economy at large and in the public finances. The seriousness of the threats involved deserves to be stressed. The two others call for the implementation of certain measures which must be worked out and put in hand without delay.

The table above gives an indication of the scale and rate of growth in the E.E.C. as a whole in the decade and a half to 1965 with projections of growth to 1970 and contrasts this with two Associate countries, the U.S.A., U.K. and Efta.
o

Bibliography

Treaty of Rome (new edition) 1967.
General Report on the Activities of the Community from 1958 (annual).
Euratom Bulletin from 1962 (quarterly).
European Community London (monthly).
Economic Growth 1960–70 O.E.C.D. Paris 1966.
Exposé sur l'évolution de la situation sociale dans la Communauté en 1965 E.E.C. 1966.
Tableaux Comparatifs des Régimes de Sécurité Sociale E.E.C. 1965.
Report of the Committee on Turnover Taxation H.M.S.O. 1964.
Guide Pratique concernant les Articles 85 and 86 du Traité E.E.C. 1963.
Securité Sociale des Travailleurs Migrants E.E.C. 1965.
Comment appliquer la T.V.A. Paris.
Études sur la Securité Sociale dans les pays de la C.E.E. E.E.C. 1964.

Trade in the Common Market Countries Walsh & Paxton. London 1965.
The Political Dynamics of European Economic Integration L. N. Lindberg. Stanford 1963.
The Schuman Plan: A Study in Economic Co-operation 1950–59 W. Diebold. New York 1959.
The Common Market's Labor Programs Mark J. Fitzgerald. London 1966.
Keesing's Contemporary Archives from 1951.
The Statesman's Year-Book 1966–67 S. H. Steinberg. London 1966.
British Agriculture and the Common Market N.F.U. London 1966.
The Challenge of the Common Market U. W. Kitzinger 1961.
Legal Problems of the E.E.C. and Efta London 1961.
The Common Market Jean Deniau. London (new edition) 1967.

APPENDIX I

Who sells most to Britain and the Common Market Countries?

The following tables show for 25 commodity groups where Britain and each country in the Common Market buy their supplies of those commodities. In the table, each country's total imports under the commodity group are given, together with the share of the exporting countries which account for the bulk of the supplies.

Supplementary notes indicate, in exceptional cases, other significant sources of the imports.

An important feature of these tables is the Export: Import Ratio shown against each commodity group. This figure provides a measurement of the strength of the domestic industry in terms of its ability to export or its dependence on imports. The figures are for the year 1965 and have been approximated.

Where — is shown in the tables, the relevant figure is nil or negligible.

203

Appendix I

Product	Importing Country	Total World Imports	PRINCIPAL SUPPLI				
			U.K.	U.S.	Bel.	Neth.	Ger
		$ Million	%	%	%	%	%
	Bel./Lux.	58	—	3		57	7
	Neth.	39	4	43	18		8
Dairy	Germany	223	—	—	10	41	
Produce	France	64	—	17	4	15	17
and	Italy	145	—	4	8	8	19
Eggs.	U.K.	583		—	—	5	—

Notes: Other suppliers include:
(1) Finland 2%. (2) Australia-New Zealand 2%, Sino-Soviet 7%.
(3) Finland 3%, Sino-Soviet 5%. (4) Australia-New Zealand 49%, Sino-Soviet 4%.

	Bel./Lux.	193	2	47		5	1
Cereals	Neth.	266	1	60	4		—
and	Germany	525	1	27	3	7	
Cereal	France	136	—	38	4	4	2
Preparations.	Italy	497	—	31	—	—	—
	U.K.	649		26	2	10	1

Notes. Other suppliers include:
(1) Argentina 8%. (2) Argentina 12%. (3) Argentina 7%. (4) Argentina 13%.
(5) Argentina 39%. (6) Argentina 7%, Australia-New Zealand 11%.

	Bel./Lux.	11	1	—		4	1
Sugar	Neth.	25	9	5	19		5
and	Germany	53	5	2	11	11	
Sugar	France	79	—	—	2	1	2
Preparations.	Italy	36	1	—	—	2	—
	U.K.	287		—	—	1	—

Notes. Others suppliers include:
(1) Cuba 14%. (2) Mexico 6%, Argentina 7%. (3) Reunion 36%, Fr. Antilles 37%.
(4) Cuba 17%, Dominican Rep. 8% (5) Australia-New Zealand-S. Africa. 25%, W. Indies 70%.

	Bel./Lux.	72	—	18		9	3
Feeding Stuffs	Neth.	129	1	33	3		6
for Animals	Germany	266	2	15	1	8	
excluding	France	117	—	36	5	6	2
unmilled	Italy	58	—	24	4	15	—
cereals.	U.K.	212		1	—	1	—

Notes. Other suppliers include (Peru, Brazil, Chile, Argentina etc.) 25% to 40% o supplies.

	Bel./Lux.	21	1	1		56	14
	Neth.	11	3	17	47		7
Miscellaneous	Germany	14	10	10	4	32	
Food	France	4	10	5	15	7	14
Preparations.	Italy	3	6	9	16	6	35
	U.K.	74		53	18	3	1

Appendix I

ARE OF IMPORTS

It.	Nor.	Swe.	Den.	Aus.	Swit.	Export Import Ratio	Notes
%	%	%	%	%	%		
2	—	—	2	1	7	73: 58	(1)
—	—	—	3	—	1	334: 39	
1	—	—	14	1	2	56:223	(2)
12	—	—	3	—	19	176: 64	
—	—	1	3	8	12	40:145	(3)
—	1	1	20	1	—	29:583	(4)
—	—	—	—	—	—	64:193	(1)
—	—	—	—	—	—	87:266	(2)
10	—	3	3	—	—	120:525	(3)
16	—	—	—	—	—	534:136	(4)
—	—	—	—	—	—	112:497	(5)
—	—	—	—	—	—	61:649	(6)
—	—	—	—	—	—	27: 11	
—	—	—	4	—	—	29: 25	(1)
2	—	—	—	—	1	8: 53	(2)
—	—	—	—	—	—	129: 79	(3)
—	—	—	3	—	—	3: 36	(4)
—	—	—	—	—	—	66:287	(5)
—	4	—	1	—	—	20: 72	
—	4	—	1	—	—	56:129	
2	1	—	3	—	—	41:266	
—	5	—	—	—	—	53:117	
—	2	—	—	—	—	11: 58	
—	7	—	4	—	—	16:212	
1	—	—	1	—	2	17: 21	
2	—	—	13	—	1	60: 11	
8	—	—	6	2	3	10: 14	
10	—	—	—	—	8	25: 4	
—	—	—	—	—	2	10: 3	
4	—	1	5	—	2	31: 74	

Appendix I

Product	Importing Country	Total World Imports	PRINCIPAL SUPPLI[ERS]				
			U.K.	U.S.	Bel.	Neth.	Ger
		$ Million	%	%	%	%	%
Hides and Skins.	Bel./Lux.	28	9	7		9	18
	Neth.	30	13	13	19		15
	Germany	189	3	14	2	2	
	France	110	—	4	1	3	2
	Italy	108	5	8	1	2	5
	U.K.	156		9	—	4	1

Notes. Other suppliers include: (1) Australia-New Zealand 23%. (2) Australia-New Ze[aland] 16%, Brazil 3%, Argentina 3%. (4) Australia-New Zealand 48%, Argentina 5%, Ur[uguay] 4%. (5) Australia-New Zealand 24%. (6) Australia-New Zealand 41%, India-Pak[istan] etc. 8%.

Pulp and Paper.	Bel./Lux.	34	—	14		2	2
	Neth.	75	1	8	2		5
	Germany	176	1	13	2	5	
	France	121	—	14	2	—	2
	Italy	139	—	18	—	—	1
	U.K.	390		8	—	—	—

Notes. Other suppliers include:
(1) Finland 24%. (2) Finland 30%. (3) Finland 14%. (4) Finland 18%. (5) Finland (6) Finland 21%, Canada 11%, other countries 23%.

Chemical Elements and Compounds.	Bel./Lux.	112	8	16		13	29
	Neth.	196	9	21	10		32
	Germany	366	5	34	6	9	
	France	278	8	27	7	7	23
	Italy	175	7	19	2	7	29
	U.K.	334		22	4	7	16

Notes. Other suppliers include Sino-Soviet countries averaging about 5%.

Dyeing, Tanning and Colouring Materials.	Bel./Lux.	34	11	7		21	38
	Neth.	39	18	5	10		42
	Germany	51	12	7	6	21	
	France	54	9	9	8	10	39
	Italy	44	9	10	1	8	39
	U.K.	44		14	2	4	27

Medicines and Pharmaceutical Goods.	Bel./Lux.	64	8	23		18	16
	Neth.	37	19	5	18		18
	Germany	61	10	2	2	14	
	France	62	15	2	3	5	18
	Italy	59	8	1	1	10	23
	U.K.	31		—	2	5	20

Appendix I

HARE OF IMPORTS

It.	Nor.	Swe.	Den.	Aus.	Swit.	Export Import Ratio	Notes
%	%	%	%	%	%		
—	2	—	1	—	—	14: 28	(1)
—	—	—	—	—	—	30: 30	(2)
2	4	4	5	1	2	31:189	(3)
1	1	—	1	—	1	42:110	(4)
—	1	—	1	—	2	13:108	(5)
2	2	2	6	—	1	15:156	(6)

—	8	39	—	—	—	8: 34	(1)
—	12	29	—	—	—	10: 75	(2)
—	4	42	1	3	—	12:176	(3)
—	6	42	—	—	1	20:121	(4)
—	3	33	—	7	1	2:139	(5)
—	13	33	—	—	—	5:390	(6)

4	1	—	—	—	1	88:112
3	—	1	—	—	2	188:196
9	1	1	—	1	5	653:366
7	1	1	1	—	8	329:278
—	—	1	—	1	4	222:175
4	3	2	1	—	7	298:334

1	—	—	—	—	8	21: 34
1	1	—	2	—	8	52: 39
2	1	1	1	3	28	266: 51
2	—	—	—	—	18	47: 54
—	—	—	1	—	15	16: 44
—	—	—	—	—	26	152: 44

3	—	—	1	—	15	30: 64
3	—	—	3	—	16	70: 37
3	—	1	4	1	26	225: 61
10	—	—	3	—	23	138: 62
—	—	1	—	—	27	60: 59
2	—	3	4	—	10	187: 31

Product	Importing Country	Total World Imports	PRINCIPAL SUPPLIER				
			U.K.	U.S.	Bel.	Neth.	Ger.
		$ Million	%	%	%	%	%
Perfumery, Toilet and Cleaning Materials.	Bel./Lux.	23	12	8		25	25
	Neth.	33	10	10	34		23
	Germany	53	8	12	8	15	
	France	62	3	9	6	7	12
	Italy	24	12	12	1	7	21
	U.K.	42		21	1	2	6

Notes. Other suppliers include:
(1) Sino-Soviet 7%.

Manufactured Fertilisers.	Bel./Lux.	52	—	—		—	23
	Neth.	26	—	1	44		27
	Germany	18	—	2	76	5	
	France	50	—	4	63	14	9
	Italy	10	—	6	14	—	13
	U.K.	54		—	3	28	23

Notes. Other suppliers include:
(1) Sino-Soviet 5%. (2) Sino-Soviet 9%. (3) Sino-Soviet 19%.

Plastic Materials.	Bel./Lux.	88	10	12		23	29
	Neth.	103	12	14	20		34
	Germany	157	8	18	8	19	
	France	122	8	19	6	9	4
	Italy	67	8	17	3	8	45
	U.K.	153		37	2	8	17

Leather and Leather Manufactures.	Bel./Lux.	30	15	9		22	10
	Neth.	33	14	9	19		23
	Germany	115	9	7	10	9	
	France	37	9	8	5	3	18
	Italy	31	21	7	2	3	19
	U.K.	73		6	1	—	2

Notes. Other suppliers include:
(1) Uruguay 1%, India-Pakistan 8%. (2) Morocco 6%, India-Pakistan 18%.
(3) India-Pakistan 13%. (4) India-Pakistan 38%.

Rubber Manufactures.	Bel./Lux.	47	8	7		30	23
	Neth.	41	11	9	30		29
	Germany	119	8	12	10	11	
	France	38	16	17	6	3	35
	Italy	28	16	28	7	2	29
	U.K.	35		24	4	3	12

Appendix I

It.	Nor.	Swe.	Den.	Aus.	Swit.	Export Import Ratio	Notes
%	%	%	%	%	%		
2	—	—	—	—	3	21: 23	
2	—	—	—	—	3	41: 33	
5	—	1	—	—	12	80: 53	
16	—	—	—	—	5	156: 62	
	—	—	—	—	9	30: 24	
10	—	—	—	—	6	105: 42	
—	—	—	—	—	—	139: 52	(1)
—	—	—	—	—	—	73: 26	(2)
—	—	—	—	—	—	156: 18	
4	—	—	—	—	—	81: 50	
	—	—	—	—	—	82: 10	
—	—	—	—	—	—	23: 54	(3)
9	—	—	—	—	1	54: 88	
7	—	1	—	—	1	118:103	
18	—	2	1	2	5	398:157	
15	—	1	1	—	2	127:122	
	—	1	—	—	2	151: 67	
6	3	2	1	—	1	226:153	
4	—	—	—	—	—	26: 30	
7	—	—	—	—	—	25: 33	
13	1	1	—	3	1	83:115	(1)
6	2	—	—	—	—	94: 37	(2)
	—	—	—	—	—	44: 31	(3)
1	—	2	—	1	1	85: 73	(4)
9	—	1	1	—	1	36: 47	
7	—	2	—	1	1	43: 41	
9	2	6	—	7	4	134:119	
13	—	3	—	1	3	141: 38	
	—	—	1	4	2	76: 28	
6	2	4	1	6	2	131: 35	

Appendix I

Product	Importing Country	Total World Imports	PRINCIPAL SUPPLIERS				
			U.K.	U.S.	Bel.	Neth.	Ger
		$ Million	%	%	%	%	%
Paper and Paperboard.	Bel./Lux.	119	5	4		31	10
	Neth.	145	3	6	21		16
	Germany	388	2	9	4	12	
	France	145	4	8	11	7	15
	Italy	71	4	21	1	3	11
	U.K.	344		13	—	3	2

Notes. Other suppliers include:
(1) Finland 16%. (2) Finland 17%. (3) Finland 23%. (4) Finland 18%.
(5) Finalnd 15%. (6) Finland 18%, Canada 25%.

	Bel./Lux.	283	4	3		33	18
Textile Yarns, Fabrics and made-up Articles.	Neth.	453	4	2	43		22
	Germany	1,015	6	3	16	15	
	France	251	8	7	18	8	21
	Italy	154	10	5	7	4	3
	U.K.	424		8	7	5	6

Notes. Other suppliers include:
(1) India 16%. (2) India 13%. (3) India 1%, Iran 5%. (4) India 1%. (5) India 1%, Hong Kong 5%. (6) India 17%, Hong Kong 11%, Iran 2%.

	Bel./Lux.	198	3	6		14	30
Iron and Steel.	Neth.	376	4	1	30		46
	Germany	827	2	2	30	7	
	France	549	3	1	35	2	46
	Italy	313	4	4	11	4	2
	U.K.	218		10	5	10	7

Notes. Other suppliers include:
(1) Sino-Soviet 2%. (2) Sino-Soviet 1%. (3) Sino-Soviet 2%. (4) Fr. A.O.C. Oceania (5) S. Africa 2%, Finland 2%, Yugoslavia 2%. (6) Sino-Soviet 9%, S. Africa 4%, Finlan

	Bel./Lux.	366	5	2		4	5
Non-ferrous Metals.	Neth.	196	9	6	34		20
	Germany	997	9	10	14	6	
	France	446	10	13	25	4	6
	Italy	299	8	19	4	2	7
	U.K.	1,029		11	2	3	2

Notes. Other suppliers include:
(1) South Africa 4%, Congo-K 48%. (2) Sino-Soviet 4%, Rhodesia 2%, Mexico 1%.
(3) Sino-Soviet 5%, Canada 3%, Australia-New Zealand 1%, Zambia 7%, Chile 12%, Peru 3%, Mexico 2%. (4) Cameroun 3%, Congo-K 5%, Zambia 10%, Chile 4%, Malaysia 1%. (5) Congo-K 8%, Zambia 9%, Chile 6%, Malaysia 5%. (6) Sino-Soviet, Zambia 20%, Chile 7%, Australia-South Africa 8%, Peru 2%.

	Bel./Lux.	588	10	13		9	40
Machinery other than Electric.	Neth.	682	13	11	9		42
	Germany	1,158	13	21	5	6	
	France	1,217	10	19	6	2	36
	Italy	552	15	19	4	2	38
	U.K.	1,037		34	2	4	2

Appendix I

ARE OF IMPORTS

It.	Nor.	Swe.	Den.	Aus.	Swit.	Export Import Ratio	Notes
%	%	%	%	%	%		
1	4	14	—	1	1	76:119	(1)
—	6	20	—	3	1	124:145	(2)
2	7	23	1	8	—	149:388	(3)
3	5	20	—	1	1	116:145	(4)
	1	20	—	8	2	48: 71	(5)
—	9	23	—	1	—	141:344	(6)
8	—	—	—	1	2	591: 283	(1)
8	—	—	—	1	1	461: 453	(2)
16	—	—	—	4	6	666:1015	(3)
20	—	1	—	1	5	717: 215	(4)
	—	—	—	1	8	638: 154	(5)
8	—	1	—	2	3	768: 424	(6)
1	2	4	—	1	—	1143:198	(1)
2	2	3	—	1	—	243:376	(2)
6	3	7	—	8	1	1417:827	(3)
5	—	3	—	—	—	966:549	(4)
	1	3	—	3	—	366:313	(5)
—	14	17	—	2	1	655:218	(6)
1	4	—	—	—	—	505: 366	(1)
3	—	2	—	1	2	129: 196	(2)
3	6	1	—	1	1	387: 997	(3)
1	4	1	—	—	1	239: 446	(4)
	2	—	—	1	2	107: 299	(5)
1	3	1	—	—	1	470:1029	(6)
5	—	2	1	—	4	422: 588	
4	—	3	2	—	5	387: 682	
10	1	5	3	3	11	3933:1158	
10	—	3	1	—	5	1064:1217	
	—	3	1	1	5	1038: 552	
5	—	—	—	—	6	2605:1037	

Product	Importing Country	Total World Imports	PRINCIPAL SUPPLIE				
			U.K.	U.S.	Bel.	Neth.	Ger.
		$ Million	%	%	%	%	%
Electrical Machinery.	Bel./Lux.	303	5	6		29	32
	Neth.	585	8	6	26		33
	Germany	505	9	18	4	17	
	France	428	9	29	4	10	27
	Italy	303	7	19	6	13	36
	U.K.	353		38	1	9	14
Transport Equipment	Bel./Lux.	616	12	8		9	38
	Neth.	578	10	7	34		26
	Germany	638	5	21	22	6	
	France	422	13	14	3	6	43
	Italy	236	15	13	4	2	36
	U.K.	306		22	15	7	15
of which passenger motor cars.	Belgium	164	8	3		15	50
	Neth.	296	4	1	50		25
	Germany	312	3	3	40	—	
	France	187	18	4	1	1	56
	Italy	107	9	—	1	1	58
	U.K.	67	—	2	14	1	39
Clothing.	Bel./Lux.	92	3	2		35	14
	Neth.	218	3	2	43		27
	Germany	428	3	2	5	8	
	France	90	6	6	8	5	21
	Italy	30	25	4	2	2	24
	U.K.	160		2	2	1	2

Notes. Other suppliers include:
(1) Hong Kong 3%. (2) Hong Kong 15%. (3) Hong Kong 4%.

Footwear.	Bel./Lux.	33	1	—		17	12
	Neth.	28	3	—	24		16
	Germany	111	1	—	3	6	
	France	23	1	—	8	2	8
	Italy	2	14	3	1	1	9
	U.K.	50		—		2	1	3

Notes. Other suppliers include:
(1) Yugoslavia 3%, Hong Kong 3%. (2) Hong Kong 26%.

Scientific Instruments, Photographic Goods and Clocks.	Bel./Lux.	80	7	12		8	36
	Neth.	106	8	19	9		37
	Germany	208	14	20	6	5	
	France	173	12	24	5	3	30
	Italy	119	6	16	4	2	33
	U.K.	201		31	4	3	15

Appendix I   213

IARE OF IMPORTS

It.	Nor.	Swe.	Den.	Aus.	Swit.	Export Import Ratio	Notes
%	%	%	%	%	%		
7	—	1	—	—	3	258:303	
6	—	1	1	3	3	623:585	
13	1	2	2	4	8	1478:505	
13	—	1	—	—	4	534:428	
	—	2	—	1	3	430:303	
5	—	3	2	1	4	926:353	
5	—	2	—	—	—	603:616	
9	—	2	—	—	—	341:578	
15	1	2	1	2	1	2858:638	
15	—	2	—	—	—	1043:422	
	1	1	1	1	1	708:236	
6	—	12	—	—	—	2027:306	
7	—	1	—	—	—	367:164	
7	—		—	—	—	39:296	
23	—	1	—	—	—	1636:312	
18	—	1	—	—	—	494:187	
	—		—	—	—	297:107	
10	—	10	—	—	—	704: 67	
14	—	—	—	2	2	148: 92	(1)
15	—	—	—	1	2	88:218	
29	—	1	—	6	3	205:428	(2)
46	—	—	—	1	2	243: 90	
	—	—	—	6	6	425: 30	
9	1	2	1	2	3	138:160	(3)
32	—	—	—	—	3	15: 33	
37	—	1	—	1	3	17: 28	
52	—	1	—	2	4	33:111	(1)
56	—	1	—	—	8	75: 23	
	—	—	—	—	5	211: 2	
24	—	1	—	—	3	42: 50	(2)
3	—	1	—	1	11	105: 80	
2	—	1	1	1	6	58:106	
7	—	2	2	2	20	548:208	
7	—	—	—	1	13	158:173	
	—	—	—	1	18	96:119	
3	—	1	1	1	15	281:201	

APPENDIX II

The extraction of statistics of Consumption, Imports and Exports of the Common Market countries by the use of Input-Output Tabulations.

In the following tables, use has been made of Input-Output tabulations (Second Edition 1965) prepared by the Statistical Office of the Commission of the European Economic Community to show, for each Common Market country, under the principal industrial groups:
(1) The value of the consumption for each product for each country. Consumption figures have been aggregated for intermediate consumption (i.e. consumption by other industries), private and public consumption and for fixed capital formation but the capital figures are shown in a separate column.
(2) The percentage which Imports of similar goods at c.i.f. prices (exclusive of import duties) bear to consumption.
(3) The percentage which Exports bear to national production.

The figures for stock variations have been disregarded, as these are marginal in any case.

The original Input-Output tabulations are in the currencies of the individual countries and these are shown for the consumption figures for each country. Because of the enormous amount of statistical calculation which Input-Output Tables involve the information is for 1959 in all countries except West Germany, (including West Berlin), for which it is for 1960. The second version of Input-Output Tables issued in December 1965 embodies a number of revisions of the tables for the same years which were issued in 1964.

FRANCE — Appendix II — Million Francs.

Product Group	Consumption Intermediate Public Private	Capital Formation	Total	Imports as % of Consumption	Exports as % of Production
Textile Fibres and Manufactures	8,138		8,138	4	25
Knitwear	1,683		1,683	2	15
Clothing, Carpets, etc.	9,936		9,936	0·6	6
Footwear	2,061		2,061	0·8	9
Pulp and Paper	4,244		4,244	13	8
Leather and Leather Manufactures	1,419		1,419	6	21
Plastics	1,639		1,639	0·4	4
Synthetic and Artificial Fibres	2,395		2,395	15	19
Chemicals	11,217		11,217	9	16
Glass and Glassware	1,051		1,051	4	22
Iron and Steel E.C.S.C.	9,293		9,293	13	28
Iron and Steel non E.C.S.C.	2,453	49	2,502	8	28
Non-Ferrous Metals and Products	4,212		4,212	28	15
Agricultural Machinery and Tractors	137	1,927	2,064	12	7
Non-electric Machinery	7,104	9,748	16,852	12	15
Electric Machinery and Equipment	4,661	2,470	7,131	5	12
Motor Vehicles	4,344	2,781	7,145	2·5	30
Precision Instruments, Photographic equipment, etc.	886	257	1,143	23	29

Appendix II
BELGIUM

Million Francs.

Product Group	Consumption			Imports as % of Consumption	Exports as % of Production
	Intermediate Public Private	Capital Formation	Total		
Textile Fibres and Manufactures	20,830		20,830	42	60
Knitwear	3,850		3,850	20	30
Clothing, Carpets, etc.	13,250		13,250	12	16
Footwear	4,310		4,310	15	12
Pulp and Paper	10,500	10	10,510	40	22
Leather and Leather Manufactures	2,720		2,720	44	35
Plastics	1,590		1,590	38	24
Synthetic and Artificial Fibres	3,960	30	3,990	67	60
Chemicals	20,340	150	20,490	50	54
Glass and Glassware	1,570		1,570	37	86
Iron and Steel E.C.S.C.	17,980	90	18,070	32	64
Iron and Steel non E.C.S.C.	2,870		2,870	25	64
Non-ferrous Metals and Products	14,120	20	14,140	82	80
Agricultural Machinery and Tractors	330	1,200	1,530	50	43
Non-electric Machinery	10,880	11,810	22,690	50	44
Electric Machinery and Equipment	8,250	6,350	14,600	40	39
Motor Vehicles	13,820	5,580	19,400	50	33
Precision Instruments, Photographic equipment, etc.	960	1,320	2,230	70	39

ITALY

Appendix II

'000 *Million Lire*.

Product Group	Consumption			Imports as % of Consumption	Exports as % of Production
	Intermediate Public Private	Capital Formation	Total		
Textile Fibres and Manufactures	796		796	7	19
Knitwear	127		127	1	26
Clothing, Carpets, etc.	525		525	15	5
Footwear	146		146	11	23
Pulp and Paper	317		317	16	3
Leather and Leather Manufactures	164	1	165	6	8
Plastics	106	5	111	2	5
Synthetic and Artificial Fibres	184		184	20	33
Chemicals	1,056		1,056	12	10
Glass and Glassware	99	12	111	14	8
Iron and Steel E.C.S.C.	539	3	542	17	12
Iron and Steel non E.C.S.C.	242	21	263	5	11
Non-ferrous Metals and Products	276		276	31	11
Agricultural Machinery and Tractors	1	77	78	14	15
Non-electric Machinery	63	457	520	28	34
Electric Machinery and Equipment	207	240	447	13	9
Motor Vehicles	125	225	350	6	31
Precision Instruments, Photographic equipment, etc.	76	33	109	45	15

Appendix II
NETHERLANDS

Million Guilden.

Product Group	Consumption			Imports as % of Consumption	Exports as % of Production
	Intermediate Public Private	Capital Formation	Total		
Textile Fibres and Manufactures	1,822	10	1,832	44	44
Knitwear	352		352	35	19
Clothing, Carpets, etc.	1,378		1,378	13	11
Footwear	341		341	8	10
Pulp and Paper	1,107		1,107	3	26
Leather and Leather Manufactures	261		261	27	33
Plastics	165		165	37	23
Synthetic and Artificial Fibres	352		352	60	74
Chemicals	2,068	15	2,083	45	45
Glass and Glassware	207	2	209	65	14
Iron and Steel E.C.S.C.	1,258	70	1,328	57	45
Iron and Steel non E.C.S.C.	215		215	50	35
Non-ferrous Metals	667		667	70	65
Agricultural, Machinery and Tractors	30	236	266	34	12
Non-electric Machinery	1,021	918	1,939	60	45
Electric Machinery and Equipment	1,376	512	1,888	50	58
Motor Vehicles	353	581	934	60	20
Precision Instruments, Photographic equipment, etc.	407	61	468	30	26

WEST GERMANY INCLUDING WEST BERLIN Million DM.

Product Group	Consumption			Imports as % of Consumption	Exports as % of Production
	Intermediate Public Private	Capital Formation	Total		
Yarn, Textile and Knitwear	14,915	193	15,108	18	9
Clothing, Carpets, etc.	8,921		8,921	4	3
Leather and Leather Manufactures	4,525	60	4,585	9	8
Pulp and Paper	6,873	15	6,888	20	6
Rubber and Asbestos Manufactures	2,980		2,980	8	13
Chemicals, Synthetic and Artificial Fibres and Plastics	18,413		18,413	14	26
Iron and Steel E.C.S.C.	13,350	33	13,383	15	18
Iron and Steel non E.C.S.C. and Manufactures excl. Machinery	15,642	6,137	21,779	5	16
Non-ferrous Metals and Products	6,449		6,449	47	21
Non-electric Machinery, Rolling Stock and Aeronautical Construction	12,275	15,387	27,662	15	29
Electric Machinery and Appliances	7,458	5,697	13,155	6	21
Precision Instruments, Optical, etc.	4,296	343	4,539	14	37

The above product headings are the only ones available for West Germany from current input/output tabulations.

APPENDIX III

Who produces most in the Common Market?

Production figures for 38 basic commodities in the Common Market, together with each country's share of the total production figures. Mainly for 1965, except where stated.

Appendix III

Product Group		Total Production	Unit
IRON AND STEEL			
Blooms, Billets, etc.		4,248	'000 tons
Angles, Shapes and Sections, heavy		5,264	'000 tons
Bars and Rods for Tube manufacture		2,003	'000 tons
Wire Rod in coils		6,789	'000 tons
Hot-rolled and cold-rolled Sheets and Plates 3 mm. and over		8,456	'000 tons
Cold-rolled Sheets, under 3 mm.		12,136	'000 tons
Tinplate		3,787	'000 tons
Steel Tube, welded and weldless		6,076	'000 tons
NON-FERROUS METALS			
Aluminium, semi-manufactures		732	'000 tons
Copper	(1964)	1,596	'000 tons
CHEMICAL PRODUCTS			
Sulphuric Acid		12,210	'000 tons
Fertilisers, Nitrogenous		4,147	'000 tons
Fertilisers Phosphatic		2,900	'000 tons
Fertilisers, Potassic		4,445	'000 tons
Paints and Varnishes	(1964)	1,711	'000 tons
Soap	(1964)	580	'000 tons
Plastic		3,480	'000 tons
PULP AND PAPER			
Wood Pulp	(1964)	3,714	'000 tons
Paper		11,069	'000 tons
LEATHER			
Light	(1964)	136	Mio. m²
Heavy	(1964)	55	'000 tons
TEXTILES AND CLOTHING			
Synthetic Fibres and Yarn		428	'000 tons
Rayon Fibres and Yarn		272	'000 tons
Woollen Yarn		538	'000 tons
Woollen Textiles		222	'000 tons
Cotton Yarn		1,024	'000 tons
Cotton Textiles		777	'000 tons
Woollen Carpets		89	'000 tons
Stockings and Socks	(1964)	1,726	million pairs
Shoes	(1964)	564	million pairs
OFFICE EQUIPMENT			
Typewriters		2,242	'000 units
TRANSPORT EQUIPMENT			
Tractors (Agricultural)	(1)	256	'000 units
Motor Cars, passenger and Commercial		5,765	'000 units
ELECTRICAL EQUIPMENT			
Domestic Refrigerators	(1964) (3)	5,569	'000 units
Washing Machines	(1964)	3,691	'000 units
Electric Razors	(1)	5,097	'000 units
Radio Receivers	(2)	4,842	'000 units
RUBBER MANUFACTURES			
Tyres		940	'000 tons

(1) Total Germany France and Italy. (2) Excluding Netherlands.
(3) Excluding Belgium/Luxembourg and Netherlands.

Appendix III

res of each Common Market Country
;ium/
embourg

	Netherlands %	Germany %	France %	Italy %
3	3	50	14	24
—	—	43	21	15
·5	·5	66	22	10
2	2	42	28	11
5	5	50	21	11
8	8	30	29	19
7	7	30	31	16
3	3	47	21	22
18	18	43	24	15[2]
—	—	47	24	19
9	9	31	24	25
11	11	33	27	22
7	7	32	29	15
neg	neg	54	41	5
7	7	43	30	15
9	9	19	28	36
6	6	50	17	24
4	4	38	38	15
9	9	38	27	20
8	8	35	31	23
10	10	25	18	43
10	10	42	19	27
14	14	29	20	32
5	5	22	24	37
11	11	23	28	30
7	7	38	26	20
11	11	35	25	20
16	16	40	11	8
5	5	38	24	30
6	6	30	38	20
—	—	60	4	36
—	—	41	36	23
1[1]	1[1]	47	25	19
—	—	42	19	39
4	4	36	23	34
—	—	61	31	8
—	—	49	26	17
—	—	36	35	20

[2]Estimated

ludes
mbled

APPENDIX IV

Population of the Common Market by country, age and sex, 1965 (in thousands).

Country	Sex	Total	Age 0–14	Age 15–64	Age 65 & over
Belgium	male	4,628	1,150	2,984	494
	female	4,800	1,098	3,012	690
	Total	9,428	2,248	5,996	1,184
West Germany	male	27,765	6,749	18,330	2,686
	female	30,823	6,422	20,168	4,233
	Total	58,587	13,170	38,498	6,920
France	male	23,768	6,339	15,251	2,178
	female	24,919	6,110	15,147	3,662
	Total	48,687	12,449	30,398	5,840
Italy	male	24,948	5,938	16,779	2,231
	female	26,276	5,790	17,661	2,825
	Total	51,224	11,728	34,440	5,056
Luxembourg	male	165	37	112	16
	female	165	35	109	21
	Total	330	72	220	37
Netherlands	male	6,090	1,774	3,786	530
	female	6,122	1,690	3,800	632
	Total	12,212	3,463	7,586	1,162
Common Market	male	87,364	21,987	57,242	8,135
	female	93,105	21,145	59,897	12,063
	Total	180,468	43,131	117,138	20,199

Source: Exposé sur l'evolution de la situation sociale dans la Communauté. 1965 (E.E.C. 1966).

Unemployment in the Common Market Countries, 1958 to 1965.

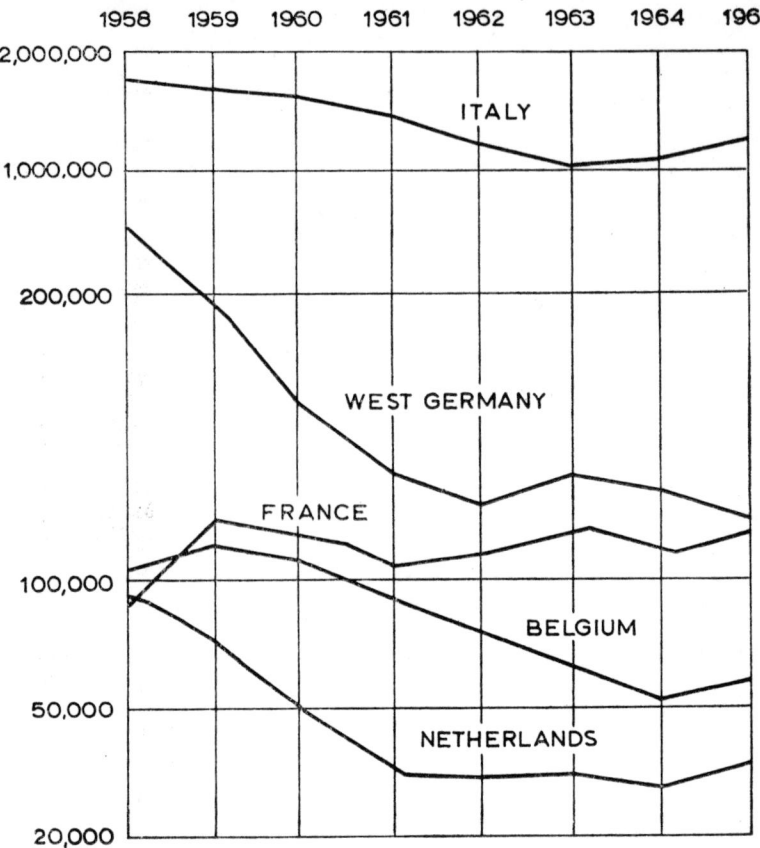

Average monthly unemployment 1963-65. '000's.

	1963	1964	1965
France	140·3	113·4	141·3
West Germany	185·6	169·1	147·4
Belgium	59·1	50·4	55·4
Luxembourg	0·2	0·045	0·046
Netherlands	33·7	30·2	34·8
Italy	1,068	1,086	1,179

Source: Exposé sur l'evolution de la situation sociale dans la Communauté. 1965. (E.E.C. 1966).

Appendix IV

Employment in the Common Market countries by occupation 1965.

	France	Germany	Belgium	Lux.	Neth.	Italy
Agriculture, Forestry, Fishing	760	370	20	1·2		1,525
Mining	286	662	95			
Manufacturing Industry of which	5,098	9,415	1,152			4,341
Foodstuffs	463	785			Breakdown not available	
Textile	455	1,324				
Wood and Wood Furniture	247					
Chemical Products	446	895		57·9		
Base Metals		1,030				
Transformation of metals	742	2,267				
Building	1,631	1,974	240			1,756
Electricity, Gas, Water, Sanitary Services	192	208	32			272
Commerce, Banking, Insurance etc.	2,051	2,997	350			
Transport and Communications	1,093	1,286	231	42·5		826
Other services except armed forces	3,253	4,475	732			3,391*
Total	14,346	21,387	2,853	101·6	3,720	12,111

*incl. Commerce etc.

Source: Exposé sur l'evolution de la situation sociale dans la Communauté. 1965. (E.E.C. 1966).

Appendix IV

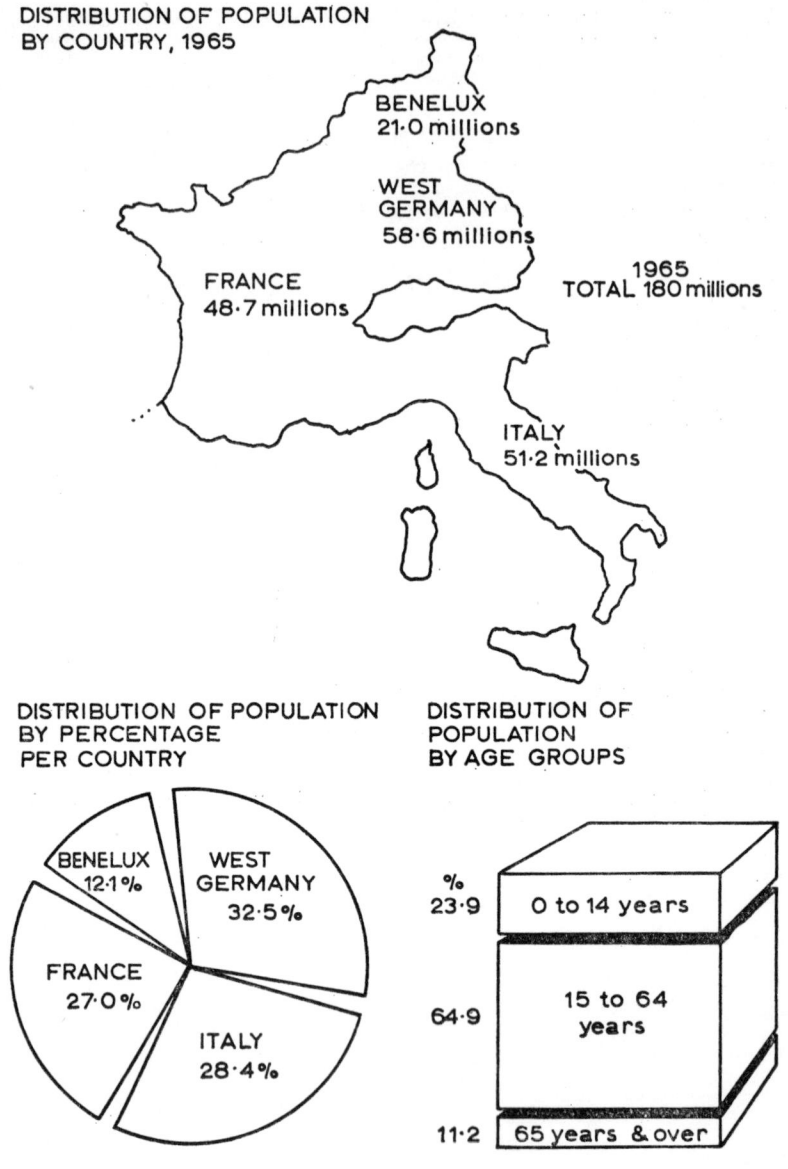

Source: Exposé sur l'evolution de la situation sociale dans la Communauté. 1965. (E.E.C. 1966).

Index

African independent states, 14
Agreements of association, 169–84
  African states, 178–81
    establishment, services, payments, capital, 180
    financial, technical, co-operation, 179–80
    general provisions, 180–1
    institutions, 180
    trade, 178–9
  Greece, 169–75
    Agricultural provisions, 172–3
    escape clause, 174
    external tariffs, 171–2
    institutions, 173–4
    internal tariffs, 170–1
    loans, 174–5
    other provisions, 173
    quantitative restrictions, 172
  Iran, 183
    trade agreement, 183
  Israel, 183–4
    trade agreement, 183–4
  Lebanon, 184
    trade, technical co-operation, 184
  Nigeria, 181–3
  Turkey, 175–8
    first stage, 176
    second stage, 176–7
    third stage, 177
    transition, first to second stage, 177–8
Algeria, 33–4
Aluminium, 100
Anglo-American loan agreement, 6
Associated African states, 181
Australia, 12
Austria, 14

Business turnover taxation, 83–99
  cascade tax, 86–8
  comparative taxation, 86–7
  excise duties, 98
  exemptions in T.V.A., 96–9
  harmonisation in E.E.C., 90–4
  purchase tax, 83, 85–6, 96–7, 99
  purchase tax levels, 85
  Richardson report, 99
  taxe locale, 89–90, 96
  taxe unique, 89
  T.P.S. tax, 88, 90, 96
  T.V.A. reduced rates, 94, 96
  T.V.A. tax, 88–99

Cambodia, 34
Canada, 12
Capital, movement of, 132
Chronology of principal events, 12–16
Coal and steel, 135–53
  common energy policy, 137
  general objectives, 136
  health, safety, social surveys, 138–41
  industrial policy, 136
  industries, 4
  loans, 136–37
  pool, Franco-German, 2
  pooling of, 2
  pooling of resources, 138–40
  production, 1, 6
  re-adaptation projects, 137–8
Common agricultural policy, 56–82
  agricultural fund, 60–1
  animal products, 61–2
  cereal prices, 62–3
  common norm price, 76
  common price level, 75–6
  common prices, individual products, 81
  constitutional crisis, 69–75
  cost-of-living index, 77
  E.E.C. commission proposals, 64–5
  E.E.C. commission proposals, contributions for 1967, 67; contributions in 1968–71, 67
  E.E.C. commission proposals, new agricultural regulation, 65–7

E.E.C. commission proposals, total revenue, expenditure, 1967-8, 67
  effect on British farmers, 81-2
  expenditure European Guidance and Guarantee Fund, 79
  final agreement, 79
  final breakthrough, 75-6
  financing European Agricultural Guidance and Guarantee Fund, 78
  free movement of produce, 77-8
  fruit, vegetables, 79-80
  grain, 61
  guide price, 76
  harmonisation of prices, 59
  intervention price, 76
  levies, 61
  management committee, 60
  objectives, 58
  olive oil, oil-seeds, 81
  products, 58
  quality standards, 58-9
  safeguard clause, 59-60
  sugar, 80
  target price, 76
  threshold price, 76
  transition period 58
Council of Europe, 7-8
Council of Ministers, 37-9
Customs Union, 8, 10, 18-19, 43, 169-70, 175

Draft Convention, 111-13
Dutch New Guinea, 34

Economic growth 190-202
  gross national product, 191
  insecurity of Balances, 194-201
  scale, rate of growth, 201-2
E.C.S.C. treaty, 135-53
  agreements, concentrations, 148-9
  commercial policy, 150-1
  financial provisions, 144-5
  general provisions, 144
  impairment, conditions of competition, 149
  investment, financial assistance, 145-6
  prices 147-8
  production, 146-7
  provisions, 142-53
  transport, 150
  wages, movement of labour, 149-50
Euratom, 34-5, 37-41
  electricity consumption, 154
  research centres, 154

European Coal and steel community, 3-5, 34-5, 37, 39-40
European Development Fund, 185-8
  finances, 186
  financial aid distribution, 188
  rules, requests, carrying out projects, 186-8
European Economic Co-operation Organisation, 6, 9
European Free Trade Association, 10-11
European Investment Bank, 61, 188-9
European Nuclear Energy Agency, 155
European Parliament, 67-9, 72
European Payments Union, 7
European Social Fund, 131-2

Free trade, 76
Free trade area, 8-11
French overseas Depts., 33-34

GATT, 46
Greece, 13, 43

Institutions of European Communities, 37-41
  administrative, Commission Social Security, migrant workers, 41
  assembly or European Parliament, 37
  budgetary policy committee, 41
  central Bank governors committee, 41
  civil service, 39
  commissions, 38-39
  consultative committee, 40
  court of Justice, 40
  economic and social committee, 40
  economic policy committees, 41
  High Authority, 39-40
  monetary committee, 41
  nuclear research consultative committee, 41
  scientific and technical committee, 41
  transport committee, 41
Iron and Steel Pool, 5
Italian Somaliland, (former), 34

Kennedy Round, 15, 27, 46-7, 57, 70

Laos, 34
Libya, 32, 34

Madagascar, 14, 178, 180
Mansholt, Dr., 62
Mansholt Plan, 15, 63-4

Index

Marshall Plan, 6
Merger of institutions, 37
Migration of labour, 129–30
Monnet, M. Jean, 1–3, 138, 140–1
Morocco, 32, 34

Netherlands Antilles, 32, 34
New Zealand, 12
Nigeria, 16, 70
Norway, 14
Nuclear development, 154–68
  admission new members, 164
  agency transaction—prices, 161
  amendment of treaty, 164
  capital investment, 167
  common market in nuclear materials, 162
  community undertakings, 159–60
  co-operation with other countries, 166
  costs of nuclear-produced electricity, 167
  dissemination of information, 157–8
  Euratom, British programmes, comparison between, 165–6
  external relations, 163
  finance, overseas territories, 164
  financial, general, provisions, 163–4
  insurance against risks, 167–8
  investments, 159
  need for nuclear energy, 165
  nuclear fuels, 166–7
  provisions for, 156–62
  provisions, other, 161
  public health, 158–9
  reactors, 166
  report, 164–5
  research, 156–7
  resources within Community, 160
  resources outside Community, 161
  security, 161–2
  special fissile matter, ownership, 162
  supplies, 160

Ockrent Report, 10
Oil products, 34

Patent, European, 113
Patents, International Institute, 112
Pig-iron production, 5

Regulations, 103–9
Republic of Ireland, 14
Rules Governing Competition, 101–9
Rules of Competition, 110

Schuman, M. Robert, 1–4, 138–41
Schuman Plan, 2, 5, 138, 140–1
Social security, 115–28
  Belgium, 120
  benefits, 121, 124
  compulsory contributions, 124
  contributions, 122–3
  convention, 115
  costs, 124
  France, 118–19
  Italy, 119–20
  Luxembourg, 120–1
  Netherlands, 120
  Self-employed workers, 124–8
  West Germany, 119
  Workers, 118
Spaak, M. 8, 69, 71, 77
Spain, 14
Strasbourg Convention, 114
Surinam, 32, 34
Sweden, 14, 47
Switzerland, 14, 47

Tariff levels, 48–55
  base metals, 48
  factory plant, equipment, 50
  household, consumer durables, 54
  mechanical handling equipment, 52
  miscell, manufactures, 54
  miscell. metal manufactures, 54
  office equipment, 52
  photographic, optical goods, scientific instruments, 52
  plastics, 52
  pulp and paper, 48, 50
  television, radio, 54
  textiles, clothing, 52
  tools, implements, 52
  transport equipment, 50, 52
  U.K. imports, 49, 51, 53, 55
Tariff structure, 43–7
  external tariff, 43–6
  free trade, 43
  U.K. tariff, 45–7
Transport, 133–4
  access to market, 133
  rate policy 133–4
Treaty of Rome, 8, 11, 17–35
  agreement on common institutions, 34
  agriculture, 21
  annexed protocols, 33–34
  approximation of laws, 26
  Assembly or European Parliament, 35

Assn. of other countries, 32
balance of payments, 26-7
basis of E.E.C., 19-24
capital, 22-3
cartels, monopolies, 24-5
chemical products, 48
common rules, 24-6
community executive, 35
community statistical offices, 35
Council of Ministers, 18-19, 21-3, 25-7, 29-30, 32-3, 35
Court of Justice, 26, 34-5
cuts, 46-7
dumping, 25
duties, 45
economic policy, 26-8
electric plant, 50
European Investment Bank, 29-30, 35
external tariffs, 20
external trade policy, 27-8
general finance, 32
general provisions and safeguards, 32-3
institutions, 18-19
internal tariffs, 20
Joint publications, 35
labour, 21-22
main principles association, 30-1
membership and association, 33
merger of institutions, 35

monetary committee, 26
overseas development fund, 31-2
allocations for, 31, contributions for, 31
overseas territories assn. with common market, 30-1
patents, 35
quantitative restrictions, 20-1
right of settlement, 22
safeguarding clauses, 32-3
scientific data, 35
seat of institutions, 35
services, 22
social fund, European, 28-9
social policy, 28-9, general provisions of, 28, wages, social insurance contributions, 28
state monopolies, 21
state subsidies, 25-6
transport, 23-4
Vanoni Plan, 33
workers' health services, 35
Tunisia, 32, 34
Turkey, 14, 43

UNRRA, 6

Vietnam, 34

Yaoundé, 15
Yaoundé Convention, 14

3 1144 00292726 6